THE SEA OF MEMORIES

A galley of "The Religion"

THE
Sea of Memories

THE STORY OF
MEDITERRANEAN STRIFE
PAST AND PRESENT

BY

Charles Moran

NEW YORK

Charles Scribner's Sons

1942

Chapter XIV of this book appeared in somewhat
abbreviated form in the United States Naval
Institute Proceedings for April, 1941.

To the memory of a gallant soul:

MARTHA DE PAU ADAMS MORAN

my wife

Preface

THE BOOK you are about to read is not history, although the tale it tells is, I trust, as accurate as history should be. It is not a book of travel, although it will take you to some strange places. Above all it is not fiction, although it may be romance. It is the story of an ancient sea, one that has witnessed the birth of western civilization and may, alas, now be witnessing its destruction. How to deal with a subject covering approximately two thousand five hundred years, involving a score or more of nations whose requirements have progressed from an elementary search for food followed by a simple desire for booty or gain, to culminate in the nerve-racking race for security and power without which no one can survive in our modern industrial world, is indeed a problem that would tax the ingenuity of any chronicler. I shall therefore make my apologies to Clio, adopt a frankly Scheherazade attitude toward the Mediterranean and tell the story, or rather some of the stories, merely because they *are* such good stories. If my selections have been wisely made, then, in spite of my unorthodox procedure, I may have succeeded in throwing some light on the part the Mediterranean has played and is still playing in the making of the world in which we live.

Such an approach, however, may not please some of my erudite readers who may consider that the span we are about to traverse, from Mythology to Mussolini, is rather a long one to attempt without careful planning. We shall, therefore, pause frequently to take a bearing, keeping in mind always that the lines thus drawn are never clearly defined and that much over-lapping must be expected. Occasionally we shall log the passing of some headland in the sea of time, although many of the landmarks we thus leave astern have a way of re-appearing, perhaps only as a mirage. To those who, like Theseus, are seeking for an Ariadne to guide them through the labyrinth, I have but one suggestion to make. Follow the thread of strife; in the last analysis it is the only certain connecting link between the various periods of Mediterranean history.

And now a word of apology to my reader. The book you are about to read is an intensely personal one. It is the result of a long familiarity which, far from breeding contempt, has bred a deep love; a love not for any one people, any single period, any particular characters, but for the sea itself, the matchless setting endowed by nature and enriched by man, in which the slow process of history was evolved. So do not look for any theorizing, which I shall leave to wiser heads, but bear with me patiently while I try to tell you what the Mediterranean means to me, hoping all the while that it will mean as much and more to you!

CHARLES MORAN.

New York, December 1, 1941.

Contents

Illustrations

THE SEA OF MEMORIES

The Pillars of Hercules

THAT the present war, which originated in the Baltic, should soon spread to the Mediterranean was probably inevitable. Distance has again failed to secure immunity. Geographical names that recall the deeds of warriors dead these many years have already appeared in the terse communiqués of the war offices; a half-forgotten past will continue to emerge from the reports of war correspondents; in short, from now on we shall be reminded daily that the Mediterranean is, above all others, the sea of memories. For those familiar with the annals of this sea the struggle will have additional poignancy.

It is always with a certain emotion that I make the historic landfall of Cape Saint Vincent. We have passed the scene of Jervis' victory over the Spanish fleet, a victory that added one more earl to the British peerage and started Nelson on his road to immortality. As we draw nearer, the angular outline of the headland breaks through the morning haze, revealing the long roll of the Atlantic beating against a perpendicular cliff crowned by a lighthouse and a flagstaff on which Portuguese colors are being raised, vertical fields of dark green and darker red surcharged with a Braganza globe, the symbol of a once mighty seafaring people. We change our course and head for Cape Trafalgar, a name of magic and tragic import, while "nobly, nobly Cape Saint Vincent to the Northwest dies away." And then, as we turn our gaze to starboard, we suddenly realize that we have left the New World definitely behind. Africa, the mysterious, like a drowsy giant is lowering at us ominously.

Antiquity is closing in on us. Past Tarifa, the weather-beaten fortress built by the Moors, whose fame is still re-echoed by our word tariff, the Pillars of Hercules await us. Calpe, the Rock of Gibraltar, lies ahead and Abyla, the modern Ceuta, can be dimly seen to the southeast. In the distance beyond we get our first glimpse of the Mediterranean. We have crossed the Sea of Experiment and are entering the Sea of Memories.

"La mythologie, ce n'est pas des bêtises," a precept I learned as a youngster in France, involuntarily comes to mind. Mythology frequently astonishes us by a symbolism that modern research transforms into knowledge. Between his tenth and eleventh labors Hercules visited the court of King Geryones, who, so runs the legend, ruled over what is now southern Spain. Among his possessions that monarch owned a herd of red cattle who had an annoying propensity for straying from their home on the range. Hercules is assigned the task of rounding them up, his eleventh labor. While so doing, just to keep his hand in, he performed a feat that outranks any of his regular labors, in historical importance at any rate. He took a mountain that was fulfilling the useful function of holding back the ocean and divided it into two pillars, Calpe and Abyla, thereby allowing the waters to rush in and form the sea we are entering. Without vouching for the accuracy of this story, this much is certain. Some thirty thousand years ago some force did that very thing, to the undoubted dismay of the race of big-game hunters and artists whose records, carefully concealed in inaccessible caverns, have so puzzled present-day scientists.

Physical geography has never been considered an exhilarating study. I shall therefore let the reader absorb his topographical facts from a map. There is, however, one detail of the physical make-up of the Mediterranean that might escape the notice of those not in the habit of consulting charts. The Mediterranean is divided into two distinct parts of about equal size, the enlargement of two swampy lakes that were united when the herculean forces of nature broke through the spur of the Atlas range that once connected Morocco and Spain and, continuing the irruption eastward, made a still wider gap in the Alpine range that once reached unbroken into Africa via Italy, Sicily and Tunis. If you will examine the soundings on a chart you will find them much less than you probably suppose, especially at the two points of strangulation in question. In fact, of the 813,000 square miles of the Mediterranean over 201,000 are within the 100-fathom mark. As·a result the Mediterranean lends itself readily to mining operations, to the great detriment of sea power in the former acceptation of the term.

The Mediterranean is practically free from tides and currents. Shoals and reefs are conspicuous by their absence. These factors made the Inland Sea the cradle of navigation, the first school of naval strategy. The classical accounts of the perils of navigation are, therefore, the consequence of superstition or of misinformation purposely disseminated by the Phœnicians who desired to discourage others from competing with them for sea-borne trade. I have taken a moderate-sized power boat past Scylla and Charybdis, in "nasty" weather at that, without incurring any danger from the mythical whirlpool through which Scylla was supposed to draw passing ships to their doom on the rocks below: "Ora exertantem et navis in saxa trahentem."[1]

Another important fact to remember about the Mediterranean is that until recently its only maritime approach was through the Straits of Gibraltar. To be sure, some rudimentary attempts at a canal connecting the Nile and the Red Sea had been made as far back as the Ptolemies but they hardly comply with our definition of a waterway, one permitting the passage of sea-going vessels. With the completion of the Suez Canal in 1869 the Mediterranean at last became a sea of passage.

An absorbing, stirring subject is the Mediterranean, full of pathos and pageantry, replete with adventure and intrigue, but

[1] *Æneid*, III, 425.

one that cannot be crowded into any definite number of acts and scenes. I trust, therefore, that I may be pardoned if I adopt the technique much in vogue with modern playwrights and treat the action as a succession of typical or pivotal episodes.

Being the oldest of the seas, historically if not geologically, the first chronicles of the Mediterranean have come down to us in a vague though highly imaginative setting; poetic in form, scriptural in expression. To distinguish fact from fancy would be a fascinating pastime but one that would take us far afield. Suffice to say that through the mist of legend two nations gradually emerge and assume familiar characteristics, recognizable to present-day minds: Greece and Phœnicia. With them our narrative begins. Both are traders but the former are warriors and artists to boot. Both ultimately succumbed to Rome, one by absorption the other by conquest. The long struggle between commercial Carthage and militaristic Rome is one that, *mutatis mutandis,* is still undecided in principle.

This first period of Mediterranean history we may, for lack of a better term, call the Classical Period. It is difficult to assign a date for its termination. The Battle of Actium is as good a date as any, as with the voluntary demobilization of the Roman Navy after that victory a change came over the complexion of Mediterranean events. Rome entered on a career of territorial expansion, over-expansion we may safely call it, in which she sowed the seeds of her own disintegration.

The next period is a confused and rambling one which, again for want of a more accurate name, we may call the Period of Disintegration. Civilization took refuge in the Golden Horn. Invaders appeared on the shores of the Mediterranean in ever-increasing numbers. *Mare Nostrum* became anybody's sea. Goths, Vandals and other strange people began to challenge the hegemony of Rome and Byzantium. The contest exhausted all involved; so much so that when the great Islamic surge that was to carry the Crescent to the gates of Tours got under way

Christianity was disorganized and divided. Again it is difficult to assign a limit to the period in question. The First Crusade is perhaps an arbitrary division point but it ushered in the vigorous counter-offensive that decided the type of Mediterranean civilization, probably for all time.

A rough and tumble period was that of the Crusades in which some distinctly unholy exploits were performed under a pious garb. From a naval standpoint the outstanding feature of the period was the revival of Italian sea power under the leadership of Genoa and Venice. Had Italy been united Europe might have been faced with another *Mare Nostrum*. Lepanto, though not strictly speaking a Crusade, marks the end of the Crusading Period. From then on, in spite of sporadic outbursts of military activity, Islam was on the defensive.

With the subsidence of the religious conflict the Mediterranean gradually drifted into the present era of international intrigue and colonial expansion for which the Germans have coined the word *Weltpolitik*. With the entry of Britain issues non-Mediterranean in origin began to influence Mediterranean events. The long struggle between France and England, much of which was fought out in the Inland Sea, is but the first of a series of which the end is not yet. The French Revolution added a new development by arousing the dormant national spirit of many nations. Wars of "liberation," of which the Greek War of Independence and the Italian Risorgimento were the most spectacular, made their appearance. The quest for political liberty, however, ultimately gave way to a more complex but equally compelling motive: the quest for economic liberty. Russia began her drive for an ice-free port, an objective for which the liberation of the Balkan Slavs furnished a convenient cloak. *Weltpolitik* was never lost sight of by the major protagonists in espousing the cause of their weaker allies. As for the minor protagonists, they were forced to seek powerful protectors to replace their former masters.

Since the dawn of history the Mediterranean has been a region in which strife prevailed. People may come and people may go, objectives may vary, methods may change, motives may differ, but the strife remains. That is why one time is as good as another in which to write about the Mediterranean. Why wait until one war is over when the post-war period is but one of preparation for the strife that is to follow? The Mediterranean has always offered to the venturesome a profusion of tempting objectives from which to choose. To those familiar with history this persistence of strife seems the logical result of a God-given geographical position rather than of man-made events, a remark that is saved from being a platitude only by the fact that its truth is so often overlooked.

But "the play's the thing," and here come the first characters.

CHAPTER I

Down to the Sea in Ships

STRANGE as it may seem, the birth of navigation was largely due to one of God's humble creatures, the tunny fish. When we stop to consider that these overgrown mackerel frequently attain a weight of four hundred pounds we can see what a windfall such a catch represented to a half-starved people. The first seafarers in the Mediterranean were undoubtedly men driven to the coast by their more powerful neighbors, deprived of their normal diet of meat and corn and thus compelled to resort to fishing. Now the tunny is decidedly migratory in his habits. He spawns in the Sea of Azov, passes through the Bosphorus, the Sea of Marmora and the Dardanelles and then roams about the entire Mediterranean. The Greek word for harpooning is $\theta v v v \acute{a} \zeta \epsilon \iota v$, which gives us a clue as to how the tunny was taken. The Argonauts, of classical fame, were probably tunny fishers armed with bronze harpoons who had tracked their prey to a backwater of the Euxine.

It was not long before one of these early seafaring people, the Phœnicians, came to realize that the sea offered greater opportunities than were contained in tunny fishing. Maritime history was about to begin. The quest for food and booty had progressed to a quest for legitimate gain. The achievements of the Phœnicians as traders need not surprise us. They were a Semitic people. Some scholars of late have advanced the rather plausible theory that it is a misnomer to speak of the Jews as a trading people. The biblical Jews were essentially a pastoral

7

people. It is the descendants of their kinsmen, the Phœnicians, now scattered over the entire globe, who constitute the nucleus of the international trading community we are wont to call Jewish. The only time in history these traders attained the dignity of national existence was during the period of Punic prosperity. The word "Phœnicians" is of Greek origin and means "the sun-burnt ones." The Phœnicians called themselves Canaanites. Many of them subsequently adopted the Jewish religion, hence the confusion. It is interesting to speculate as to how much trouble Europe would have been spared had Phœnicia survived in some form to our day to serve as a haven for all Semitic people.

Unlike the Jews, the Phœnicians were a venturesome sea-faring people. Herodotus tells us that, starting from the Red Sea, they circumnavigated Africa. The voyage, which was made in the seventh century, B.C., took three years to accomplish and necessitated a landing on the African coast each autumn in order to grow a crop of corn to be used on the ensuing summer cruise. Not until 1486 was this performance equalled when Bartholomew Diaz rounded the Cape of Good Hope. Whether the Phœnicians ever ventured across the Bay of Biscay in search of Cornish tin is, however, extremely doubtful, legends to that effect notwithstanding. "Thou breakest the ships of Tarshish with an east wind," says the Psalmist. If the Phœnicians had difficulty in weathering the prevailing east wind of the Mediterranean what chance would they have had, especially when heavily laden with metal, in one of the stiff blows of the Bay of Biscay?

Although the leading Punic cities of Tyre and Sidon in time attained a state of ostentatious prosperity that deeply incensed the prophet Ezekiel, they started life very modestly on islands and did not extend to the mainland for some time. Sidon in Hebrew means "fishery," a name that bears out the tunny-fish theory. The first seaports of the Mediterranean were located not on estuaries or in land-locked bays but on islands. Convenience was discarded in favor of safety. Traders by sea had no intention of putting themselves at the mercy of landsmen with ill-defined notions of *meum et tuum*. For the same reason they long preferred open roadsteads to snug harbors for ports of call. Their boats, being light, could always be drawn up on shore. The beach of Phaleron was used in preference to the Piræus for many centuries as giving a better chance for a "get-away." Trading operations in antiquity can hardly be said to have been conducted in the bosom of confidence. Kidnapping of customers and plundering of traders were all too frequent.

The scrupulous honesty of the Phœnicians, however, gradually made them welcome all over the Mediterranean. The method they pursued in smaller communities is amusing. After unloading their wares on the beach—a practice their descendants still continue in the Cyclades—they retired to their ships in the offing. The natives then drew nearer, inspected the goods and placed alongside of them what they considered a fair purchase price, usually gold or other metals. The Phœnicians then returned and if satisfied with the purchase price departed with it; if not satisfied they withdrew again as a sign that the price must be raised. This process was repeated until a meeting of the minds occurred or an impasse was reached.

The trade routes along which the Phœnicians plied began at Tyre and Sidon, the termini of the caravan routes of Asia Minor. The Ægean being pretty well under Greek control, the Phœnicians made straight for the Malta passage. There they established themselves solidly at Carthage, "Kart-hadasht," the New City. The date and circumstances cannot be fixed with any accuracy, fortunately for Virgil, as it enabled him to indulge in a bit of romancing which is one of the glories of Latin literature but hardly a contribution to history. The new settlement soon extended its sway as far as Leptis to the east and Hippo to the west besides crossing over to Sicily and founding

Panormus and Lilybæum (the modern Palermo and Marsala) as well as several lesser towns. Then, passing on to the next strategic point, the Phœnicians secured the Straits of Gibraltar and spread out as far as Carthagena on the Mediterranean and Gades (the modern Cadiz) on the Atlantic, the latter city being the Tarshish of biblical fame. With the innate sense of naval strategy that characterizes trading nations the Carthaginians occupied the Balearic Isles as well. "Junior" had by this time completely outstripped his parents.

The commercial instinct *érigé en système* is what gave Carthage her strength. An uncanny skill in supplying wants, in creating them first if necessary by transforming a luxury into an indispensable commodity, resulted in the astonishing network that tapped every known source of supply and reached every known market. Her sea-borne traffic laid the foundation of our modern economic life and in their efforts to develop that traffic the Phœnicians began the scientific study of navigation, a science they were careful to keep to themselves. One of the reasons for their success as carriers was that they had mastered the art of night sailing, of laying a course by the stars. A curious, secretive people!

Greek navigation on the contrary was a "point to point" affair with twelve hours "on" and twelve hours "off." Homer gives us a vivid account of a mutiny that occurred when Odysseus, after safely passing Scylla, attempted to compel his crew to continue on instead of pulling up on a beach for a good night's rest. The spokesman on that occasion was one Eurylochus, the first of a long line of "sea-lawyers" bent on upholding "seamen's rights."[1]

The Greeks of Homer's time apparently had the sportsman's contempt for a man "in trade," a contempt undoubtedly increased by the fact that the distinction between a trader and a pirate was long a shadowy one. Euryalus, who at one time

[1] *Odyssey*, XII, 279–287.

held the wrestling championship of Phæcia, taunted his ship-wrecked opponent Odysseus with being a mere trader who did not look like an athlete.

> A wandering merchant he frequents the main,
> Some mean seafarer in pursuit of gain,
> Studious of freight, in naval trade well skill'd,
> But dreads th' athletic labours of the field.
> —Pope's translations.[2]

It was not until the sixth century that the Greeks overcame this prejudice sufficiently to establish trade routes of their own. Leaving the African coast to their Phœnician competitors, except for Cyrene in Libya and Naucratis on the Canopic mouth of the Nile, neither of which cities was ever important politically, Greek merchants preferred to ply between Asia Minor and the islands of the Ægean and to follow the sinuous shores of southern Europe. Greek trade was never as venturesome as Phœnician trade and was mostly confined to the Greek states and colonies.

The origin of the Greek states is bewildering owing to the fact that four distinct stocks, the Ionians, the Dorians, the Æolians and the Achæans, long struggled for supremacy. In Homer's time Greece was predominantly Achæan. When therefore we are told that the Achæans were really not Hellenic the average student gives up in despair. The ancient Greeks were continually accusing each other of not being "one hundred per cent" Greek. A map showing the territorial distribution of the various stocks is a veritable crazy quilt. When we come to the Greek colonies the situation is still more intricate. It is hopeless to attempt to remember by whom the many Greek outposts were founded. They dotted the entire shore of the

[2]*Odyssey*, VIII, 163–164. Homer's lines are as follows:

φόρτου τε μνήμων καὶ ἐπίσκοπος ᾖσιν ὀδαίων
κερδέων θ' ἁρπαλέων· οὐδ' ἀθλητῆρι ἔοικας.

Euxine, they were strung along the southern coast of what is now France and Spain. Nice, Marseilles, Tarragona, Sagunto were among them. Beyond Sagunto lay the Carthaginian "sphere of influence."

The most important of the Greek colonies, however, were those in southern Italy and eastern Sicily, the famous Magna Græcia of antiquity, whose monuments are still among the most perfect specimens of Greek architecture. Greece proper contains no temples so well preserved as those of Pæstum. Standing alone in a desolate plain whose population has long since fled, the effect they produce on the traveller is one of astonishment and melancholy. Croton and Sybaris are but names today, the latter still re-echoing the tales of wealth and luxury for which the vanished Greek civilization of Italy was noted. At the time of its capture by the Normans Naples was still essentially a Greek city. It was in Sicily, however, that the main struggle of Greek history, the Athens-Sparta feud, was to be decided and thereby hangs one of the most stirring stories in the annals of the Mediterranean.

Of all the thunderbolts in history the one that struck a barber shop on the waterfront of the Piræus was probably the most startling. Business was progressing as usual one morning in the last weeks of 413 B.C., when a stranger, obviously a seafaring man, sat down in one of the chairs. After many days at sea he required considerable attention before venturing to appear in the gay metropolis whose glistening monuments could be seen a few miles inland. It is a pity we do not know his name. Plutarch describes him merely as "a certain stranger." As he was ministering to the wants of his customer the Attic Figaro began his usual "pumping" process. Conversation naturally drifted to the all-important topic, the war in Sicily. Here the stranger, being a tactful, considerate fellow, ventured to express the hope that none of the barber's kin were among the slain or, worse yet, among the prisoners.

"What sayest thou?" exclaimed the barber.

"Why, dost thou not know?" answered the stranger. "The Syracusans have destroyed the entire Athenian fleet. Those who escaped the slaughter are penned up like so many wild animals in the quarries of Achradina!"

"By Zeus . . ." The rest was lost on the stranger as the master, leaving the apprentice to finish the job, was "running at top speed to the upper city before others could learn the news." Breathless he accosted the Archons. The evil tidings, however, had travelled almost as fast as the barber. Soon the city was in an uproar, the market in a panic. Classical markets could apparently "break" as well as their modern successors. The Archons lost no time in having the stranger arrested. What was he trying to do? Why, "discredit the administration," obviously. Summoned to give the source of his information the stranger was at a loss. It was current news where he came from. That did not satisfy the Archons, so he was put on the rack. The stranger grimly stuck to his story, or rather the story stuck to him, for after a while messengers arrived and he was released from torment. It was all too true! One of the greatest disasters of history had befallen Athenian arms.

The invasion of Greece during the reign of Darius had been undertaken as a reprisal for the help Athens had extended to the Ionian cities of Asia Minor in their struggle against that Persian conqueror. The victory of Marathon had brought the first invasion to an inglorious close. It was not until ten years later that Xerxes dared attempt to avenge that defeat. The very size of the new expedition convinced the Greek states that more than the humiliation of Athens was contemplated. Xerxes had carefully timed his invasion to coincide with a Carthaginian attack on the Greek colonies and had enlisted the support of the Egyptian fleet in his operations against Athens. For once the Greeks forgot their mutual rivalries. Without in any way belittling the prowess of the Spartans at Thermopylæ, it must be conceded that if Greece was saved from becoming a Persian satrapy it was due to the naval victory of Salamis in which Athens played the outstanding part.

Salamis had demonstrated the strength of the Athenian navy. It was therefore but natural that Athens should assume the lead in the confederacy that was to guard Greece from further attacks by Persia. The Delian League, although its headquarters were on the small island of Delos, was essentially an Athenian institution in which the lesser maritime states were admitted, or coerced, to membership either as allies or as contributing members. As the danger of attack from without lessened, the League developed into a thalattocracy designed to give Athens the monopoly of sea-borne trade. Mutterings of discontent were soon heard. Ionic Athens saw her hegemony threatened by Doric Sparta.

While Athens was tightening her hold on the sea Sparta was lining up her allies on land. The crazy quilt was undergoing a drastic simplification. If all the Ægean, including Thessaly, was in the Athenian column, the entire Peloponnesus, with the exception of Achæa, was banded together by Sparta. Across the Gulf of Corinth, Ætolia, like Achæa, endeavored to remain neutral. Bœotia sided with Sparta. Greece was preparing for the first great war that was to bring sea power and land power to grips.

The situation has an extremely modern ring. For some years the future enemies bided their time, increased their armaments and sought allies. Athens made a defensive treaty with Corcyra (the modern Corfu), a strong naval base and Corinth's bitter enemy, also with Rhegium (the modern Reggio) and Leontini in Sicily. The grain supply of the Peloponnesus was now at the mercy of the Athenian fleet. Peace was at the mercy of an incident. Corinth, angered by the Athenian alliance with Corcyra, was urging Sparta to launch a campaign in defense of "the freedom of the seas." She was joined by Ægina, who, besides chafing under the heavy taxation her membership in the League entailed, had another grievance in that she had not secured from Athens the home rule promised her. Megara had an even more practical cause of complaint. The high-tariff party at Athens was ruining Megaran trade.

The comedies of Aristophanes, in a way, are the "revues" of the day in which current events are humorously but scathingly paraphrased, the characters in the public eye pitilessly lampooned. Aristophanes was a moderate who believed in compromise. Had he lived in our country during the early sixties he would have been dubbed a "copperhead." Turn to *The Acharnians* and see what happens to a Megaran farmer who tries to sell his wares in the Athenian marketplace. He is promptly denounced as a smuggler, his produce is confiscated. A consignment of wicks is likewise seized on the ground that the wicks are surely intended to set fire to the docks. Sabotage is not a recent discovery. Informers abound. A privileged Bœotian trader, after disposing of his goods, is looking around for something to take back home that is plentiful in Athens but scarce in Bœotia.

"I tell you what," suggests Dikæopolis, "pack up an informer!"

"He is rather small," the Bœotian objects as he sizes up the proposed return cargo.

"True," answers Dikæopolis, "but every inch of him bad!"

In 432 the town of Potidea in Chalcidice revolted. That gave Sparta her chance. She served an ultimatum on Athens that no self-respecting state could tolerate. Pericles held his ground, Sparta declared war. The Spartans, like some modern nations, fully expected to win with a "Blitzkrieg." The Athenians, however, retired to the fortified Athens-Piræus position and dug themselves in. By a series of brilliant naval victories, Chalcis, Naupactos, Sphacteria, the Athenian navy swept the Spartans from the sea. Then, a stalemate. By 421 both sides were ready for a peace which turned out to be only a truce, as it satisfied neither side.

In the meantime Aristophanes was playing to sold-out houses. Several of his plays have been successfully revived recently; they require no revision to be understood. To begin with we have the high cost of living. In *The Wasps* a son clamors for some figs, a common enough article of food in pre-war days. "How can I buy figs with my paltry pay, I have enough trouble buying bread and fuel!" exclaims the father. "Stop poking at that wick! It is easy to see *you* do not have to pay for the oil!" Every one is hard-up. In *The Birds* the King describes how once he was a man "and had creditors, and did not pay them, just like you and me," turning to the audience. And yet because a good catch of fish is brought in peace negotiations are broken off. "We want no peace, let the war continue," shout the Mr. Britlings in *The Peace*. All the stock evils of modern war are present. Soft jobs for favored officers, dearth of domestic servants, the slaves having escaped to the enemy, no young men to be seen in the streets, lesbianism rampant. Line after line of bitter sarcasm does Aristophanes reel off, for all of which the reader can supply a modern counterpart.

There is one feature for which the reader will not find a modern counterpart. That Aristophanes could in war time apply to the leader of the war party such an expression as "a whale who keeps a public house and has a voice like a pig on fire" and not go to jail speaks volumes for the spirit of liberty that prevailed in Athens at that time. In *The Knights* Demosthenes is casting around for a successor to Cleon and hits upon a sausage-maker.[3]

"But I know nothing, friend, beyond my letters and those I know badly," says the sausage-maker.

" 'Tis a pity you know anything," answers Demosthenes.

[3] It is amusing to note that the slang for sausages in Athens was "dogs"!

"How can I manage the state?" the sausage-maker insists.

"That's easy," says Demosthenes. "All you have to do is to keep on doing as you do now. First make a hash of everything, then get everything into a stew," etc.

There was one subject, however, on which even the great humorist could not be funny. The crowding of refugees in the fortified area led to abominable living conditions. Within a year black death was stalking in the streets of Athens. In spite of the suffering of the civilian population and the "butcher's bills" the war party in both camps remained adamant. By a curious fatality the two warmongers, Cleon the Athenian and Brasidas the Spartan, both fell in action at Amphipolis thus paving the way for the peace which Nicias negotiated in 421.

The war had produced one unexpected result. In Sicily the Greek cities, irrespective of previous affiliations, adopted a "plague on both your houses" attitude. Under the leadership of Hermocrates a Pan-Sicilian Congress convened at Gela and proclaimed a "Monroe Doctrine" with "Sicily for the Sicilians" as a slogan. Athens being the maritime state was the one to suffer from the movement. Sparta heartily approved of the plan; so did Carthage, for obvious reasons.

The peace was to be of short duration. Corinth and Bœotia refused to adhere to it *ab initio*. Its terms were never lived up to by either Sparta or Athens. Within a year the Spartan-Bœotian allies found themselves facing a new line-up of "democratic states," Athens-Argos-Mantinea-Elis. As can be seen, Athens had made some recruits on the Peloponnesus, thanks to the eloquence of Alcibiades. The victory of Mantinea in 418 again demonstrated the efficiency of the Spartan military machine.

And now we come to the turning point of the war. The city of Segesta on the northern coast of Sicily was one of the few Greek settlements to remain loyal to Athens. As a result she found herself threatened by Syracuse. Segesta appealed to

Athens for help. Nicias, the Athenian commander-in-chief, was a typical professional soldier. Plutarch tells us that he spent long hours in the War Office working hard. After hours he refused to discuss military matters with politicians or gossips. As a result he was none too popular and no match for the smooth-tongued amateur strategist who had evolved a plan for winning the war by attacking the enemy on a new front. Alcibiades was probably the inventor of the "side-show." This particular one was not the Dardanelles but Sicily. If Athens could conquer that island she would deal a blow at Carthage, whose intervention in the war was becoming a nuisance, and secure additional forces for the struggle at home. In vain did Nicias recommend fighting it out along the old lines, the expedition was enthusiastically voted.

Thucydides has graphically described the tragedy that ensued. The bare facts are as follows. The expedition, consisting of 134 triremes, besides transports carrying 5000 men, arrived off Syracuse in April 414. The fleet blockaded the city by sea while the army began erecting a wall on the land side, which you can still see. Nevertheless the Syracusans received a welcome auxiliary, the Spartan general Gylippus, who stopped the Athenians circumvallation by building a cross wall. Alcibiades having been recalled to answer a charge of sacrilege, Nicias continued the siege and before long was clamoring for reinforcements. Demosthenes with seventy-three vessels was accordingly sent out, but still the siege dragged on, until on August 27, 413, the Syracusans got a boom across the small neighboring harbor the Athenians were using as a base. Gylippus had accomplished one of the few successful "bottling up" operations in the annals of naval warfare. Abandoning their ships and the siege the Athenians now tried to escape overland. They were captured to the last man. Demosthenes and Nicias, in spite of Gylippus' plea, were butchered in cold blood. The survivors were cast into the quarries of Achradina. Now they are pleasant sunken gardens. At that time they must have been sun-scorched wastes littered with sharp stones. Did any survive to tell the tale? Yes, those who knew the verses of Euripides. War had not dulled the Sicilian Greeks to the extent of not respecting Greek poetry.

> When Athens' army fell at Syracuse,
> And fetter'd thousands bore the yoke of war,
> Redemption rose up in the Attic Muse,
> Her voice their only ransom from afar;
> See! As they chaunt the tragic hymn, the car
> Of the o'ermaster stops; the reins
> Fall from his hands; his scimitar
> Starts from his belt; he rends the captive chains
> And bids him thank the bard for freedom and his strains.[4]

It was the news of this disaster that had filtered through to the barber shop in the Piræus. That any one in Athens could have a spark of humor left seems unbelievable, yet in *Lysistrata* Aristophanes has given us one of the most spicy and rollicking farces that ever got by the censor. Lysistrata, the "disbander of armies," had devised a new plan to make the men stop fighting. She enlisted the *monde* and the *demi-monde* of Athens in a "sit-down strike" that failed. Through temperamental weakness some of the conspirators turned strikebreakers! Behind the daring humor of the lines Aristophanes was endeavoring to deliver a message. Stop the war and unite! His preaching fell on deaf ears. The war continued.

Again the Athenian navy proved the better, but Arginusæ was to be the last Athenian victory. The Spartans had at last developed an admiral, Lysander. Falling upon the Athenian fleet at Ægespotomi while the crews were on shore, he captured or destroyed all but eight ships. The next year Athens was compelled to submit to a humiliating peace.

[4] *Childe Harold*, canto iv, 16.

The Peloponnesian War was over. Historically it settled nothing but a quarrel between two Greek states. Carthaginian power it left intact. It had, however, proved one thing: the inherent weakness of the Greek political system.

CHAPTER II

The Adventures of a Certain Young Man

SOME TIME in the early part of the year 401 B.C. a young Athenian, who judging from appearances had not turned thirty, was slowly climbing the steep path leading to the oracle of Delphi. Although spring was still some weeks off, the road was sun-beaten and the glare, reflected by countless marble temples and statues, blinding even to his young eyes accustomed as they were to the hunting field. By his dress and demeanor he was evidently a gentleman. Curly dark hair, hazel eyes and regular features enhanced an athletic bearing that bespoke a boyhood spent in the open air. Even in a country noted for the good looks of its men and women you would have noticed him. What crisis in his life was impelling him to seek to lift the veil with which the Gods conceal the future from mere mortals? It must have been some difficult problem that confronted him since his teacher and friend Socrates had confessed his misgivings and had advised him to seek divine guidance.

Although Athens was still the intellectual center of the world, the sun of Athenian power had passed its zenith. The theatre of Dionysius still rang to the impassioned verse of Æschylus, Sophocles and Euripides or rocked with laughter at the biting wit of Aristophanes, the paintings of Zeuxis and the sculptures of Phidias were still the models of the artistic world, but Salamis and Platea were memories, the glory of the Persian War had given way to the stern reality of defeat. Syracuse and the loss of the great armada had cast a gloom that could not be dispelled even by the philosophers who were now coming into their own. "No," said the young man to himself, "no opportunity can be found today but overseas."

There was nothing new or startling about the situation in which young Xenophon found himself. History has often been made by men in just such a predicament. Yet in the present case conscientious scruples made Xenophon hesitate. A few years previously he had struck up a friendship with an attractive young soldier of fortune, a Bœotian, Proxenus by name. In fact, Proxenus had stayed for a while in Xenophon's house while he was studying in Athens. Then his roving spirit got the upper hand and he disappeared. Now Xenophon gets a letter from Proxenus, written from Sardis—of all places! He had entered the service of young Cyrus and enthusiastically assured his friend that a brilliant future awaited him if he will only join him in Sardis. Serve under a Persian, the hereditary enemy! Enlist in a corps of mercenaries composed largely of Spartans! It was but recently that Athens had taken a terrible licking from Sparta in the Peloponnesian War. Although Sparta had raised the armies, the money had been supplied by Persia. Athenian raids on Sardis during the Ionian War that preceded the Persian invasions had now been avenged.

Cyrus, however, was not to be confused with the ordinary run of Persian potentate. He had been carefully educated, was thoroughly imbued with the Hellenic spirit; in short he was an "enlightened" ruler. Had he lived in the eighteenth century he would have been dubbed with that very vague quality known as "philosophic." What was Xenophon's alternative? The life of a country squire on the estate of his father, a man of limited means whose farm at Ercheia was about twelve miles distant from Athens. That thought settled the matter. Before Xenophon reached the tripod of the sibyl he had made up his mind. After all, it was only a matter of a few years and he could return to Attica with enough money to maintain the position to which his father's family entitled him. How many emigrants have succumbed to the same spirit of optimism! So instead of consulting the oracle on the wisdom of accepting the opportunity offered by Proxenus, Xenophon merely inquired to what god he should sacrifice in order to ensure a prosperous outcome of his odyssey.

Why should Cyrus be quietly increasing his armaments? They were suspiciously formidable for the comparatively simple task of policing the province of Ionia which he still governed by virtue of the authority granted him by his late father, Darius the Bastard. Wars of succession are among the oldest known to mankind. They arise from the attempt of some ambitious pretender to upset the established rules of succession or from the obstinacy of some "legitimate" monarch in insisting that such rules, being divine in their origin, may not be upset. A war of that type was now brewing in the Persian Empire. The Persians have contributed one rather unique theory to the doctrine of legitimacy. According to their philosophy regal attributes cannot be imparted to a prince unless his father be actually on the throne at the time the heir apparent is born. An application of this rule would exclude Cyrus' elder brother Artaxerxes from the succession whereas Cyrus could qualify thereunder. For reasons history has not recorded Darius decided to set aside this rule by what modern historians would call a "pragmatic sanction." That Cyrus was raising an army to prevent his brother from enforcing so "unconstitutional" an act as the one his father had promulgated was a fact of which Xenophon was in blissful ignorance when he landed at the busy seaport of Ephesus. His alert mind must have been keenly interested in the sights he beheld. Swarthy Saracens with their turbans, brown-bodied Egyptians from the grain ships and on all sides the ubiquitous Phœnicians with curly beards, beaked noses and sharp eyes unloading tin and other wares imported from fabulous distances.

After a brief stay in Ephesus Xenophon resumed his journey and arrived at Sardis, a massive fortress whose crenelated towers stood out boldly against the cloudless sky. Waterfowl from the Caÿster were still perching on the walls, as in Homer's time.[1] Some three hundred years before the town had been destroyed by a roving band of merciless savages, the Cimmerians, whose pallor seemed to reflect the Arctic ice from which they were said to have come, the first of a long line of invaders that were to descend on the older civilizations of the Mediterranean. Under Crœsus the damage was repaired, thanks to the wealth for which that plutocrat was famous. Sardis had been the starting point for the invasions launched by Darius the Elder and Xerxes. Now it was once more humming with activity as Cyrus had mustered an army of over 100,000 men whose tents and picket lines spread over the fertile plain.

As Proxenus had predicted, Xenophon quickly fell under the spell of the young Persian prince and soon found himself on the staff of his friend whose Bœotian contingent formed part of the command of the Spartan general Clearchus among whom were the immortal Ten Thousand. Artaxerxes, however, was not asleep. His wily old satrap Tissaphernes, who ruled over the province of Caria to the south, bore Cyrus an old grudge. Although Cyrus had given the rebellious Pisidians as his objective the sly old fox was not deceived and rode from Miletus to Susa to warn Artaxerxes. The advantage of surprise was therefore lost.

On March 9, 401, Cyrus and his army began the march in-

---

[1] Τῶν δ , ὥσ τ' ὀρνίθων πετεηνῶν ἔθνεα πολλά,
χηνῶν ἢ γεράνων ἢ κύκνων δουλιχοδείρων,
Ἀσίῳ ἐν λειμῶνι Καῦστρίου ἀμφὶ ῥέεθρα

Iliad, II, 459–461

Pope's translation of this passage is as follows:
    Not less their number than th' embodied cranes
    Or milk-white swans in Asius' watery plains,
    That o'er the windings of Caÿster's springs
    Stretch their long necks, and clap their rustling wings.

land, or Anabasis, with which all schoolboys are familiar, that
is those of the days when classical studies had not been discarded
for more important subjects such as—well, what has been
put in the place of the classics? I shall abridge ἐντεῦθεν ἐξελαύνει
and the parasangs and merely "touch the high spots." After
three days of marching under a blazing sun the army reached
the Meander, over which the engineers threw a pontoon bridge,
and entered a large game preserve belonging to Cyrus. The
Greek officers enjoyed a day's sport in this park, or paradise to
give it its Greek name. The enlisted men staged an athletic tournament. Cyrus himself bestowed the prizes on the winners. Tena-
cious of their customs, these ancient Greeks! A few more
marches and *das ewige weibliche* made its appearance. Queen
Epyaxa arrived with enough money to pay the mercenaries who
were already clamoring. Xenophon suspected that Cyrus and
the queen συγγενέσθαι, for which the usual translation "had
intimate relations" will do! A realistic review was held ending
with a charge by the Greek hoplites, to the dismay of the
queen and her barbarian escort who promptly fled for their
lives. Loud laughter from the Greeks! Through the Cilisian
Gates, an imposing mountain pass, and the army was once
more on the seacoast, at Tarsus. Here trouble seemed imminent
as Epyaxa's husband, Syennesis, blocked the way with an army.
Everything went off smoothly, however, thanks to Epyaxa, who
is not the first, nor the last, woman to patch up a truce between
her husband and her lover. Tarsus is, of course, the birthplace
of Saint Paul. Here he got his first start in life, not as an Apostle
but as an army contractor. Tents were his specialty.[2]

We are now in the month of July. For some time past mutterings had been heard among the foreign contingents. The
real object of the expedition was beginning to dawn upon them.
War on the "Great King"—as the King of Persia was com-
monly called in Greece—was rather more than they had bar-

[2]Acts 18:3.

gained for. Clearchus finally arranged matters. The method he employed was good then and now. He raised the pay of all hands and the march was resumed. After crossing the Euphrates at Thapsacus rugged country was encountered. Wild asses abounded, also flocks of ostriches. Omar Khayyam mentions the wild asses centuries later. The usual riots between the various Greek troops kept Clearchus busy. One particularly odious treason was discovered. The culprit, a Persian Orontas by name, entered the tent in which the court-martial was sitting, never to be heard from again. "No grave of his was ever seen," Xenophon grimly recorded.

At last the army of Artaxerxes was reported. Cyrus called his officers together and gave his final instructions. Liberal rewards were promised to all in the event of victory. "My father's realm," he assured them with oriental grandiloquence, "extends to the south to a region where men cannot dwell because of the heat and to the north to where they cannot dwell because of the cold. I fear not that I shall not have enough to give but rather that I shall not have enough friends to whom to give." Here Clearchus, with typical Spartan contempt for the barbarian, asked: "Do you think, Cyrus, that your brother will fight?" Ancestral pride dominating his hatred for the brother who was seeking to defraud him of his kingdom, Cyrus replied: "If he is a son of Darius and Parysatis and a brother of mine, by Zeus, he will fight!" This prediction was to be abundantly verified.

On September 3, 401, the armies met on the memorable field of Cunaxa. The Greeks, of course, carried everything before them. On seeing the enemy line they "automatically" broke into a charge. The native Persians on either side fought with magnificent courage. The two brothers sought each other in personal combat. Before they could reach each other Artaxerxes was severely wounded; Cyrus was unhorsed and disappeared. Sunset put an end to the slaughter. The Greeks slept supperless on their positions and awaited news of their chief, in vain. The next morning the body of Cyrus was discovered under a pile of slain. The Greeks retired to an entrenched camp and pondered on their plight. Hundreds of miles from the sea, short of supplies, in a hostile country, abandoned by their late allies who hastened to make peace, their situation was indeed desperate.

Obviously, the only salvation lay in trekking the long distance separating them from the Greek cities on the southern shore of the Euxine. At first Artaxerxes seemed anxious to get his formidable enemies out of his dominions. He accordingly furnished food and guides and the northward march began over a difficult country criss-crossed by irrigation ditches. The evil genius of the Greeks, however, was the old villain Tissaphernes. His conduct grew more and more suspicious. Fearing an ambuscade Clearchus, despite the protests of his more prudent officers, decided to "have it out" with the satrap and requested a parley. He persuaded twenty-two officers, including Proxenus, to accompany him. The hours passed and the anxiety of the Greeks grew apace. Finally, just before sundown, one lone officer, mortally wounded, staggered back with the sickening tale of treachery. From then on all pretense disappeared. The Greeks had to fight a series of rear-guard actions which, on a small scale, recall the retreat from Moscow, with this difference: the Greeks brought their force through substantially intact. Being unable to cross the rivers they were compelled to seek the headwaters. Savage mountain tribes, the Carduchi among others, hovered around and picked off the stragglers. A body of Rhodian slingers did heroic work beating off the raiders. Centuries later General Wolfe, shortly before his death on the Plains of Abraham, admitted that he had learned the art of Indian warfare from Xenophon's account of the guerilla tactics of the Carduchi. Through the snows of the Armenian mountains the retreat continued. The cold was intense. Xenophon tells of coming upon a party of Greeks who had discovered a hot spring and were warming themselves. When ordered to move on, the snow-blinded, frost-bitten wretches begged Xenophon to put them out of their misery. The incident affected him deeply.

Xenophon's part in the retreat, or Katabasis, began very modestly. In telling of one of the early councils of war he refers to himself as "a certain young man." As time went on his influence increased until he was chosen as leader. As the danger lessened, however, the "democratic" spirit of the Greeks reasserted itself and a number of "Commissars" were appointed to give Xenophon the benefit of their opinions. Being unable to appreciate the beauty of this primitive form of Bolshevism he resigned his command. Before doing so he had the satisfaction of fulfilling his mission. As the head of the column was scaling Mount Theches, Xenophon from his position in the rear heard a shout. Expecting another skirmish he urges his horse forward. The babel of voices becomes more distinct: Θάλαττα! θάλαττα! The sea! the sea! The entire force breaks into a run, even the pack animals. Officers and men, with tears in their eyes, embrace one another and erect a cairn to mark the spot.[3]

The country and the inhabitants became more hospitable as the Greeks skirted the Euxine. A curious adventure befell the wanderers in the Colchian villages. Coming upon a number of beehives the men proceeded to gorge themselves. The honey being made from the laurel rose common in Asia Minor intoxicated them. It took three days to recover in some cases. On the march to Cunaxa Xenophon had noted the aromatic wormwood, or apsinthion. Little did he know what that was capable of in the way of intoxication! On reaching Trapezus the Greeks, forgetting their fatigue, held another athletic festival in honor of Zeus and Heracles. Perhaps sports do form character after all! Over six thousand had come through the gruelling ordeal alive.

[3]The episode has furnished Heine with the theme of his poem *Meergruss.*

I shall omit the details of the homeward journey. With difficulty was the necessary shipping found to ferry the lost battalions to their various destinations. The danger over, discipline relaxed badly. Moreover the Greek cities did not extend to their fellow-countrymen the welcome they had a right to expect. The Euxine and the Troad had passed under barbarian rule and "generals" of the type we now associate with Latin America held ephemeral sway. From them offers of colonization were received. For a while Xenophon served with a Thracian adventurer, Seuthes, an unpleasant experience. In the meantime the cities of Ionia which, with the exception of Miletus, had sided with Cyrus were again in danger of Persian reprisals. Sparta was appealed to for help and Xenophon found himself once more in a corps of mercenaries. Service with the Spartans, however, proved remunerative, which was more than could be said for service with Persian pretenders. From now on the Spartan army was his home. Athens was only a memory. His old friend Socrates had been forced to drink the hemlock and the Academy was closed. "Corrupting the morals of youth" was one of the charges. In other words, Socrates would not surrender academic freedom to please the oligarchy that now ruled Athens. The Peloponnesian War had resulted in the usual loss of civil liberties. Having no desire to return to Athens under such conditions Xenophon accompanied the Spartan army home and served in the war against Athens and her ally Thebes. His native city thereupon exiled him but his adopted country voted him an estate near Scillus.

Xenophon's last years were spent writing the works that have immortalized his name. They brought him at least one satisfaction during his lifetime as well. His two sons were allowed to return to Athens to be educated. The elder, Gryllus, named for his grandfather in accordance with Athenian custom, served in the army and actually fought against the adopted country of his father. The Greeks were certainly liberal-minded in such matters. One day Xenophon, now an old man, was sacrificing when a runner was seen approaching. Removing the garland from his head he awaited the news. Gryllus had fallen at Mantinea, gallantly fighting to the end, the messenger thoughtfully added. Long residence in Sparta had given Xenophon the austerity of a Doric column. "I knew my boy was mortal," was the only comment he made as he replaced the garland and continued the sacrifice. He was soon to rejoin his first-born. His death occurred in 356 or thereabouts; his age around seventy-five.

If I have dwelt on one episode of Greek history it is because it furnishes an involuntary but pitiless exposure of the defects of the Greek people. The intellectual and artistic supremacy of Greece in antiquity needs no apologist. Its influence survives to this day. Why must such outstanding cultural achievements, such courage and endurance, be neutralized by shortcomings which, though obvious to the modern mind, seem to have escaped Xenophon, keen observer though he was? During his campaigns in Asia Minor Xenophon was frequently treading on ground that should have been Greek territory, yet it never occurred to him that the Ten Thousand, instead of fighting the battles of a Persian pretender, could have been employed in a far nobler cause, the redemption of the Greek cities of Ionia which had revolted from Athenian rule during the Peloponnesian War and as a result were once more under Persian domination. True, the Greeks were of heterogeneous stocks, but no more so than many other people who have forged their national unity. The suicidal wars between the states, the factional feuds within the cities, seemed perfectly natural to Xenophon. He himself fought against his native city and allowed his son to fight against his father's adopted country. Nor was his attitude an isolated case. Alcibiades, rather than meet the charges brought against him, deserted to Sparta and took up arms against Athens, then returning home after his vindication resumed his Athenian citizenship and, what to us is incomprehensible, was allowed so to do.

The lack of national spirit among the Greeks was probably due to the presence of several powerful cities in a small area, a situation that invariably retards national unity. If Italy remained asunder until our times it was largely due to a similar state of affairs. Xenophon had sensed the solution when he sang the praises of the autocratic government of Cyrus the Elder. A King in the modern acceptation of the word, some one who is more than a tribal chief, was needed before the Greek states could be welded into a nation. "There's such divinity doth hedge a King." When such a monarch at last appeared in Greece it was in Macedonia, a state not wholly Greek in origin or in customs. Under Alexander Greece attained an expansion that few nations, ancient or modern, have equalled but it was essentially a military one, hence transitory. Conquest never solidified into dominion. The monarchical principle he typified remained, however, as a permanent contribution to Mediterranean history. Eastward, not westward, the empire of Alexander spread. In so doing Greece forsook the Mediterranean. Alexander went so far as to disband his navy, except for a paltry twenty vessels chartered from Athens. We shall have to look elsewhere for the next power that was to mold human destinies in the Mediterranean.

CHAPTER III

Mare Nostrum

TRADERS are always at a disadvantage when they go to war. Their commerce makes them vulnerable. War entails a far greater disruption of normal activities for them than for a self-contained nation. Moreover, the lure of gain does not make for discipline. Military service is unpopular in trading nations, who would much prefer to equip a navy than to submit to conscription. Unfortunately mercenaries and militia are poor substitutes for regular national levies.

While Carthage was developing her commercial system the Italians were forging a state built on agriculture and manpower. The origin of the various people who were ultimately united under the hegemony of Rome is as intricate as that of the Greek people. What is more, the story has been obfuscated by the pseudo-historical works of Livy which, although delightful reading and the source of untold literary and artistic effort, may be dismissed practically *in toto* so far as historical accuracy is concerned. All of which, however, does not alter the fact that Livy has had a considerable influence on history, as the French Revolution with its somewhat childish aping of non-existing Roman qualities has illustrated.

Without venturing on the uncertain ground of legendary history this much is certain and important. With the exception of the Etruscans, who reached Italy around 800 B.C., the early inhabitants of Italy were essentially landsmen. Even the Etruscans abandoned seafaring after settling in the Italian peninsula.

We need not go into the details of the wars by which the Latins established their supremacy. For a while Rome was governed by Etruscan kings, the Tarquins Macaulay has sung. After their expulsion the Roman republic had to contend with another powerful foe, the Samnites, a tribe of mountaineers who inhabited the Apennines. Three wars did Rome wage against them. Peace was finally concluded in 290, the Samnites, in recognition of their bravery, being admitted to the status of allies.

These threats eliminated, another formidable enemy appeared. The Greek city of Tarentum, alarmed by the rapid advance of Rome southward, called upon Pyrrhus, King of Epirus, for aid. In 281 Pyrrhus landed with an army of 25,000 men and some elephants. An able soldier of fortune, bent on repeating the exploits of Alexander, to whom he was related, he might well have blocked Roman expansion had he received the whole-hearted support of the Greek cities of Magna Græcia. This was obviously more than any one could expect. He began by defeating the Roman army at Heraclea but at such cost as to give rise to the expression "Pyrrhic victory." "One more such victory and we are lost," was his famous comment. Two years later he scored one more such victory at Asculum, after which he decided to give the Roman army a wide berth, so crossed over to Sicily with the idea of driving out the Carthaginians. The Romans, however, came to the assistance of their future enemies. After three years of futile campaigning in Sicily Pyrrhus returned to Italy. The Greek cities, however, were heartily sick of him and his high-handed methods. A decisive defeat at Beneventum sent him back to Epirus in disgust, elephants and all, where he soon met a violent death. Before leaving Italy he made one prophetic remark: "What a battlefield I am leaving to Rome and Carthage!"

As can be seen, the first contacts between Rome and Carthage had been friendly. As far back as 509 a trade treaty had been entered into between the Etruscan kings and the Punic cities. Rome and Carthage, however, were proceeding on converging courses, not only geographically but economically. The strain upon the Roman farmers resulting from continual military service was more than even that hardy stock could stand. Roman agriculture declined. Corn had to be imported from overseas. No wonder the grain ships had a goose carved on their sterns. They too were saving the capitol.

The clash was brought about by Carthaginian designs on Sicily, an important source of food supply that Rome could no longer afford to see in hostile hands. In 264 a band of Campanian mercenaries who were garrisoning Messina for Hiero II of Syracuse mutinied and appealed to both Rome and Carthage for help. The Carthaginians arrived on the scene first, seized the city and then committed one of the greatest strategical blunders of history. They allowed Rome to land a force. The Roman commander soon found a pretext for arresting the Carthaginian admiral and compelling him to withdraw. As a result both Syracuse and Carthage declared war. Hiero soon tired of the struggle, however, leaving Rome and Carthage to fight out the epic endurance test Pyrrhus had foreseen. All attempts to oust the Romans from Messina failed. The initial blunder weighed heavily on all subsequent Carthaginian operations.

The first Punic War is an illustration of a fact that is often overlooked. A non-maritime people can, if they have the will to conquer, adapt themselves to naval warfare. It was not long before Rome realized that in order to defeat Carthage her communications with Africa must be interrupted. The ingenuity Rome displayed in creating a navy is instructive. Using a stranded Carthaginian quinquereme as a model the Roman shipbuilders performed the *tour de force* of building 130 replicas in the astonishingly brief period of sixty days! What was more, knowing that their foot soldiers were immeasurably superior to the mercenaries Carthage employed, the Romans equipped their vessels with a new device which in the first engagement worked one of the most complete surprises in the annals of naval warfare. The device consisted of a boarding bridge which revolved on the bow so as to permit grappling the enemy abreast as well as ahead. Old-time sailors shook their heads and predicted that if the *corvus*, as the new invention was called, missed the opposing ship its weight would capsize the Roman galley. But the landlubbers whom Caius Duilius commanded at Mylæ had not the slightest intention of missing their opponent and the Roman marines did the rest.

Of the six naval engagements fought during the first Punic War the Romans were unquestionably the victors in four. And yet during the twenty-four years of fighting required to conquer Sicily the Roman losses afloat reached the ghastly total of 700 vessels. The reason? The Romans were indifferent sailors. The Roman generals continually overruled the advice given by seamen. Their approach to the subject had that contempt for seamanship that characterized Napoleon. As a result storms took a larger toll from them than did the enemy. In one storm alone they lost 284 ships, yet such was the obstinate perseverance of the Roman people that all losses were promptly replaced. One fleet of 200 vessels was paid for by popular subscription. Cost what it may, Rome was going to "see it through."

It was not long before Rome had isolated the Carthaginian army in Sicily, was expelling the Carthaginian garrison from Corsica and landing troops on African soil. Although the expedition to Carthage, after an easy victory over the local militia, came to grief thanks to a Greek general, Xanthippus, and his well trained cavalry and better trained elephants, by 241 Carthage was ready for peace. The price was nothing less than the relinquishment of all claims to Sicily besides a huge war indemnity. The most important event of the period, however, passed unnoticed. While Hamilcar Barca was harassing the Roman armies in Sicily from his impregnable fortress on Mount Erecte a son was born to him whom he named Hannibal.

The widely scattered empire of Carthage now began to reveal its inherent weakness. Defeats affected the loyalty of the colonies. Sardinia revolted in 239 and the mercenaries threw themselves into the arms of Rome, whose armies occupied the island. Hamilcar was in no position to retaliate, so bided his time and made one of the most astonishing adaptations of history. Sea power had failed him so he switched to land power. The last years of his life—he died in 228—were spent organizing the armies his son was to use with such telling effect and consolidating Carthaginian rule in Spain. Hannibal continued the task and in 219 captured the Greek city of Saguntum which, like many other Greek cities of the Mediterranean, had passed into the Roman sphere of influence. The second Punic War ensued.

The spectacular invasion of Italy via Gaul is the converse of the naval campaigns of the first Punic War. If a military people can take to the sea, by the same token a seafaring people can resort to military action. Thanks to his father's careful preparation Hannibal was able to forestall Rome. The initiative, instead of lying with the power in command of the sea, had passed to the power in a position to start promptly on land operations. The choice of the theatre of war was a clever one, as the Gallic tribes to the north of the Roman dominions could be counted on for co-operation. Again the military mind hoped to win by a "Blitzkrieg." Hannibal was willing to lose 14,000 men in the Pyrenees and 26,000 more in the Alps if thereby he could give Publius Cornelius Scipio the slip and arrive suddenly in Cisalpine Gaul. Others have reasoned in the same way and succeeded. Hannibal failed. Why? Because Roman morale remained unimpaired in spite of such crushing defeats as Lake Trasimenus and Cannæ. The cautious tactics inaugurated by Fabius "Cunctator" kept the Roman forces intact. Hannibal could survey the defenses of Rome but they were too stoutly held to be stormed. Cut off from any base he soon found himself roaming about Italy trying to stir up revolt.

The force Hannibal had succeeded in bringing across the Alps, some 26,000 men, was obviously too small to defeat Rome, now that surprise had failed, unless he could secure the assistance of some disgruntled ally. Hannibal was aiming at nothing less than the disruption of the Roman confederation which at that time was far from presenting the solid front it afterwards assumed. Capua seems to have been the only place to have responded, so thither he went, an unfortunate move if we are to believe the tales of his army succumbing to the "delights of Capua." Slowly but surely he was being driven into the lower end of the peninsula.

A revolt in Syracuse for a while promised to turn the tide in favor of Carthage but when Syracuse fell in 212 that hope vanished. For three years the city held out, thanks to the genius of Archimedes, a scientist who devoted his spare time to military engineering. He had constructed some remarkable artillery, both long range and rapid-fire, that kept the Roman fleet at bay. When the Roman army at last broke into the city they found the absent-minded mathematician working out some abstract geometrical problem. His angry rebuke to the soldier who disturbed the figures he had traced on the sand: "Noli tangere circulos meos!" cost him his life. Archimedes is best remembered, however, by an anecdote, probably apocryphal, as to how he perfected his method for detecting the presence of alloys in precious metals, a subject that had been troubling King Hiero. The increased bulk produced by the addition of baser metals caused a greater displacement of water for the same weight. This discovery he made while in a bath, whereupon he became so excited that he ran home, without stopping to dress, shouting *Eureka!* "I have found it!"

But to return to the Carthaginians. In 209 Carthagena, the

principal Punic city of Spain, was captured by a young general, Scipio, soon to be surnamed "Africanus." Nevertheless Hannibal's brother Hasdrubal invaded Italy with a second army in 207 but the Romans, by a skillful use of their interior lines, prevented a junction of the two forces. In 202 Scipio was given command of an expedition against Carthage. Reluctantly Hannibal was forced to give up his Italian plans. The defense of the capital required his presence in Africa. The battle of Zama settled the war.

The terms imposed on Carthage again were severe. She lost all her African possessions, including the wheat-growing region around Tunis, and paid a heavy indemnity. The terms included a provision against the use of elephants, those early tanks, in warfare; probably the first instance of "outlawing" a weapon the victor had difficulty in combating. The peace treaty came very near to being rejected by the Carthaginian senate. Young Hasdrubal led the opposition, who objected to Rome stigmatizing Carthage as the "aggressor." So the "Schuldlüge" is as old as that! If the treaty was approved in the Roman senate, many of whose members were afraid of a Carthaginian comeback and wanted even stiffer terms, it was due to the insistence of Scipio. Like most great soldiers he had a secret admiration for his able opponent and, leaving hatred to politicians and plebeians, forced a ratification of the armistice terms he had concluded. Unfortunately for Carthage, Cato, who was both a politician and a plebeian, visited the Punic capital on a mission some years after Zama. To his horror he found that Phœnician trade was once more thriving. The third Punic War we can dismiss summarily. It was merely an exhibition of spite inspired by the tirades of Cato. "Delenda est Carthago!" Carthage, already defeated, was now destroyed.

Why did Carthage fall in spite of the ability of her generals and her admirals? Apologists of the "blue water" school of naval strategy attribute the result entirely to the loss of the so-

called command of the sea. As a matter of fact the war between
Rome and Carthage was not really one between sea power and
land power. Both contestants at one time or another held the
advantage on one or the other element. The struggle was one
between a warlike people, whose strength was based on discipline, and a commercial people, whose strength was based on
the wealth they derived from trade. In the last analysis, between
belligerents at all evenly matched, victory is largely a question
of the will to win.

Few periods of history are so completely dominated by the
personality of one man as are the Punic Wars by Hannibal.
What interests us as much as his campaigns is his character.
Dread him, hate him, as they did, his Roman contemporaries
have not succeeded in blackening his name. Among the Greeks
he had many admirers, thanks to whom we have pretty good
evidence. His alleged cruelty, on analysis, proves to have been
no greater than the prevailing customs of his time. His so-
called greed was merely the financial acumen inherited from his
Semitic ancestors. He was a man of temperate habits who never
drank more than one pint of wine at a time. His attitude toward
women surprised friend and foe alike. Robert E. Sherwood's
delightful hit, *The Road to Rome*, is not wholly fanciful.
There is something intensely modern about his career. He was
an early example of the brilliant commander required to make
out as best he could with irregular troops, foreign mercenaries and weird auxiliaries of every hue, grudgingly allotted
to him by selfish financiers who desired the fruits of victory but
wanted others to do the fighting. After a lifetime spent battling
for his country Hannibal, like many another soldier of a lost
cause, took the thorny road of exile that leads to service in a
foreign army. But his relentless enemies were on his track and
demanded of King Prusias of Bithynia the surrender of his
drillmaster. Prusias "straddled" the issue by closing his eyes
while the Romans prepared to seize Hannibal at Lybissa. When

his servant warned him that a strange body of armed men was approaching he quietly swallowed the draught he habitually kept ready. "This will save the Romans the worry of waiting for the death of an old and hated man," he exclaimed. He was sixty-five when he unlocked the door that admitted him to immortality.

The Mediterranean became *Mare Nostrum* after the elimination of Carthage. The only challenge Roman naval supremacy was to meet came from an unexpected quarter. The civil war between Octavian and Marc Antony that followed the murder of Julius Cæsar was decided on September 2, b.c. 31, at the Battle of Actium, the first of several battles fought in that strategic area where the Gulf of Corinth and the Adriatic join the Ionian Sea. Antony had enlisted the support of the Greek ruler of Egypt, Cleopatra, one of the most misrepresented characters of history. Leaving aside her morals, which were probably no better nor worse than those of many of her subjects, Cleopatra must be given credit for considerable political wisdom. Her alliance with Antony would, if victorious, have shifted the axis of Roman power to Alexandria centuries before it was shifted to Constantinople.

The threat to Rome was a serious one, as Egypt was in a position to furnish a fleet, thanks to the engineers at the court of the Ptolemies, besides ample funds and supplies. The Egyptian fleet numbered approximately 300 vessels, over half of which were battleships equipped with high turrets and powerful catapults. Their very size was their undoing, moreover they were undermanned. The Roman vessels, some 250 in number commanded by Agrippa, were lighter, hence faster and handier. Their tactics were to crash through the banks of oars, thus crippling their unwieldy opponents, and then use the ram, being careful to avoid being grappled and boarded. To the credit of Cleopatra it should be said that she showed both courage and wit during the engagement, in which she took part with seventy galleys, probably the only case in history of a woman commanding a fleet in action. Seeing that the heavy Egyptian ships could not gain enough momentum to damage the Roman galleys, she hoisted sail and charged under full canvas. The move, although a clever one, did not seriously injure the enemy who were able to maneuver and avoid the charge. After breaking through her force was to leeward and could not be brought into line again. Cleopatra thereupon withdrew, closely followed by Antony. The extent of the Roman victory was purposely exaggerated by Octavian, although the losses among the Egyptian fleet had been considerable. What was more important than the material losses was the loss of prestige. The failure of Antony's plans affected the loyalty of his generals, who had watched the battle from the shore. They hastened to make peace with the victors, leaving the lovers to their tragic fate.

After Actium the Roman navy was reduced to a mere police force for want of opponents, in which respect the Romans followed the example of Alexander. Rome became once more an essentially military power. *Mare Nostrum* was no longer an issue.

CHAPTER IV

The First Invaders

THE URGE to "spend the winter on the Riviera" is really a very old one. It is surprising how in the very dawn of history intruders are found hovering around seeking an opportunity to settle in the sunlit lands of the Mediterranean. In this connection it is well to remember that it is a misnomer to speak of "Mediterranean races." The Mediterranean race is one of the three great families of men who have peopled Europe, the other two being the Nordic and the Alpine. That they were the most venturesome of the three is proven by the fact that in prehistoric times they overran such distant countries as Ireland. In speaking of the men who lived around the Mediterranean I shall therefore adhere to the word "people" to avoid a misuse of the word "race."

The earliest authentic case of a northern invasion seems to have been the Cimmerian, of which the destruction of Sardis was an episode. Homer has given us a fantastic description of Cimmeria which suggests the Arctic regions, a land where the sun never pierces the mists, where darkness is perpetual.[1] This

[1] ἔνθα δὲ Κιμμερίων ἀνδρῶν δῆμός τε πόλις τε,
ἠέρι καὶ νεφέλῃ κεκαλυμμένοι· οὐδέ ποτ᾽ αὐτοὺς
Ἠέλιος φαέθων καταδέρκεται ἀκτίνεσσιν,
οὔθ᾽ ὁπότ᾽ ἂν στείχῃσι πρὸς οὐρανὸν ἀστερόεντα,
οὔθ᾽ ὅτ᾽ ἂν ἂψ ἐπὶ γαῖαν ἀπ᾽ οὐρανόθεν προτράπηται,
ἀλλ᾽ ἐπὶ νὺξ ὀλοὴ τέταται δειλοῖσι βροτοῖσι.
—*Odyssey*, XI, 14–19

Pope's translation of this passage is as follows:

There, in a lonely land, and gloomy cells,
The dusky nation of Cimmeria dwells;
The sun ne'er views th' uncomfortable seats,
When radiant he advances, or retreats;
Unhappy race! whom endless night invades,
Clouds the dull air, and wraps them round in shades.

land has been identified by some as the Jutland peninsula but
this identification rests on no more solid ground than a similarity of names, Jutland being the home of the Cymbrii. Herodotus gives us more authoritative data and assigns southern Russia as the Cimmerian habitat, a location that is borne out by the
name Crimea. From his account the Cimmerians were undoubtedly a Tartar tribe related to the Scythians. During the seventh
century these savages crossed the Hellespont and for one hundred years ravaged Asia Minor. The Persians finally drove
them out with the help of the Scythians.

For a while the Euxine and the Mediterranean were free
from invasions of this nature but the Greeks had the Persians
to contend with. History has been rather unfair to the Persians.
The Greeks have branded them for all time as barbarians. As
a matter of fact the Persians were an old and highly civilized
people and should not be confused with the wild auxiliaries they
drafted for their wars with the Greeks. Persian civilization was
of course inferior to Greek, especially in spiritual matters, but
had the Mediterranean come under Persian influence it would
not necessarily have reverted to barbarism. When relegated to
their own country the Persians continued to develop an art and
culture of their own. Politically, they could teach the Greeks.

The next invaders were the Gauls, whose sacking of Rome
has given rise to considerable legendary history. The Roman
Senate dying to a man at their posts without any loss of sena-
torial dignity, Brennus casting his sword in the scales as he
uttered the famous "Væ Victis," gallant young Camillus finally
driving off the barbarians. What a pity that not one word of
Livy's story will bear analysis, outside of the bare fact that in
the year 390 some Gallic tribe did pillage Rome. In 279 another Gallic tribe known as the Galatians invaded Thrace,
twenty thousand strong, then made an unsuccessful attack on
Delphi and were defeated at Thermopylæ. The next year they
appeared before Byzantium. Fortunately about that time they

received an invitation from the King of Bithynia to assist him in his wars, so passed over into Asia Minor where they again proved troublesome neighbors by settling athwart the trade route from Mesopotamia to the Ionian cities. Augustus finally incorporated them into the Empire (64 B.C.) to which regime they remained loyal. It was to the descendants of these raiders that Saint Paul addressed his inspired Epistle, thereby bestowing on them an odor of sanctity with which secular history would never have honored them.

The northern wastes, however, still held plenty of sun-hungry hordes who were casting covetous eyes on the lands whose temperate climate and natural resources promised an easier mode of life. More than three hundred years before the Christian Era a Greek by the name of Pytheas started from Marseilles, then a Greek colony, on a voyage of exploration that entitles him to be considered the Marco Polo of antiquity. Equipping at his own expense an expedition, he boldly sailed through the Pillars of Hercules and entered the dreaded Ocean. After touching at Cadiz, he skirted the coasts of Spain and France and crossed over to Britain. Here he indulged in an extended walking tour, the first of its kind on record. His observations are interesting. He noted the tin mines on the islands off Cornwall. The British fondness for ale surprised him. A large island said to lie to the north aroused his curiosity although he was unable to reach it. He gave it the name of Thule. As he mentions a twenty-four-hour solstice it may have been Iceland[2] but it is more likely to have been Mainland, one of the Shetland group. So far Pytheas has been most truthful. When he comes to describing the arctic regions, or "the sleeping place of the sun" as he picturesquely calls them, he falls into the fancifying that has since befallen some other arctic explorers. According to Pytheas, earth, air and water are all blended in

[2]Of course Iceland not being within the Arctic Circle the solstice is never quite twenty-four hours.

the Arctic into a gelatinous mass resembling a jelly fish; an amusing idea but not one we should expect from a scientist who had correctly analyzed the causes of tides and made astonishingly accurate observations of latitude. It is more than likely that he penetrated into the Baltic. One thing is certain. He came into contact with the Goths, or Guttones, in Scandinavia and noted the amber these people gathered along the coast. On his return home he published an account of his travels which unfortunately has come down to us only through transcriptions. Little did his readers suspect that the Guttones were one day to play an important part in Mediterranean affairs.

It was not until about 180 A.D., that the Goths began to move southward. By the beginning of the third century they had progressed as far as the Black Sea. Constantine defeated them in 336. Shortly thereafter (c. 370) they split up into two distinct branches, the eastern or Ostrogoths and the western or Visigoths. The Ostrogoths remained north of the Danube and so fell under the sway of the Huns until they regained their independence under their great king Theodoric. It was the Visigoths who took the warpath under Alaric and sacked Rome in 410. Continuing south, Alaric suddenly died and another beautiful legend took root. The river Busento was turned from its course by some of his followers who, after burying their leader in the river bed, elected to follow him to Walhalla. The facts are less romantic. The captives who had dug the King's grave were murdered. Dead men tell no tales. Alaric's grave has not yet been found.[3]

The Visigoths had by this time compelled Rome to admit them to the status of allies. As such they helped repel the Huns, among whom they found their cousins the Ostrogoths. The Visigoths then overran southern France (419), where they founded the Kingdom of Toulouse, and Spain. A severe defeat

[3]The episode has furnished the theme of a poem by Platen, *Das Grab im Busento*.

at the hands of Clovis at Poitiers in 507 cost them the greater part of their French possessions. They did manage nevertheless to maintain themselves in southwestern France, thanks to a timely diversion by the Ostrogoths under Theodoric. In the old *Cité* of Carcasonne you can see the mighty fortress they built. It was not until 724 that the Saracens drove them from France. The kingdom they founded in Spain was, as we know, the back-bone of Christian resistance.

The rough edges were gradually being worn off the Goths by constant contact with Roman civilization. Theodoric spent ten years of his early youth in Constantinople as a hostage and had been carefully educated. Under his rule the two branches of the Goths were reunited and the high-water mark of Gothic power reached. The Visigothic domains in France and Spain were added to the territory Theodoric already held in northern Italy and Ravenna became the capital of a Gothic kingdom (493). Under Totila the Gothic surge swept over all Italy and in 548 actually touched Sicily. By that time, however, the Goths had become badly over-extended and as a result were unable to withstand the attacks launched against them by the Eastern Emperors.

Strangely enough, the fraction of the Gothic people to re-tain their distinctive traits the longest was a small colony of Ostrogoths who had settled in the Crimea. In 1562 a traveller from the Low Countries met two of their ambassadors in Con-stantinople and made interesting investigations concerning their language. In 1750 a Jesuit priest from Vienna ransomed a Gothic galley slave from that settlement. The good church-man was considerably pained to find that his protégé was still worshipping trees! Gothic Christianity, like that of all the Ger-manic tribes, was only skin-deep and tainted with Arian heresy. It is therefore not surprising to learn that Gothic architecture, an essentially ecclesiastical form of the art, had nothing to do with the Goths. It is merely evidence of the fact that their importance in the empire had been such that anything non-Roman came to be known as Gothic.

The invasions of the Vandals, another Germanic tribe, coincided with that of the Goths and frequently did the two clash. The Vandal surge soon resolved itself into an attempt to conquer Spain. It took the Vandals only thirty years to cover the distance between the Oder and the western Mediterranean, a journey of about one thousand miles. The name Andalusia perpetuates the memory of their occupation. About 429 Genseric received an invitation from Bonifacius, the Roman governor of Africa, to settle in his province and assist him in his none too loyal plans. The proposition appealed to Genseric who was making heavy weather in his struggle with the Goths who had plans of their own concerning Spain. Eighty thousand men, women and children were accordingly ferried from Julia Transducta, the modern Tarifa, to Tangiers. The guests, as might have been expected, soon set themselves up as masters. Within a year all but three cities, Carthage, Hippo (the present Bone) and Cirta (the present Constantine) were in their power. Hippo, of course, was the see of Saint Augustine, who died there during the Vandal siege. In 435 the emperor Valentinian III confirmed the Vandal occupation, reserving to Rome only the city of Carthage. Four years later that last stronghold was seized without declaration of war.

The Vandal reign in Africa lasted nearly one hundred years, during which time it is hard to find one creditable action to set to its credit. Genseric began by putting piracy on a paying basis, thereby forestalling the Sacacens by several hundred years. His outstanding performance, however, was the systematic looting of Rome in 455. Eudoxia, the widow of Valentinian, was rash enough to call on Genseric for help to regain the throne of her husband. Genseric responded and landed near Rome. He met with no resistance as the army was away on a futile campaign against the Goths. A few years before, Attila, King of the Huns, had passed that way while on one of his forays, on which occasion Pope Leo I had dissuaded him from sacking Rome. He was now called upon to try his eloquence once more. Attired in his pontifical robes the Pope awaited Genseric before the dilapidated city walls. Genseric, though himself an Arian, dismounted and listened courteously. All he would agree to was to respect the churches, a precedent few conquerors, heretic or orthodox, have followed. The city itself was parcelled out among the army who, while strictly respecting the inhabitants, proceeded to remove everything moveable and some things not usually considered so, such as mosaics and Eudoxia herself. With a thoroughness that would have done credit to any modern archæologist, the loot was packed, boxed, crated, labeled and catalogued. Then the creaking oxcarts wended their way to the waiting fleet. When after two weeks the army of ants departed Rome looked like a skeleton. Among the spoils were the famous seven-branched candlesticks Titus had brought back from Jerusalem. It was not the last time that Rome was to see her treasures removed, as any visitor to the Louvre may have noticed. The term "Vandalism," however, owes its origin to another bit of thoroughness, the persecution of the Catholic Christians. Justinian finally came to the rescue of his co-reli- ·gionaries in 533 when he sent Belisarius to rid Africa of these barbarians.

The only province of Italy today to re-echo the name of its northern conquerors is Lombardy. The Lombards first came into contact with the Romans in the year 5 A.D., when Tiberius invaded their habitat in the lower basin of the Elbe. Their early history is shrouded in some uncertainty and seems to have consisted mainly in desultory warfare with other Germanic tribes. *Chi va piano, va sano*, apparently was their motto. In any event they were careful not to cross swords with such formidable opponents as the Romans until Roman military power had been broken by the struggle with the Goths. In 569 the Lombard king Alboin formed a coalition with some Saxon tribes and descended into the great plain at the head of the Adriatic and extended their dominions to include the duchies of Spoleto and Benevento. It was not a change for the better when Belisarius drove the last remnants of the Goths across the Alps, where they lost their identity among the Asiatic tribes who were raiding Europe. The Goths, had they been assimilated instead of expelled, would have strengthened the Italian stock. Not so the Lombards who took their place. No more cordially detested people ever invaded the lovely land of Italy.[4] They remained impervious to civilization and were in constant conflict with the Papacy. Several attempts were made to rid the country of their unwelcome presence. As far back as 568 the Merovingian King Childebert II had been urged by the Pope and the Emperor to prevent the Lombard occupation from becoming permanent but after six years of fighting Childebert was compelled to admit defeat. In 753 Pope Stephen II induced Pepin "the Short" to make another attempt. This time the Franks met with some success but it remained for Pepin's son Charlemagne to do things in a big way by combining a domestic quarrel (his divorced wife Desiderata being the daughter of Desiderius, King of the Lombards) with a desire to pose as the Defender of the Faith. Responding to the call of Adrian I, Charlemagne put an end to the Lombard rule. In so doing he paved the way for a new chapter in history, the Holy Roman Empire, an institution that was to last in one form or another until the 512th page of Mr. James Bryce's book. The Lombard rule had been the longest of any of the tribes who had crossed the Alps into Italy, over two hundred years. The name "Lombard Street" is of course a misnomer. It was the Florentines who spread Italian banking throughout Europe.

[4]The hatred of the Italians for their Lombard conquerors is set forth in the colorful opera of Montemezzi, *L'Amore dei Tre Re*, on the play by Sem Benelli.

With the advent of the Franks the Exarchate of Ravenna became another of the memories that charm the wanderer through the byways of Mediterranean waters. For nigh on two hundred years after its capture by Belisarius in 540 Ravenna had been the seat of the governors sent out by the Eastern Empire. Then it fell to the Lombards. Pepin soon rescued it and presented it to the Pope (754). It is the pomp of the East, however, that Ravenna reflects, not on the grandiloquent scale of Byzantium, to be sure, but with all the fidelity of a miniature, all the clarity of a cameo. San Vitale is aglow with mosaics in which Justinian and Theodora, nobles and ladies in waiting, eunuchs and warriors, still gaze on us through an indefinable atmosphere derived from contact with eastern modes of life. The vague nostalgia inseparable from all attempts at reproducing a distant homeland permeates Ravenna. Nature seems to have conspired with man to intensify the sadness that rests heavily on the once opulent city by transforming it into a Herculaneum of Gothic and Byzantine art. The lagoons have long since yielded to the outpourings of the rivers. Ravenna is dead. No wonder Dante chose Ravenna as an asylum in which to dream his sombre visions of life beyond the tomb. The migrations of works of art often speak volumes of history. Among the monuments of a vanished past to find a new abode after Ravenna became a Papal city were the statues of the Twelve Apostles that stood guard over the mausoleum of Theodoric the Great, a massive circular tomb that suggests a monolith carried hundreds of miles by some glacial drift which has long since receded. As Theodoric had been an Arian he was not entitled to so sumptuous a sepulchre. Besides, thought Charlemagne, the statues would look better in his new palace at Aachen. Obviously, the region needed purification, so the Pope removed the body of the Gothic Cæsar and consecrated a non-heretical sanctuary in the famous rotunda. His body was discovered by workmen excavating in the neighborhood of the church some eighty years ago. Before it could be rescued it had been stripped of its gorgeous golden armor. Only a few pieces were recovered.

As can be seen, we have come a long way from the days when the Mediterranean was *Mare Nostrum*. A steady process of disintegration has seriously impaired the prestige of Imperial Rome. In this the Roman conquests had been a two-edged sword. They had shown the barbarians the road to Rome, much as modern nations are doing today with their African and Asiatic allies. If only the mistakes of history, once made, would serve as a warning instead of a model! If the original Mediterranean culture is to survive some more vigorous champion than Rome must be found.

CHAPTER V

The Golden Horn

OST PRESENT-DAY travellers approaching Istanbul from the Sea of Marmora confess to a feeling of disappointment. In many respects the first glimpse of the city suggests San Francisco: hills covered with small wooden houses resembling those that survived "the fire" interspersed with commonplace apartment houses. All disillusion, fortunately, is soon dispelled by the distinctive feature of the skyline, the countless minarets guarding like lofty sentinels the domes of the mosques. The "golden" quality we had been led to expect, however, is conspicuous by its absence. Numerous river steamboats are belching forth black smoke as they nose against the Galata bridge awaiting a load of passengers in which commuters predominate. Beyond the bridge a narrowing stretch of muddy water, on which the most prominent objects are the rusty remains of the Turkish navy, extends to Eyoub, the dreamy burial ground and sanctuary dear to Pierre Loti. Let us not indulge in idle regrets because we expected Byzantium or Constantinople and have found Istanbul but rather ponder over these three names, which should be proof enough that we are entering the most historic harbor in the world.

Byzantium was a Doric colony. In 657 B.C., an expedition from Argos and Megara commanded by a navigator called Byzas founded a city at the entrance of the Bosphorus in obedience to the Delphic oracle who told them to settle opposite "the land of the blind." This typically sibyllic message embodied an uncanny strategic sense. The first settlers had been so blind as to the importance of the site of Byzantium that they overlooked it in favor of an inferior location on the Asiatic shore, the roadstead of Chalcedon, the modern Scutari. In fact strategy seems to have played a surprisingly negligible part in the location of primitive cities and for many years Byzantium was of far less importance than the other Greek colonies of the Euxine and Asia Minor that did not begin to have its possibilities as a citadel.

The independence of Byzantium was short-lived. It was one of the first of the Greek cities to fall to the Persians and soon thereafter suffered severely as a result of its participation in the Ionian revolt. Pausanias, the victor of Platea, restored the city and the eloquence of Xenophon saved it from a visitation by the Ten Thousand. By 340 Byzantium had become powerful enough to withstand, with the help of Athens, a two-year siege by Philip of Macedon, and during the reign of Alexander a certain amount of autonomy was retained.

Byzantium next came under Roman influence and sided with the Empire in the wars against Philip III. In 196 A.D., Septimus Severus deprived the city of its privileges and dismantled the fortifications as a punishment for having espoused the cause of his rival, Pescennius Niger. In 269 Byzantium received a visit from the Crimean Goths and, being defenseless, was unable to prevent the Gothic vessels from entering the Mediterranean. Claudius Gothicus is entitled to the credit of being the first ruler to sense the strategic importance of the Bosphorus. He decided to make Byzantium a bulwark of Roman power. The dawn of a glorious era was at hand. For some time past the Roman emperors, who were succeeding one another with bewildering frequency, had been losing contact with the Roman people and had shown signs of preferring other residences in their vast domains. The decisive step which resulted in the transfer of the imperial government to Byzantium was the work of one of the most remarkable characters in history, remarkable not so much for any inherent qualities as for the influence his decisions were to have on posterity.

Constantine I, known as the Great, was born at Naissus, the present Serbian town of Nish, probably in 288. His father Constantius seems to have been the typical Roman governor who, thanks to the devotion of his troops, had managed to assume regal powers. His mother was an innkeeper, Flavia Helena, better known to the Christian world as Saint Helena, a dignity she earned by her efforts in converting her illustrious son. Constantine, therefore, owed his existence to a banal intrigue in a little garrison town, not a very auspicious start for a career. During his youth he accompanied Diocletian and Galerius on their travels and campaigns, more or less as a hostage for the good behavior of his father. He finally contrived to escape from his quasi-captivity by suddenly commandeering all the post horses in the neighborhood, a resourceful stratagem that rendered pursuit impossible. Crossing Europe at breakneck speed he joined his father at Boulogne just as he was about to sail over to Britain to repel an invasion of the Picts and Scots. Shortly thereafter (306 A.D.) his father died at York and the army proclaimed Constantine his successor. Now begins one of the most extraordinary filibustering expeditions of history. Constantine decided to wrest the imperial crown from his less forceful rivals and within six years he made himself master of the eastern and western empires. Legend ascribes his success to the fact that before attacking Rome he persuaded his troops that he had beheld at high noon a flaming cross in the sky emblazoned with the words: Ἐν τούτῳ νίκα![1] The conversion to Christianity that followed this apparition was probably responsible for his seeking a residence less impregnated with paganism

[1]"By means of this ye shall conquer!" The Greek preposition ἐν is frequently mistranslated to mean "in"; a mistake that accounts for the arguments as to how John the Baptist administered the sacrament of baptism.

than Rome. Again relying on a vision he chose Byzantium and on May 11, 330, was duly inaugurated in his new capital which he dedicated to the Virgin Mary and named New Rome.

The empire he founded was destined to last until 1453 and to number no less than seventy-four emperors. Into this labyrinth we shall prudently refrain from entering any more than necessary. The story, if told, would be only a monotonous repetition of palace conspiracies in which profligacy, treason and cruelty play all too prominent a part. Even Constantine's reign was sullied by the execution of his son Crispus on charges brought by his stepmother Fausta. The belated discovery that these charges were unfounded led Constantine to condemn his wife to a similar fate. Let us rather remember the artistic and intellectual splendor that was Byzantium, the defender of the priceless heritage of Greek and Roman culture.

Roman imperialism possessed one characteristic that goes a long way toward atoning for the subjection it imposed. The desire to preserve the values of the conquered people is ever-present. A certain respect for Greek civilization was part and parcel of the Roman system of administration. The Greek language was always considered as having equal rights with Latin in the Eastern Empire. The reward for such fairness was the dazzling blending of the two cultures that was Byzantium. The early history of Constantinople, as Byzantium was called after the death of Constantine, is unfortunately one long struggle to regain the former boundaries of the Western Empire, to oust the invaders who had encroached on Rome, rather than to resist the incipient attacks that were threatening the Eastern Empire itself. This failure to discern accurately which of several menaces was the most serious in the long run was quite as disastrous as the violence that characterized the internal politics of the realm.

The high-water mark of Byzantine power was attained during the reign of Justinian. A glance at the map at the time of

his death in 565 will show that the Eastern Empire had temporarily regained all of Italy, Sicily, Corsica, Sardinia, Illyria,
Greece, Thrace, the southern coast of Spain, the Balearic Isles,
all the northern coast of Africa, Egypt and Asia Minor to the
boundaries of Persia. This extraordinary "come-back" was
largely the work of one man, Belisarius, one of the greatest soldiers of antiquity. If we are to believe a legend Belisarius' suc-
cesses aroused the distrust of the Emperor. The famous general,
blinded and penniless, begging in the streets of Constantinople,
has been a favorite subject for artists and poets. That he may
have aimed at founding a kingdom of his own on the ruins of
the kingdoms he had uprooted is more than likely. Thanks to
his ability the Vandal power had been completely destroyed
in Africa, the Goths driven out of Sicily, Naples and Rome and
their King Vitiges taken prisoner at Ravenna. As might be expected, these results had not been accomplished without seriously weakening Roman military strength. In spite of his victories, Justinian's reign was a failure in that it left both the
Western and the Eastern Empires in such a state of prostration
as to render the tasks of invaders easy.

In the meantime events in the Balkan peninsula were assuming a distinctly modern tinge. The problems of present-day
Europe are much older than is generally assumed. We shall
omit the Huns and the Avars, as these tribes were mainly bent
on pillaging; such settlements as they made were not along
the Mediterranean. The latest batch of invaders did not come
from the north but from the northeast. The Slavs soon disclosed
an intention of establishing themselves by the sea. Slavic historians have denied that the Slavs were an Asiatic people. As
their immigration into Europe took place fifteen hundred years
before the Christian Era we may concede that point. Their first
attempts at migrating were not very successful. They succumbed
to the Goths wherever they came in contact with them, so much
so that the name Slav came to be synonymous with slave. As a

result of this inferiority the Slavs advanced cautiously behind the Teutonic invaders. A primitive people of a decidedly backward mentality, but tricky like most savages. Early chroniclers assure us that they were able to lie concealed for hours in lakes and rivers breathing through a reed extending to the surface. At the opportune moment the waters suddenly became alive with a dripping but doughty swarm of warriors ready to attack. In 581 A.D., the Slavs invaded Thrace and pushed their incursion into the Peloponnesus, exterminating the rural population as they progressed. Their descendants, as we know, still inhabit portions of the Balkan peninsula, which they thus thoroughly prepared for colonization.

The next invaders are also "headliners." The Bulgars were a Turanian people akin to the Tartars. The fact that they gradually adopted the Slavic language has caused them to be classed as Slavs, incorrectly so as their inability to live in peace with the Slavs has repeatedly proven. Their original habitat was the region between the Volga and the Ural Mountains. In 679 they invaded the province of Mœsia, the corner adjoining the Euxine south of the Danube, and absorbed its Slavic population. Shortly thereafter they advanced to the gates of Constantinople and secured the confirmation of their conquests. Greeks, Slavs, Bulgars, the elements of a Balkan war are steadily gathering. When we consider the historic intricacy of the problem that confronted the mapmakers, we can hardly call them the peacemakers, at Versailles it is a wonder that they did not make more of a mess than they did. We still need a fourth to start the game but the Turk is not far off and is longing to take a hand.

The casual student is astonished at the number of people whose origin is attributed to Asia and amazed by the fact that one and all usually deny any Asiatic affiliation. Apparently no nation in Europe wants to be beholden to Asia, an antipathy that today is in a fair way of becoming mutual. Without entering into any discussion as to whether the Turks were of Mongolian extraction, this much is certain. By the sixth century they had established themselves in the region around the Caspian Sea and by the latter part of the eleventh century they had occupied the greater part of Asia Minor and come into contact with the Arabs, whose religion they adopted and whose nominal rulers they eventually became.

While the Turks were steadily progressing toward their ultimate goal, Constantinople, matters were going from bad to worse in that city. Shortly before the Fourth Crusade a series of brutal palace revolutions had taken place. One of the evicted parties appealed to the French crusaders, promising an amalgamation of the Eastern and Roman churches in return for aid in capturing the city. The Crusaders thereupon stormed the walls. In vain did Innocent III remind his faithful of their duty to rescue the Holy Land from the Infidel, the prize was too rich to let go. The Latin Empire thus founded by Baldwin, a descendant of Charlemagne, lasted from 1204 to 1261 when Michael VIII Paleologue re-established the Greek Empire.

For nearly two hundred years the Paleologue-Cantacuzene dynasty strove to maintain themselves against the growing power of the Turks. Obviously, the only way this could be accomplished was by enlisting the support of the Western Church. So John VII Paleologue made the journey to Florence and agreed to a reconciliation of the two churches. There is a legend to the effect that he rode his charger into the Duomo that Brunelleschi had just completed. A proud, handsome prince he must have been, judging from the frescoes of Benozzo Gozzoli in the Riccardi palace. He is portrayed as one of the three Magi Kings whose cavalcade, resplendent in jewels and golden trappings, is wending its way through a delightfully medieval Tuscan countryside bearing gifts to be placed in the Manger. The spirit of disunion, however, was so ingrained in the Greek mentality that the Florentine accord was disapproved by the Eastern bishops. When Nicholas V sent Cardinal Isidore to Saint Sophia to celebrate the first Latin mass the fanatical population cried out: "Rather than be Latin would we be Turks!" To be sure the nightmare of the Fourth Crusade furnished some justification. The Byzantines were soon to have their wish. On May 29, 1453, Mohammed II rode into Constantine's basilica. On one of the marble columns the visitor is shown a red stain resembling a hand, well above the reach of any man even when mounted. It was owing to the corpses strewn on the inlaid floor that "the Conqueror" had been able to make his mark at that height, so runs the story. The body of the Byzantine emperor was found under a pile of slain. By a bitter irony he was called Constantine, the thirteenth of his name[2] and the last of the Eastern Emperors. The booty taken was disappointing; the Fourth Crusade had attended to that.

The charm of Turkish art is undeniable. A more daringly beautiful structural conception than a minaret it would be difficult to imagine. At first sight all minarets look alike, but examine each one separately and you will see that apparent uniformity really conceals some finely shaded differences. Turkish art is highly elusive. It will surprise you at times with details of ornamentation that reveal the influence of the Italian renaissance, some vine or acanthus leaf design enclosing the façades of a "sebil," as fountains are called in Istanbul, some delicate tracery on the stele of a sultan. It takes repeated visits to the mosques before you realize that their designers have successfully solved the difficult problem of varying the model of Saint Sophia which was imposed on them although they could not hope to surpass it. One of the architectural devices employed was the color scheme, a subtle effect as any one who has felt the grotto-like spell of the Blue Mosque of the Sultan Ahmet will remember.

[2]Some confusion has crept into the numbering of the Constantines. I could not resist the temptation of·adopting number XIII, which is probably the correct one.

And yet, what thrills the Western visitor is not the victorious Crescent crowding the skies with exotic outlines but the visions of a stupendous past that vanished when Christianity was driven from the land that saw it grow to power. Justinian and his court, the glitter of jewels on robes of purple, the refulgent splendor of the vestments, the hundred-eyed lamps reflected in the glistening columns of marble and porphyry, the perfumed incense slowly rising before the brilliant mosaics that glorify the triumph of the most humble of conquerors, the Kyrie Eleison reverberating beneath the majestic dome! Amid such memories the Turk seems out of place, in spite of his long tenure, as out of place as the canons who drone the Roman liturgy in the Mosque of Cordoba. The supplications of those whose piety has built a shrine leave an aura that defies the exorcizing of subsequent intruders. In vain the Moslem inclines the axis of prayer rug and mihrab toward the Holy City of Mecca, the spiritual axis of Saint Sophia he cannot alter, our world has revolved around it too long. In Turkish Istanbul the Christian still feels as though he were ’Εις τὴν πόλιν,[3] in the city whose learning gave us the Civil Law, whose wisdom molded the Catholic Faith, whose strength was the refuge of a civilization that made our Western World. Putting aside all sentiment however, in spite of the memories of its Christian past that greet us on all sides, the Golden Horn has by now pretty definitely become the Sublime Porte.

[3]This derivation has been criticized by many who claim that Istanbul is a corruption of Constantinople.

CHAPTER VI

"Gesta Dei per Francos"

THE TRAVELLER as he wanders through the countless sanctuaries of Christian Europe continually comes across the recumbent effigy of a knight in a coat of mail having one foot crossed over the other. What a tale of daring, of high hopes probably unfulfilled this simple gesture denotes. Some younger son driven by primogeniture to seek in a distant land the position denied him in his native land. And yet after all his struggles there he lies, no richer, though undoubtedly wiser, than when with the enthusiasm of youth he gallantly "took the Cross." If hardships courageously endured can purchase the salvation of his soul, he surely rests in peace.

In the region west of the Euphrates there dwelt in classical times a group of nomadic tribes whom the Greeks called Σαρακήνοι or Saracens. An imaginative people whose dominant trait was a profound religious sense. In our times General Gordon admired their descendant, the Arab, because "he is not ashamed of his God." Interesting though the early history of the Saracens would be, we shall bridge the intervening centuries to a point where they make their first contact with the Mediterranean. In the interval they had come under the influence of a great motive force, Mohammedanism. Abubekr, the successor of the Prophet, was the leader to set the religious fanaticism of the Moslem to work. His objective was to capture Syria from the Christians. On his death in 634 the task was fairly well under way. The Eastern Emperor Heraclius, taken completely by surprise, had been defeated. He came back to the charge, however, with a larger army and in 636 met the Saracens, then commanded by Abubekr's successor Omar, at the Yarmuk

River. Again the Saracens were victorious. Jerusalem itself fell after a feeble resistance. The Saracens then turned northward. In 670 they appeared before Constantinople. Although formidable on land, they were slow to adapt themselves to naval warfare. The superior tactics and material of the Greek fleet proved more than they could cope with. The attack was resumed eight successive years but "Greek Fire"[1] remained irresistible. The Byzantine rule in Syria and Palestine, however, was doomed.

[1]"Greek Fire" is one of the few cases in history of a carefully guarded military secret; as a result considerable uncertainty exists concerning its exact composition. The only formula that has come down to us was discovered in a library in Munich in 1863 and is probably only one of many used at various times. That the use in warfare of the petroleum in which the Caspian basin abounds long antedates the Byzantine Greeks is evident from the fact that such warfare is portrayed in numerous Assyrian bas-reliefs. The innovation embodied in Greek Fire consisted in the addition of an ingredient, probably quick-lime, which caused the inflammable matter to ignite when exposed to the salt of the sea and the oxygen of the atmosphere, a process that has been resorted to recently in the flares of the "man overboard" lifebuoys. Callinicus, a Syrian engineer in the employ of the Emperor Constantine Pognatus, seems to have been the first to improve the technique of Greek Fire, thereby making it a formidable weapon of naval warfare. The mixture was pumped through a tube located below the water line, the first instance in history of submarine tactics. Occasionally the mixture was projected through the air by means of a syphon, in which case salt water was sprayed on the muzzle of the syphon to cause the liquid to ignite, the first instance in history of a "Flammenwerfer." The efficacy of Greek Fire in destroying the Saracen fleet at Cyzicus was impressive. Philippe Auguste, who saw it used at Saint Jean d'Acre, apparently secured the formula and used it himself to destroy the English fleet at Dieppe in 1193. In more recent times some form of Greek Fire seems to have been submitted to three French rulers: in 1702 to Louis XIV, in 1758 to Louis XV and later to Napoleon I. Each time the idea was rejected as being contrary to the Law of Nations. During the Napoleonic Wars the British employed a device known as the "Congreve Rocket" to set fire to ships at anchor, without any great success, be it said. In 1825 a French naval officer, Montgéry, planned to build a boat specially designed for using Greek Fire, or a modern equivalent. The introduction of the ironclad did not prevent one British shipbuilding firm, Wigzel, Halsey & Co., from experimenting with a similar vessel as late as 1878!

The occupation of the Holy Land by a fanatical anti-Christian power naturally made the position of the Christian churches in and around Jerusalem a difficult one. The complaints of returning pilgrims gradually aroused popular anger throughout Christendom so that when Peter the Hermit in 1095 preached the First Crusade a mob estimated at 600,000 began assembling in various parts of Europe bent on rescuing the "holy places" from the Infidel. It cannot be too strongly stressed, however, that the leaders of the expeditions were actuated by less idealistic motives. Stripped of all romanticism, the Crusades were a curious blending of religious fanaticism, a common failing, and a desire for lucre, a still more common failing. In this connection one uncensored letter from the front is worth quoting. "My dear wife," it reads, "I already possess twice as much gold as I have taken along with me. And this is only the beginning. We are not there yet."

One cynic, Konrad Bercovici, has summoned up the Crusades as follows: The Venetians learned the secret of several dyes which they afterwards used to good advantage in their textile industries; the Genoese revised the calendar to conform with the solar year established by the Arabs; the English improved their knowledge of the compass which was to point the way to their empire beyond the seas; the Germans imported a Moslem captive whose descendant, Goethe, became the glory of their literature; and the French brought back a new venereal disease; all at the cost of several million lives! Obviously, that is not the whole story. The West returns intellectually the richer for every contact with the East.

The Crusades were really a succession of campaigns of which only the more important have been dignified by a number. Two of them, the First and the Fourth, profoundly affected Mediterranean history and are the only ones we need consider.

The First Crusade was undertaken by three different contingents. The main body was recruited by Godfrey de Bouillon in the valleys of the Meuse and the Moselle. At the same time a second force was assembled in Genoa by Robert of Normandy and Hughes de Vermandois while the Norman princes Bohemond and Tancred organized a third in Naples and Sicily. The Kingdom of Jerusalem, of which Godfrey de Bouillon was elected king, was the result of the joint effort of these three armies. Although theoretically international in organization the Latin Kingdom, so called to distinguish it from a Greek Kingdom to the north, was predominantly French in composition. It was really a confederation in which Jerusalem occupied a position somewhat similar to that of Prussia in the late German Empire. Jerusalem was the efficient military state.

The other states, three in number, were: Antioch, the principality Bohemond had carved out for himself; the County of Edessa, founded by Baldwin of Flanders; the County of Tripoli, founded by Raymond de Toulouse. Edessa was shortlived. Tripoli soon became a fief of Jerusalem. For a while considerable rivalry existed between Jerusalem and Antioch. The prestige of the Holy City, however, was such that recruits were continually flocking to the Bouillon standards. Jerusalem prospered while Antioch dwindled.

Occupying a narrow stretch of territory between Armenia and the Sinai peninsula, the Latin Christians were literally between the devil and the deep sea. Two subsequent Crusades failed to strengthen their hold on the conquered land. In 1187 Saladin recaptured Jerusalem. Saint Jean d'Acre, the last remaining Christian fortress, fell in 1291. After the expulsion of the Crusaders from Palestine the Christians who remained were thrown on the tender mercies of their conquerors. The shifting of the center of Mohammedanism to Constantinople, however, brought a change in their status. Francis I, having concluded an alliance with the sultan Soliman, assumed the protection of all Christians *in partibus*. So great had been the prowess of "the Franks" that Christian and Moslem alike looked to the French monarchs as the executors of the defunct Latin realm. The "Capitulations" of 1535 are among the most curious documents of history and are probably the most long-lived of treaties. Louis XIV had them renewed and strengthened. They were so much part and parcel of French foreign policy that the Convention continued the protection the monarchy had extended to all Christians, going so far as to raise the Tricolor flag over missions and chapels at a time when church edifices in France were being given over to a weird secular pantheism.

The machinations of Russia to substitute herself for France as the sole protector of Christianity in the Holy Land was one of the causes of the Crimean War. The Second Empire has been blamed for plunging France into a conflict whose origin, on its face, seemed nothing more than "une querelle de moines." As a matter of fact much more was at stake. The prestige Russia would have acquired by assuming the role of Defender of the Faith would have upset the balance of power in the Mediterranean that old-fashioned diplomacy considered the foundation of European peace, and not without reason. The role of France had nevertheless declined to the protection of a few missions when the Third Republic, at the turn of the century, decided to abandon a foreign policy so much at variance with the course being pursued at home. The first World War, however, was to bring about a startling change of heart.

The month of October, 1918, was an animated one for the old Roman province of Syria, accustomed as it was to sudden variations of fortune. General Allenby, with a picturesque army of Britishers, Colonials, Indians and a French contingent, to say nothing of an Armenian corps recruited in Cyprus and a camel corps organized by Colonel Lawrence "of Arabia," was advancing at last after overcoming a stubborn Turkish resistance. On the 7th the population of Beirut was eagerly gazing southward looking for the dust clouds that would herald the approach of the victors when a rather unexpected apparition caused all eyes to turn toward the sea. Six columns of black smoke!

Six small warships soon dropped anchor in the harbor and proceeded to carry out their instructions, which were "to make as imposing a demonstration as possible." From a naval stand-point the demonstration was disappointing. The second-raters France could spare for the operation measured up rather poorly with the British cruisers familiar to the Syrians. France, how-ever, had unconsciously demonstrated one thing, the mystical appeal of the Levant to the French mind, an appeal that Ad-miral Castex has accurately summed up as consisting of "historic memories inadaptable to the present, sentimentality unconnected with reality, stereotypes bequeathed to us by the generations that have preceded us and, finally, a touch of snobbishness."

On October 8 a division of the Indian Army, the Meirut divi-sion, entered Beirut, "amid the plaudits of the inhabitants," according to the British account. Ten days later the same divi-sion occupied Tripoli in Syria. The six French gunboats fol-lowed their allies, or should we say their rivals, cheek by jowl and after "demonstrating" at Tripoli pushed on to Latakia and Alexandretta.

"The lands of the Orient," Pierre Lyautey once remarked, "leave in the heart as well as in the mind a philtre that will last as long as life itself. The spell of forgotten goddesses captivates our senses and our reason. The landscapes and the monuments are settings animated by a subtle magic." There's the rub! France could not forget. Strictly speaking, the French action in Syria was out of order. It ran counter to the spirit, if not the letter, of the Anglo-French accord of 1904 whereby France, in exchange for a free hand in Morocco, withdrew from the eastern Mediterranean. But the countless monuments of France remained, mutely testifying to what the old chroniclers called "the acts of God performed by the Franks."

They greeted her sailors as they ran along the coast. At Sidon the fort and breakwater constructed by first Crusaders and repaired by Saint Louis were still jutting out to sea. Beirut had long been one of the principal seaports of the Frankish Kings of Jerusalem. The Ibelin family had held court there in an atmosphere of feudal austerity tempered with oriental luxury. A traveller of the thirteenth century has given us a description of the vaulted halls on which some unknown artist had painted clouds and sky in the manner to be found in many a Mediterranean villa today. The mosaics of the courts, the pool in which "a dragon seemed to be hunting wild animals who were spouting water," aroused his wonder. Tripoli, of course, was the residence of "la Princesse Lointaine" whose beauty a long line of troubadours, including Rostand, have sung. Her castle, now overrun by a swarm of Syrian families, is still standing.

The French contingent of Allenby's army must have been reminded of their homeland as they beheld every few miles some *château-fort* essentially French in design. On a similar hike in their own country they would have found but few that were not in ruins. Richelieu had done a thorough job. The ones in Syria, on the contrary, were in most cases intact. Probably most of the French men-at-arms who were once more marching through "la Syrie Franque" were surprised. One man in the British Army was not. Lawrence had chosen for his thesis subject at Oxford: "The Influence of the Crusades on the Medieval Architecture of Europe." Ten years before he had tramped from one end of Syria to the other photographing and noting details of fifty odd Frankish castles with a thoroughness that would have done credit to Ruskin. Most of them were the work of builders imported from Normandy. "Why should the Normans be such inventors in military architecture," he asked in one of his books. "They were rather asses otherwise!"

No sooner had Turkey entered the war than the French began casting longing eyes on the land their Crusaders had once conquered and in December, 1914, dispatched a squadron to the coast of Palestine, thereby raising a troublesome question of seniority. Great Britain good-naturedly consented to place her vessels under a French Vice-Admiral. Numerous plans for intervening in "les Échelles" were considered by the French naval command. They finally boiled down to a blockade of the Syrian coast, proclaimed in order to enhance French "prestige," and the occupation of the islands of Ruad and Castellorizo, the latter move having been made without consulting the British.

The most serious threat to Franco-British harmony, however, came from the military branch. On November 13, 1915, the French military attaché in London presented the following astonishing memorandum: "Should the British government be considering a disembarkment of troops in the Gulf of Alexandretta in order to cut the railway to Palestine, they will have to take into consideration not only the economic interests but also the moral and political position of France in these countries. French public opinion could not be indifferent to any operations in a country it considers as destined to form part of the future Syrian state; and it would require of the French government not only that no military operations should be undertaken in this particular country without previous agreement between the allies, but also that, should such action be taken, the greater part of the task be entrusted to French troops and the French generals commanding them." That France had more pressing problems confronting her is evident from the fact that she was utterly unable to furnish the troops in question. The army that had occupied Syria was, as we have seen, British except for a small French contingent. France, however, had gained her point.

We shall pass over the negotiations whereby France acquired her Syrian mandate from the League of Nations. A complicated government was set up consisting of a Syrian state, capital Damascus, the Republic of Lebanon, capital Beirut, the Government of Latakia and the Sanjak of Alexandretta. Lebanon adopted as its flag the French colors with a cedar tree surcharged on the white field. Whether this satisfaction to French pride compensates for the trouble the mandated territories are causing is another matter. The conflict with the Emir Feisal, the rioting at Damascus, the disappointing trade results would indicate that France would be better off if she heeded Admiral Castex's warning to "close the history book and open an atlas." But in spite of this sound advice can we blame France for heaving a heavy sigh of regret?

After the fall of Jerusalem the succession became hereditary in the Lusignan family of Cyprus, one of the Bouillon clan, who thereafter carried on in that island the kingship that had been lost on the mainland until Venice relieved Catherine Cornaro, the last Queen of Cyprus and herself a Venetian, of a purely titular crown far too heavy for her fair brow.[2] The Lusignans could never reconcile themselves to the loss of Jerusalem. One of them, Peter I, actually made an attempt to recover Palestine only to meet death at the hands of an assassin in 1369. He began by founding a new order, the Order of the Sword. Guillaume de Machaut has given us a quaint picture of this last Crusader.

> Quand ce roi étoit bien armé,
> Bien monté et bien acesmé,
> La lance en poing, l'escot au col,
> Il n'y avoit ni sage, ni fol,
> Qui ne dit, à grand murmure:
> Ce roi est né en l'armure![3]

[2]The House of Savoy claims the Kingdom of Cyprus, Jerusalem and Armenia, not from Catherine Cornaro but by inheritance from one of the Lusignans.

> [3]When armed and mounted, on his way,
> With shield in place and lance in hand,
> No fool, no sage, in all the land
> But could be heard to say:
> 'T was thus he saw the light of day!

If any of the French naval officers who were "demonstrating" at Tripoli pushed their explorations a few miles inland up the Oronte River they came upon a sight that must have made them long to draw their swords and follow in the footsteps of King Peter. The valley through which the river flows is known as the "Trouée de Homs." It is the passageway in the coastal range by which Tripoli reaches into the hinterland of Syria. At the summit of the pass stands the famous "Crac des Chevaliers," the fortress of the Knights Hospitalers. One of the kings of Hungary called it "The Key to the Christian Lands." It is perhaps the most perfect medieval castle ever built, one of the few that has a complete "double enceinte." Its size permitted it to house a large force of knights who for one hundred and thirty years defended the approach to Tripoli from their impregnable aerie. The lofty towers whose walls are thirty feet thick have earned for the "Crac" the name of the "Castle of the Jinns." The simple shepherds who until recently were its only tenants could not understand how human beings could have built it. When it was finally captured by the Saracens it was by a questionable *ruse de guerre*. They exhibited a forged order from the Grand Master directing the Knights to retire to the coast. The castle was thereby saved from damage and is now being restored by the French government. Moat, dungeon, *chemin de ronde*, majestic halls, the chapel with its tasteful ornamentation, in short the whole military and ecclesiastical art of the medieval French architects can be studied here.

On one of the columns of the cloister some governor has graven a Latin motto that is still legible. "Sit tibi copia, sit sapientia, formaque detur; inquinat omnia sola superbia si commetetur," which may be translated freely as follows: "May abundance be thine, may wisdom be thine; may health be granted thee; but beware of pride which debases everything it touches!" Prophetic words that call to mind Admiral Castex's dictum about snobbishness. Will France neglect the work so well begun by her zouaves and *chasseurs d'Afrique* to pursue the mirage of a kingdom once conquered by her *preux chevaliers* but now lost these many centuries? The new chapters of the "Gesta Dei per Francos" had better be written in Africa than in the legendary realm of the Crusaders.

One of the reasons for the failure of the Franks to maintain themselves in Palestine was the quarrelling that soon broke out among the leaders of the Crusades. By the time of the Third Crusade the crusading spirit was definitely dead, as the feud between Richard, Cœur de Lion, and Philippe Auguste and Richard's subsequent kidnapping by his co-Crusader Leopold of Austria was to prove. The Fourth Crusade, perhaps the most important single event in Mediterranean history, was a crusade in name only. In order to understand it we must go into a rather modern subject, transportation.

The First Crusaders showed a marked preference for the overland trail. It enabled them to live on the country they traversed. As the enthusiasm for the cause waned the inhabitants began objecting to the disorderly hordes that were browsing on them. The Third Crusaders found it advisable to go by sea. Strange as it may seem, the two nations that were later to engage in a long struggle for the control of the Mediterranean were then so deficient in sea power that they relied on shipping chartered from the Genoese and the Venetians. It was in recognition of the eighty galleys furnished by the Genoese Bank of Saint George that Richard adopted that saint as the patron saint of England. The Phœnician instinct, now represented by the Italians, was to have its innings. We are in the habit of thinking that the war profiteer is a modern development. History probably contains no example of profiteering equal to that of the Venetians during the Crusades.

The only permanent contribution the Huns made to Mediterranean history was an entirely accidental one. In the year 452 Attila sacked the city of Aquilea. Such of the inhabitants as escaped the massacre decided to put themselves beyond the reach of further raids by joining the fishermen living in the islands of the lagoons. Other cities followed the example, among them Padua, whose emigrants chose the island of Riva Alta, or Rialto, the modern Venice. As the danger lessened some of the newcomers returned to their former homes on the mainland but the Lombard invasion of 568 sent most of them scurrying back to their islands, this time for good. The Phœnician idea concerning the advantages of islands was about to receive its most glorious application. By the time Belisarius started his campaign to expel the Goths from Ravenna, Venice had acquired sufficient importance as a maritime state that her aid was sought by the Byzantine Emperors. The friendly relations thus established, the reflection of which can be seen in Venetian art, enabled Venice to resist the attempts of Pepin to force her into the Frankish Empire. By the time of the First Crusade Venice shared with Genoa the sea power of the Mediterranean. By the end of the Third Crusade Venice had established a chain of trading posts throughout the Levant, among them posts at such important places as Tyre and Sidon. Venice had fallen heir to the trade of the Phœnicians.

The big chance, however, came with the Fourth Crusade. For some time past relations between Venice and the Byzantine Empire had been strained, due to commercial rivalry. Relations between the Normans and the Empire had been hostile from the start. No sooner had Robert Guiscard established himself in Naples than he began casting longing eyes on the Byzantine possessions across the Adriatic. In 1080 the Normans captured Durazzo. Italian designs on Albania long antedate Fascism. To save Larissa from a similar fate the Emperor went so far as to call upon the Turks for help. The stage was all set for a profitable bargain between Venice and the leaders of the Fourth Crusade, in which transaction the Norman Crusaders acted as go-between.

The evolution of the plan is an illuminating study. The possibilities of Egypt, the gateway to the Far Eastern trade, appealed strongly to the Venetians. They accordingly persuaded the Crusaders to begin by conquering that country. To this the Crusaders readily assented and contracted for the passage of 4500 horses, 9000 knights and 20,000 men-at-arms, for which the charge was to be 85,000 silver marks[4] and one half the conquered territory. On reaching Venice the Crusaders found to their dismay that they were supposed to pay the passage money before embarking. This, of course, they were unable to do. The Venetians thereupon agreed to remit the prepayment in exchange for aid in capturing Zara, a Dalmatian town then in the possession of Hungary. Zara was taken in due course (1202), after which success the Crusaders evolved a similar plan of their own.

Why bother about Jerusalem, which had long ceased to be "the Golden"? Why not found a Latin Empire at Constantinople instead of trying to revive the Latin Kingdom of Jerusalem? If Venice would forget about Egypt and assist in this undertaking the Crusaders would increase her share of the spoils to one half plus one quarter. On this basis an agreement was reached and, since there is honor among thieves, scrupulously lived up to. Venice remembered Egypt long enough to collect a fat fee for diverting the Crusaders. Constantinople was captured in 1204. The Greek churches were pillaged, the priests massacred, the nuns raped; after which Baldwin of Flanders (not to be confused with the First Crusader of that name) was installed as Latin Emperor. When the smoke cleared away the Venetians had acquired most of the Cyclades and the Sporades, a foothold in the Bosphorus, the best harbors of the northern Euxine and the island of Crete, a record for one campaign never equalled. What was left of the Greek Empire was split up into three fractions: the Empire of Nicea, the Empire of

[4]The mark was a weight, not a coin, equal to about ninety ounces.

Trebizond and the Despotate of Epirus. The Latin Empire, which in spite of its name was a purely French enterprise, was destined to be short-lived, but never again was Byzantium to regain its former might. That in wrecking the Eastern Empire, of which the Greek Empire was but the successor, they were weakening the power best fitted to resist the Turks was the last thing that was worrying the French freebooters. The Balkan problem now troubling Europe undoubtedly owes its origin to the Fourth Crusade.

To sum up. The Crusades, especially the ones we have been considering, have contributed some of the most colorful pages of French history. Nevertheless they represent little more than wasted energy and misdirected effort. The tales of her chroniclers is all France has to show today—that and an army marooned in Syria and unable to strike a blow for France in her hour of need.

CHAPTER VII

Some Reflections on a Most Conspicuous Object

QUELLES terres n'avons-nous pas conquises et perdues!" the French historian Buchon once exclaimed.[1] So numerous are the vanished realms that were at some time ruled by French princes that history has all but forgotten two of them. On one of my wanderings in Mediterranean waters I was running along the coast of Morea bound from Ithaca to Katakolo, the small harbor from which Olympia is most readily reached. On approaching the Zante Canal I scanned the headland of Cape Glarenza looking for what the "Pilot," as the efficient publications of our Hydrographic Office are called, referred to as "a remarkable hill on which is the castle of Tornese, ancient Chelonitis, 875 feet above the sea and a most conspicuous object." As the landmark in question came into view my wonder grew apace. Imagine some *château-fort* of France, but architecturally perfect without any restoration by Viollet-le-Duc, placed on the summit of a bald mountain overlooking the Ionian Sea, every tower and crenellation set in bold relief against the limpid background of the Grecian sky. There it stood, the fortress built by Geoffrey II de Villehardouin! As late as 1825 when Ibrahim Pasha invaded the Peloponnesus during the Greek War of Independence it was still intact, a

---

[1] J. Alexandre Buchon (1791–1846) specialized in Byzantine history. We are indebted to him for the publication of the *Chronicles of Morea*, a contemporary history by some unknown but well-informed author.

monument to the might and glory of Medieval France. Deserted but not destroyed, the impression it creates is first one
of surprise, then of bewilderment. Here a dynasty of conquerors held court, drank deep, jousted and made love to their
ladies fair and then vanished. In vain I searched my memory
for some characters with which to people those vast halls, some
silhouette to fit into those gaping windows, but here was a
whole chapter of Mediterranean history concerning which my
mind at that time was somewhat of a blank. And no wonder.

Few periods in history have been so neglected as the story of
Greece between 146 B.C., when Rome took control after the
Achaian League had attacked her ally Sparta, and 1821, when
Archbishop Germanos raised the standard of Greek independence at Kalavryta. But, as one classical student inquired of Professor Krumbacher,[2] what possible good can come of studying
Greek history after the Greeks had become so degenerate as to
put the accusative case after the preposition $ἀπό$ instead of the
genitive? A comedy entitled "A Midsummer Night's Dream"
would indicate that the greatest of playwrights was familiar with
Medieval Greece, so if Shakespeare found it worth while to
study the period perhaps we will not be wasting our time in
giving it a glance.

Again we must turn to the Fourth Crusade. Among the fortune hunters who flocked to the standards of Baldwin of Flanders was a northern Italian, Boniface de Montferrat. As a reward
for leading the attack on Constantinople, when the spoils were
divided he was allotted Salonika and a large part of Greece still
under the nominal sway of the Eastern Empire. In 1204 Boniface started to reduce his realm into possession, a task in which
he could count on a certain amount of help from the Greek people, as the Archontes who ruled in the name of the Emperor had
become petty tyrants more efficient in wringing taxes from their

[2]Carl Krumbacher (1856–1909), the author of numerous works on Byzantine history.

subjects than in leading an army. After marching through Thessaly to Larissa, Boniface defeated the Archon Sgouros, a brutal military dictator, at Thermopylæ, a spot that seems to have been an obligatory battlefield in Greek wars until nature, by adding three miles of plain to the coast, deprived it of its pass-like conformation. Sgouros retired to his mountain lair at Akra Corinth and Boniface entered Athens, which he bestowed on one of his followers, Othon de la Roche, the son of a Burgundian nobleman. Shortly thereafter Othon captured Akra Corinth.

The trade of *conquistador* was one that could be practiced in those days by any one possessing the qualities of leadership and courage. The freebooters then swarming in the Levant were amply supplied with both qualities, plus the incentive a chronic lack of funds is apt to produce. Among them was Geoffrey de Villehardouin. The family was an old one in Champagne. Geoffrey's uncle was a chronicler of note who has left us a quaint description of the Fourth Crusade. In a way, he was the first of a long line of war correspondents, with this qualification however. He participated in the events he described. "Oncques ne fut plus riche saccagement," is how he tersely summed up the plundering of Constantinople. The hazard of a storm compelled Geoffrey to put into the port of Modon in Messene, the southwestern quarter of the Peloponnesus. Here he struck up a friendship with the local Archon who suggested a joint conquest of the neighboring province of Elis. As might be expected, this fitted nicely into Geoffrey's plans. All went well for a while and rapid progress was being made when, unfortunately, the Archon died and his son, whether through patriotism or lack of scruples we do not know, refused to carry out his father's bargain. The more fool he! Geoffrey, thoroughly angry, decided to call on Boniface for help. After a six days' journey he reached Nauplia, where he found an old friend and fellow-countryman, William de Champlitte. After some hesitation Boniface gave

his consent and the two allies sallied forth to conquer a kingdom. One hundred knights and a few men-at-arms constituted
their entire force. The ensuing campaign sounds like the exploits of Cortez or Pizarro. One battle was all that was necessary. The little Frankish force, which now numbered about 600
men, defeated an army of Greeks and Slavs ten times their
number. By 1212 the entire peninsula was in Frankish hands
with the exception of Modon and Korone, which fortresses the
Venetians with the assistance of the Teutonic Knights were to
hold for many years longer, and the harbor of Monemvasia,
which the Empire had converted into a miniature Gibraltar.
The Malmsy wine, to which the Duke of Clarence (for whom
Cape Glarenza was named) has given a tragic celebrity, was
grown around Monemvasia.

All that remained for Geoffrey to do now was to oust his
partner. Here luck played into his hands. While on a visit to
France Champlitte died. According to feudal law, in order to
make good his inheritance the claimant must present himself
in his fief within a year and one day. Geoffrey craftily arranged
with the Venetians to detain the heir at Venice and at Corfu
until the time limit had expired, whereupon he was proclaimed
Lord of Achaia. It was under the reign of his son Geoffrey II
that the castle of Clermont, to give it its real name, was constructed. The name Tornese was applied to it later by the Italians and owed its origin to the fact that *livres tournois*, i.e., coins
bearing the effigy of Saint Martin of Tours, were minted by the
Villehardouins. Thither flocked young noblemen from all over
France. "Some came to amuse themselves," the Venetian chronicler Marino Sanudo tells us, "others to pay their debts and
others because of the crimes they had committed." As can be
seen, all the elements of a successful colony were present. Eighty
knights with golden spurs did Geoffrey keep as his retinue. His
wife was the daughter of the Latin Emperor Peter of Courtnay
from whom the Earls of Devon are descended.

On the death of Geoffrey II his brother William succeeded to the title. Born and bred in Greece, he was more of a Greek at heart than a Frenchman. Under his rule the dynasty acquired the pride that usually precedes a fall. His escort often consisted of one thousand horsemen. So formal did his court become that in France *Lacédémonie* became *La Cérémonie,* no pun being intended. Boccaccio mentions a lordly Prince of Achaia in his Decameron. In short, William was suffering from a disease that has proven fatal to many a prince; "la folie des grandeurs," the French call it. He began by engaging in a typical Hellenic war against Guy de la Roche, the Lord of Athens, then was rash or loyal enough to espouse the cause of his father-in-law, the Greek Despot of Epirus, who was then at war with Michael VIII Paleologue. He was defeated and taken prisoner at the battle of Pelagonia in Macedonia, and was sent to Constantinople. The matter of his ransom was referred to a Parliament of Ladies. So great had been the losses among the knights that the chatelaines had to take their husbands' places. The fortress of Monemvasia, which William had recently captured, and two other strategically situated posts were agreed upon, thereby giving the Empire a foothold in Morea once more.

William died without male issue and his daughter Isabelle succeeded him for a short but animated reign. Her life furnishes one of the best arguments possible in favor of Salic Law, which, unfortunately, did not obtain among the Franks of Morea. She married three times. Her first husband was a son of Charles of Anjou, the Angevine King of Naples. After his death she married Florenz of Hainault, by whom she had a daughter, Matilda, who married Louis of Burgundy. Her third husband was Philip of Savoy,[3] an attractive spendthrift who is remembered for a tournament he staged near Corinth which ranks among the most sumptuous in the annals of chivalry. To complicate matters still further a child of Isabelle's younger sister

[3]The King of Italy still claims the title of Prince of Achaia.

married a Catalan adventurer, Fernando de Majorca. All of these various stocks put forth claims and several of the claimants met with tragic ends. Matilda perished miserably in the Castel dell' Uovo at Naples. With her death the Villehardouin dynasty became extinct. Such, briefly stated, was the astounding reign of a family of adventurers who succeeded in establishing so brilliant a replica of their feudal homeland that Morea came to be known as New France.

It was the less brilliant Burgundian court at Athens that attracted the attention of Chaucer in "The Knight's Tale" and of Shakespeare. Bottom and his amateur company performed "the most lamentable comedy and most cruel death of Pyramus and Thisbe" before Theseus, the mythical duke of the very real duchy of Athens. It remained for the German poet Goethe, however, to contribute the most controversial allusion to Medieval Greece in literature.

In the second part of "Faust," Act III, the following lines occur:

> I hail you Dukes, as forth ye sally
> Beneath the rule of Sparta's Queen!
> Now lay before her mount and valley,
> And you shall share the kingdom green!
>
> Thine, German, be the hand that forges
> Defense for Corinth and her bays;
> Achaia, with its hundred gorges,
> I give thee, Goth, to hold and raise.
>
> Toward Elis, Franks, direct your motion;
> Messene be the Saxon's state;
> The Normans claim and sweep the ocean
> And Argolis again make great![4]

TRANSLATION OF BAYARD TAYLOR

[4]The original is as follows:
> Herzoge soll ich euch begruessen,
> Gebietet Sparta's Koenigin.
> Nun legt ihr Berg und Tal zu Fuessen
> Und euer sei des Reich's gewinn!

Until recently an exegesis of this passage would have been difficult. Now it is obvious that Goethe must have read the *Chronicles of Morea*, which Buchon published in 1825, about the time Goethe was writing the second part of Faust. The passage is worth examining, as seldom has so much history been crowded into a few lines. When, however, Goethe assigns to the Germans the defense of the Isthmus of Corinth he is stretching an ethnic theory beyond any reasonable limits. The Burgundians were originally a Germanic tribe, as the Nibelungenlied proves, but the province now known as Burgundy became part of France in 613. The followers of Othon de la Roche were essentially French and the duchy he founded must be considered another of the many colonies France scattered along the Mediterranean during the Crusades. On the other hand Boniface de Montferrat was probably of Gothic extraction but long residence in northern Italy had made his family distinctly Italian. Moreover Achaia soon passed from the Montferrat family to the Villehardouins. That the Villehardouins were Frankish Goethe admits; it would have been difficult to deny it! His reference to Messene as being Saxon is again a curious claim. Modon and Korone were two good harbors and the usual ports of call for vessels bound for the Holy Land. The Venetians were essentially a trading people and not much given to good works. They accordingly were only too glad to entrust the care of pilgrims to the Teutonic Order, whom they had no reason to fear as political rivals, which was more than could be said for the Templars and the Knights of Saint John. The fact that

---

Germane du, Corinthus' Buchten
Verteidige mit Wall und Schutz!
Achaia dann mit hundert Schluchten
Empfehl ich, Gote, deinem Trutz.

Nach Elis ziehn der Franken Heere!
Messene sei der Sachsen Los!
Normanne reinige die Meere
Und Argolis erschaff er gross!

the Teutonic Knights maintained "hospitals" at the two ports in question, however, hardly makes Messene Saxon. Goethe's mention of the Normans reminds us that their navy had made a none too successful attempt at ridding Greek waters of the plague of pirates. The island of Ægina within sight of Attica was long a den of corsairs and a voyage down the Gulf of Corinth, even when Burgundian power was at its height, was described as "a voyage to Acheron."

An interesting field for Pan-Germanism did Goethe suggest nevertheless in his usual imaginative language. The suggestions he made are not wholly academic today. If the "new order" in the Mediterranean is to include an outlet for Greater Germany it is difficult to see where it can be except in some territory now occupied by Greece, in which event a little perversion of history may prove a convenient opening wedge.

What became of the two French states we have been considering? The Angevine Kings of Naples soon seized the realm the Villehardouins had conquered. The Duchy of Athens, after being overrun by the Catalans, how and when we shall see presently, passed to the Aragonese Kings of Sicily. Frankish dominion was ephemeral. There is something pathetic about the castles the French have left as monuments of their daring invasion of Greece. Could those stones but speak they would tell the tale of men unafraid who played for high stakes and after an early run of luck lost their winnings and vanished.

CHAPTER VIII

Soldiers of Fortune

A YOUNG and beautiful girl with hair as black as jet, her eyes as velvety as those of a gazelle, her arms bare to the elbow resembling those of the Venus of Arles, moved with restless impatience and tapped the earth with her pliant and well-shaped foot so as to display the pure and well-turned leg in its red cotton stocking with gray and blue clocks." Surely you have not so far forgotten the novels of your youth as not to recognize one of the causes of the trials and tribulations Edmond Dantès endured before he emerged triumphantly as the Count of Monte Cristo. Mercedes, you will recall, lived in the Catalan village near Marseilles. Whence came these people who for a while played an important part in Mediterranean affairs, only to retire to their own country leaving little trace of their passage other than the memory of their ruthlessness?

Again we find that classifying a nation is not an easy task. We shall leave aside the original population and the inevitable visit of the Roman legions, and come to the Visigoths who, as we have seen, occupied what is now Catalonia in the fifth century and gave their name to the country. Catalonia is a corruption of Gothalania. Catalan, however, is distinctly a romance language, more so than Spanish, which still retains many words of Germanic etymology. It is a derivative of the Provençal, a language that is now a mere philological curiosity recently resurrected by the poet Mistral. Catalan, on the other hand, is a living tongue spoken by over four million people in Spain and the Balearic Isles, a situation that can be explained only by the fact that Catalonia was a fief of the Counts of Provence, the Berenguers. The association of the two provinces was therefore a close one until Raymond de Berenguer married the heiress to the crown of Aragon in 1137, after which Catalonia was absorbed by Spain while Provence drifted into the French camp after the marriage of Charles of Anjou with Beatrice de Berenguer. Provençal survived in a modified form in Catalonia but ultimately died out in France.

The Catalans have recently made the front page as a glaring example of a submerged nation, a complicated subject into which we need not delve except to point out that, of all the provinces that go to make up the heterogeneous Spanish state, Catalonia is the one to have shown the most centrifugal force. During the reign of Louis XIII the Catalans voluntarily threw in their lot with France and as late as 1823 took up arms in an attempt to assert their independence. What we are interested in, however, are the early adventures of the Catalans beyond their own borders. Catalonia during the period we are about to consider was an integral part of Aragon. A warlike people with an aptitude for shipbuilding, they were frequently employed by the Aragonese kings as mercenaries. As such they assisted in the conquest of the Balearic Isles and of Sicily. The latter campaign furnished them with an opportunity of carving out a short-lived empire of their own.

At no time have the rulers of Spain made a serious attempt to strengthen their position in the Mediterranean. Spanish ambitions have always been directed elsewhere. As a result Spain's influence on Mediterranean history has been practically nil. Sicily and Naples, which devolved upon the Aragonese crown as a result of the vagaries of feudal succession, were allowed to pass to younger sons, sometimes even to illegitimate sons, and were thus lost to the Spanish realm. The Catalan effort, which constitutes the only appearance of Spaniards in the Levant, received no effective aid from home. Had it been supported

Mediterranean history might have been very different, the fate of Spain other than it has been.

The problem of the demobilized soldier is not a new one. Always a difficult one, it is doubly so in the case of mercenaries who obviously have no civil life to which they can return after their employers have no further use for their services. A desperate set of men, ready to follow any chief who can promise them the only existence for which they are fitted, the unemployed mercenaries of the Middle Ages were the material from which bandits and pirates were recruited. Sometimes, however, a romantic chapter can be put to their credit.[1] Such was the story of the Catalan Grand Company, whose passage through the lands we have been contemplating I shall now relate.

The achievements of the Catalans are so intimately connected with the personality of their first leader, Roger de Flor, that we had best begin by considering him. Much uncertainty surrounds the parentage and birth of this picturesque character. Some historians claim that he was born at Tarragona on July 14, 1262. In spite of this definite assertion, for which I have never found any good authority, it is much more likely that he was born at Brindisi of noble parents, his father being the falconer of the Hohenstauffen Emperor Frederick II, his mother an Italian lady. That makes the great Catalan leader à German; *tant pis*. Flor is evidently a latinization of Blum. Perhaps the Catalans retained enough of their Gothic traits not to consider that in serving under a German they were serving under a foreigner.

The childhood of Roger coincided with the bitter struggle between the Swabian rulers and Charles of Anjou, brother of Saint Louis, for the Two Sicilies. The Papacy had long claimed the Kingdom of Naples by virtue of the so-called Donation of Constantine, a document whose authenticity is open to serious

---

[1]See the thrilling novel by A. Conan Doyle, *The White Company*, for the experience of some English mercenaries.

doubt. It was first bestowed by the Holy See on the Norman house of Hauteville in recognition of their services in defeating the Saracens. Later the Normans added Sicily to their domain by expelling the Moslem from that island. The Hauteville line, however, soon passed into the distaff. Frederick II of Swabia was the logical heir, as he had married Costanza d'Altavilla, the daughter of Roger II. His accession would mean that the Neapolitan fief would be in the hands of the Imperialists, the last thing Rome desired, so the Popes began casting about for some one to accept the fief and reduce it into possession. Innocent IV finally persuaded Charles of Anjou to undertake that difficult task. Conradin, a grandson of Frederick II, had no sooner inherited the crown of Naples than he was decisively defeated by Charles at Tagliacozzo (1268). Shortly thereafter Charles put him to death after a farcical trial. Roger de Flor's father perished at Tagliacozzo, leaving his wife and son in abject poverty, all their estates having been confiscated.

Fortunately for Roger, a galley of the Knights Templars, the *Alcon,* put into the harbor of Brindisi when he was sixteen years old. The captain, a Frenchman named Vassail, took a fancy to the sturdy young orphan and offered to enlist him, a favor that was gratefully accepted. After cruising with his protector for several years, during which time he displayed courage and ability, he was duly admitted to the Order as a "fray sargento," or Esquire. In due course he rose to the rank of captain of a galley. His connection with the Order was to end in a rather unsatisfactory manner. While serving in the defense of Saint Jean d'Acre in 1291 he was shrewd enough to see that the fortress could not resist much longer. Collecting a number of followers, and as much personal property as he could lay his hands on, he made a hasty exit just before the victorious besiegers entered the city. Charges were, of course, brought against him and he was expelled from the Order. His defense was that he had merely endeavored to save such Christians as he could from the fury of the Moslems. On the whole, the evidence is against him. For a while he had to avoid falling into the hands of his accusers. His detractors aver that during this period he took to piracy, a charge that is not supported by any convincing testimony. What is certain, however, is that from this time on he was frankly a soldier of fortune.

When he returned to Italy the Hohenstauffen regime was a thing of the past. Charles had tightened his hold on both kingdoms. In Naples the Swabians had never been too popular and Charles had many supporters. In Sicily, however, the French were cordially hated. In 1282 the population of Palermo staged one of the most thorough political house cleanings on record, the famous Sicilian Vespers, and then offered the crown of Sicily to Peter III of Aragon, who had married another Costanza, the daughter of Manfred whom Charles had likewise defeated, at Benevento in 1266. Peter's claim was none too good, as Manfred was not of legitimate birth. Moreover, Peter was promptly excommunicated. He nevertheless drove the French out of Sicily but on the mainland Charles managed to maintain Angevine rule. Warfare between the Angevines and the Aragonese became chronic. The situation was an ideal one for a soldier of fortune. Roger began by offering his services to the Angevines, but Robert, surnamed the Wise, then Duke of Apulia, was not much impressed by the appearance of the applicant and his companions and declined the offer. Nothing daunted, Roger applied to the Aragonese King of Sicily, Frederick I (Peter's successor), who promptly accepted the ex-Templar and gave him the rank of Vice-Admiral. For three years Roger had the satisfaction of making the Angevines rue the day they had spurned him. But all good things must come to an end. In 1302 a truce was made between the Aragonese and the Angevines. The war was at an end, for the time being, but not the problem of what to do with Roger and his veterans.

Frederick was nothing if not resourceful on this occasion.

He persuaded Roger that it would be a shame for so gallant a band to waste their time in garrison duty when a first-class war against the enemies of Christendom was in progress. The Greek Emperor Andronicus II Paleologue was having trouble a-plenty with the Turks and would welcome such doughty warriors as Roger and his companions. Frederick would supply the needed vessels, a cheap price to pay for getting rid of the Catalans. The forces Roger commanded consisted of Catalans, Aragonese and a curious contingent of light infantry from the Sierras known as Almugavares. Thoroughly alive to the value of his army, Roger despatched ambassadors to Constantinople to submit his terms, and rather stiff ones they were. Double pay for his men; for himself the title of Megaduke and the hand of one of the royal princesses. His terms were promptly accepted. Nicephorus Gregoras, the Byzantine chronicler, assures us that Roger was "as welcome as though he had come from heaven." The Catalan Grand Company was thereupon formed and with one accord Roger was elected leader. A fleet of thirty-six vessels, among them eighteen galleys, had meanwhile been assembled at Messina and the armada carrying 1500 regulars and 4000 Almugavares was soon on its way. After a stop at Monemvasia, Roger dropped anchor in the Golden Horn in September, 1303.

Although welcomed by the Greeks, the Catalans received a cold reception from some unexpected rivals, the Genoese. After their expulsion from Constantinople the Paleologues crossed the Bosphorus and established themselves at Nicea, leaving Baldwin and the Venetians in control of their former capital, and bided their time. The Venetians, however, were soon to learn that backing "the winning side" can be extremely expensive. What was true in 1918 was true in 1204. There was simply no end to the amount of money Baldwin required to "consolidate" his rule. With each additional loan the quality of the security lessened. As a last resort he pledged the person of his son, Baldwin II, rather doubtful collateral to say the least. The corruption and inefficiency of the Latin Emperors was such that by 1261 the Nicean Greeks saw an opportunity of recapturing Constantinople. The help of some maritime power seemed essential, however. Venice being on the black list, the Nicean Emperor turned to her rival Genoa. In 1261 a formal treaty was entered into at Nymphæum, whereby Genoa, in exchange for naval co-operation, received valuable trading privileges. Within fifteen days of the ratification of the treaty Michael VIII Paleologue succeeded in taking Constantinople before the arrival of the Genoese fleet. The Genoese were nevertheless allowed to found a colony at Pera and began a pacific penetration of the Empire. Their methods have a decidedly modern sound. They entrusted their interests to the Bank of Saint George. The reports of the Constantinople branch to the home office have been preserved and compare favorably with the famous Fugger letters. Genoa was the power behind the throne when Roger arrived in Constantinople.

The astounding adventures of the Catalans now commenced. Maria, a niece of Andronicus, married the Catalan leader as per contract. Of course, being a princess, she is described as beautiful and clever. She was fifteen years old and the daughter of Azan, the exiled Czar of Bulgaria. The wedding festivities, unfortunately, were marred by the first of a long series of brawls that were to prove the undoing of the Catalans. Hostilities seem to have started when two Genoese made disparaging remarks about the outlandish dress of one of the Almugavares. Swords flashed and the fight soon grew to a riot. Before order was restored the Genoese commander, Rosco del Final, was killed together with a large number of his fellow-countrymen, three thousand, some accounts say. Andronicus wisely concluded that the sooner he could ship his quarrelsome allies off to war, the better. Roger and his army, reinforced by some local levies, were accordingly landed on the Asiatic side of the Sea of Marmora, near Cyzicus. The Turkish forces in the neighborhood were taken completely by surprise, not even knowing the name of their new and terrible enemy. Four galleys laden with spoils were despatched to Constantinople, the most valuable share being reserved for the bride of the Catalan general, then, the season being well advanced, the army went into pleasant winter quarters. Maria joined her conquering hero at Cyzicus.

An unbiased account of the events of the next two years does not exist. If we are to believe Ramon de Montaner, who was the Xenophon of the expedition minus the detailed accuracy, the Catalans had to contend with trickery bordering on treachery from the outset. If we are to believe the Byzantine chronicler Pachymeres, Roger was more concerned with levying tribute than with combating the Infidel. Both versions are probably correct. The idea of establishing an independent empire was undoubtedly in Roger's mind from the day he set sail from Messina. The authority of the restored Greek Emperors was so shadowy that the plan seemed tempting. In fact the only serious opposition Roger was to encounter came from Greek governors who harbored similar plans of their own.

The opening of the campaign of 1304 was delayed by the inevitable dissensions between the allies. The first rift occurred when Michael, the son of Andronicus, objected to the Catalans leaving their winter quarters until they had settled with the inhabitants for the supplies they had consumed during the winter. Montaner affirms that these debts had been paid in full. Given the high-handed way in which mercenaries usually dealt with the populations on whom they were quartered it is more than probable that Michael's complaint was well founded. The matter was never adjusted and Michael left for home in high dudgeon after sowing the seeds of discord that were to yield a crop of bloody riots. Among the native contingents was a corps of Alans, an uncouth tribe of Mongolians, from whom the emperors were in the habit of recruiting their "shock troops." Open warfare soon developed between the Alans and the Catalans. The casualties exceeded those of the prior conflict with the Genoese. The son of the Alan commander George was among the slain.

The expedition finally got under way, the first objective being Philadelphia, then the largest city in Asia Minor. After defeating the Turks at Germe Roger entered Philadelphia in triumph. In spite of the urgent appeals from the Greeks of Tripoli Roger neglected to come to their rescue and headed in the opposite direction bent on levying tribute from the cities still in the possession of the Greeks. Turning south he then descended upon Nymphæum, Magnesia and Tyria on the Caÿster. The cranes of Homer must have stared at these strange invaders! Ephesus and the seaport of Anaia were visited after which the Catalans penetrated the Cilesian Gates through which the Ten Thousand had passed. By the end of the summer Roger had occupied nearly all of Anatolia and had reached the Taurus mountains. In every encounter the Catalans had swept the field. Roger's fleet had meanwhile captured Chios, Lesbos and Lemnos. Roger thereupon went into winter quarters in the cities and prepared to consolidate his conquests the following year.

The campagn of 1305 was to be less satisfactory. The exactions of the Catalans had aroused the opposition of the Greeks. Magnesia was the first city to throw off the Catalan yoke. The Greek army was now clamoring for action against their rapacious allies. In a quandary as to what to do Andronicus sent orders to Roger to return north. As the siege of Magnesia was meeting with stout resistance, thanks to the courage of the Greek governor Attaleiotis, Roger was glad for an opportunity to save his face so, gathering his plunder, he started north. On reaching the Hellespont he crossed over and established an armed camp at Gallipoli.

As might be expected, some heated interviews took place between Andronicus and the Catalan leaders in which Roger prudently refrained from participating. In order to meet the pay roll of the Catalan army Andronicus had been compelled to put a tax on wheat and to cut the salaries of government officials by one third. The royal plate had been pawned. And yet here was Roger demanding more money when a bag full of angry despatches from Asia Minor had been received showing that the Catalans had collected one million byzants[2] in illegal levies. The military situation, however, was such that Andronicus did not feel that he could dispense with his expensive allies. The Turks had taken the field once more now that the Catalans had left. Matters were finally adjusted and Roger given the title of Cæsar and the government of Asia Minor provided he would try to relieve Philadelphia again.

Roger de Flor had, however, fought his last battle. The Genoese had not forgotten their grievance. The Greek nobles were indignant at what they considered the pretensions of an overbearing upstart. In oriental countries less is required to seal a man's doom. Before starting on his new campaign Roger visited Adrianople to pay his respects to the Emperor. On leaving the palace he was set upon by George and assassinated. The Alan had avenged his son. The three hundred horsemen who had escorted Roger were then attacked by the Alan soldiery. Only three made good their escape to Gallipoli to tell the tale.

The self-control of the Catalans on learning of the murder of their chief was exemplary. They sent a formal deputation to the Emperor to sever the alliance and to declare war. Although holding a safe-conduct from Andronicus they were waylaid and killed. Wholesale massacres of Catalans laid low all who were not fortunate enough to gain the camp at Gallipoli. The infuriated survivors slaughtered the inhabitants of Pernithos in reprisal. Now the Genoese joined in the fray. Their fleet destroyed the Catalan squadron.

The closing years of the Catalan Grand Company do not make pleasant reading, although it will remind the reader of the

[2]A byzant was the equivalent of three-fourths of an ounce of gold.

plight of the Greeks after the murder of Clearchus. On the death of Roger discipline began to deteriorate steadily. The company gradually split up into bands that fought their way through the Balkan peninsula, burning, pillaging, killing as they went. In their defense let it be said that they had been driven to banditry. In 1309 an attempt to storm Salonica was decisively repulsed. The next year the remains of the company entered the service of Walter de Brienne, Duke of Athens. They soon quarrelled with their new employer and after killing him offered the Duchy to the Aragonese King of Sicily. For over fifty years the Catalans governed Athens in behalf of the Sicilian crown. On settling down, however, they lost much of their ferocity, merged with the prior occupants and soon ceased to play an important part in Mediterranean history. Catalan contribution to the story of the Inland Sea had been a tale of violence unrelieved by any spark of idealism, one whose only redeeming feature was the indomitable courage of the Catalan soldiery.

The traveller in Naples who can tear himself away from Vesuvian influence long enough to search the records of her historic past will discover memories of some of the characters who participated in the events I have described. The Castel Nuovo, the frowning bastille designed by Charles of Anjou after the models of his homeland, still dominates the harbor, a monument to the ruthless conqueror whose vengeance sent young Roger roaming over the Mediterranean. In the nearby church of Santa Maria del Carmine a simple stone back of the high altar tells the pathetic story of the last of the Hohenstauffen kings. It is inscribed R.C.C., standing for "Regis Corradini Corpus." In the Capella della Croce, before whose portals the boyish ruler was executed, the block is preserved. The church of Santa Chiara contains the tomb of King Robert, whose failure to appreciate Roger hardly justifies his being surnamed "the Wise." It is a masterpiece of Italian Gothic. But search the sea from the Pillars to Palestine and you will fail to find a church or castle commemorating these roving soldiers of fortune. The terror their name once inspired is the only memory they have left. Their struggles have been in vain. In a few fishing villages founded by some of their more peaceful navigators an occasional Catalan name still survives, but today Mercedes would no longer be wearing the traditional red cotton stockings with gray and blue clocks.

CHAPTER IX

"The Religions"

I̲N̲ ̲O̲U̲R̲ ̲W̲A̲N̲D̲E̲R̲I̲N̲G̲S̲ around the Mediterranean we have lost sight of Hercules, who, if we are to believe the legend, provided us with our cruising ground. It is therefore with pleasure that we pick up traces of our benefactor. When last heard from Hercules was rounding up the cattle of King Geryones. As a reward that monarch gave him the pick of the herd. Choosing a few likely specimens Hercules transported them to Rome and put them out to pasture in a pleasant little valley between the Aventine and the Palatine hills. Before many days had elapsed Hercules noticed that they had not overcome their habit of straying. Four bulls were missing. After searching diligently he was about to give them up as lost when the lowing of one of the herd was answered from a cave half way up the side of the Aventine. The giant Cacus,[1] who lived on that hill, had seized the four bulls and, pulling them up the slope by their tails, had concealed them in a cavern which he carefully blocked with a rock. Hercules had seen the tracks, but as they were heading away from the hill had not thought of searching in that direction. Our western cattle thieves apparently invented nothing new when they reversed the shoes on their horses. In a towering rage Hercules strangled Cacus. The Aventine, once rid of the notorious cattle thief, became the pleasing suburban quarter of vineyards and villas that delights the visitor today. A quiet, peaceful region in which the wan-

[1]See *Æneid*, VIII, 241.

derer will find many memories of the early days of the church. Unfortunately we cannot indulge in such reminiscences, they would lead us away from our subject, the Mediterranean. One sleepy little garden, however, is directly connected with our subject. While waiting for the caretaker to answer the bell let us take a preliminary look through the keyhole. It is quite proper to do so, in fact it is one of the sights of Rome. The peep-show thus enjoyed reveals an avenue of arched bay trees centered directly on the dome of Saint Peter's. The garden gate being opened we enter upon a well-kept terrace overlooking the Tiber. A picturesque dilapidated villa stands in one corner of the grounds. It is the priory of the once formidable Knights of Malta. There is little about the surroundings to suggest the bellicose order that long battled the Infidel. A few tombstones in the adjoining church of Santa Maria Aventina and some indifferent portraits of Grand Masters in the main hall of the villa. We must seek elsewhere in order to evoke a glorious past.

The actions of the Crusaders, whatever may have been their original motives, are hard to reconcile with any spirit of disinterestedness, once they were launched on their campaigns. Not so with "the Religions," as the orders to which the Crusades gave birth are called. Taken as a whole, their record is an inspiring example of discipline and devotion that goes a long way toward redeeming the sordid features of these extraordinary expeditions. In the long struggle between the Cross and the Crescent the Knights of Malta played an outstanding part, so much so that in time the term "the Religion" came to be applied to them alone. As regards length of service they long outlived their brothers-in-arms. We shall therefore consider them last.

In view of the fabulous wealth the Templars are said to have accumulated it is somewhat surprising to learn that their official name was "The Poor Knights of Christ and of the Temple of Solomon" (Pauperes Commilitiones Christi Templique Solomonici). The origin of the order was due to the pious thought of a Burgundian knight, Hugo de Paganis. Assisted by a French knight, Godeffroi de Saint Omer, he founded in 1119 an order whose object was the protection of the countless pilgrims who were flocking to the Holy Land now that it was under the control of the Latin Kings. From the outset the Knights Templars were a combatant military company whose motto, "First to attack, last to retreat," is somewhat suggestive of the U. S. Marine Corps. The order was especially enjoined to enlist the "rogues, perjurers and adulterers" who were streaming into Palestine attracted by the hope of salvation and the prospect of plunder. No wonder it was a Templar who made the famous pass at Rebecca in *Ivanhoe!* That the order succeeded in converting such unpromising material into valiant defenders of the Faith is not the least of its accomplishments. The distinctive mark of the Templars was a red cross on a white mantle. Their outstanding contribution to Mediterranean history was the defense of Saint Jean d'Acre.

The subsequent downfall of the order is one of the controversial subjects of Medieval history. In spite of their vows of poverty, the Templars accumulated considerable wealth from gifts and bequests and, strangely enough, from their own business operations. Their holdings in real estate throughout Europe, from Denmark to Spain, from Cyprus to Ireland, has been estimated at 9000 manors. In an age when banking was little understood, when interest was universally condemned as usury, they managed to rival the Jews and the Italians. Soon "the Temple" in London was enjoying the same unpopularity as "Wall Street" in New York now enjoys. To make matters worse their business dealings brought the Templars in constant contact with the Crown. Medieval kings were troublesome borrowers. They could always discharge their debts by charging their creditors with some crime. That was exactly what happened to the Templars in 1312.

Obviously, the suppression of so powerful an institution as the Templars could not be accomplished, even in the days of arbitrary royal authority, unless the order had lost the support of the Church and forfeited the sympathy of the laity. The special privileges the Templars had wrung from the Papacy were responsible for their failure to secure help from Rome in their hour of need. Clement V was not averse to seeing the proud order brought to heel. To seal the Templars' doom all that remained to be done was to blacken their reputation. Their greed had already cost them the loyalty of their tenants. History does not contain a record of calumny equal to that of which the Templars were the victims. That they were guilty of licentiousness which hardly tallied with their vows of chastity might have been overlooked. What the superstitious masses could not pardon were the charges of sorcery, sacrilege and idolatry to which the secrecy surrounding the rites of the order lent credence. One of the charges against the order was their alleged worship of Mahomet, or "Mahom"; hence our word "mummery" to denote a mock religious ceremony. As for the secrecy it was merely a survival of the usual precautions guarding military information.

The hideous story of confessions extorted by torture, of wholesale burnings, need not be retold. Dante refused to believe the accusations and correctly analyzed the motives behind them.[2] The plain truth is that the Templars' undoing was due to the fact that after the fall of Saint Jean d'Acre the order

---

[2] *Veggio il nuovo, Pilato si crudele,*
Che cio nol sazia, ma, senza decreto
Porta nel Tempio le cupide vele. Purg. XX, 92.
Longfellow's translation of this passage is as follows:
I see the modern Pilate so relentless
This does not sate him, but without decretal
He to the Temple bears his sordid sails.
The "modern Pilate" is of course Philip le Bel. The order survives today in England in a modified form.

ceased to fulfill any useful function. They first transferred their headquarters to Cyprus, which they had purchased from Richard I of England. Richard had captured Cyprus on his way to the Third Crusade as a reprisal for the attempt the Emperor Isaac Comnenus had made to kidnap Berengaria when she came to that island to marry Richard. The Templars soon tired of Cyprus and sold the island to Guy de Lusignan, the titular King of Jerusalem. From that time on the Templars became the object of envy if not of suspicion. Soon their order was suppressed, their property confiscated, their members persecuted. The Knights of Saint John inherited some of their churches. The various crowns, however, were the chief beneficiaries. Before passing judgment on the Templars let us weigh the following facts. At the battle of Gaza in 1244 the number of Templars engaged was about 300 of whom only 18 survived to tell the tale. The 600 Templars composing the garrison of Safed chose death in preference to apostasy. Nearly all the defenders of Saint Jean d'Acre perished. Surely any body of men who could thus fight to the last ditch could not be guilty of all the crimes with which they were subsequently charged.

Brief mention must be made of two purely national orders. The Teutonic Knights we have already met at Messene. As far back as 1128 we find a German hospital in Jerusalem. At first placed under the control of the Hospitallers, the Teutonic Knights soon established their independence and maintained headquarters at Saint Jean d'Acre. After the fall of that citadel the order moved to Venice. In 1309 the German knights transferred their headquarters to Marienburg and thereafter ceased playing an important part in Mediterranean affairs. They made one contribution to the saga of the sea. The black cross that appears in German flags is the cross of the Teutonic Knights.

Another purely national order was the English order of Saint Thomas the Martyr, named in honor of Thomas à Becket.

Data concerning this order are rather vague. Its headquarters were at Saint Jean d'Acre where it maintained a hospital, *i.e.*, a house of refuge for pilgrims. In 1231 Peter des Roches, Bishop of Winchester, visited the Holy Land and placed the order under the Templars. He arranged, however, for their having a church of their own and ultimately bequeathed them 500 marks. Their badge was a red cross charged with the traditional scallop on a white mantle. They seem to have maintained a respectable force, about 5000 men-at-arms and owned considerable property in England and Ireland, also a church and a hospital in London. After the fall of Saint Jean d'Acre they too retired to Cyprus and soon faded out of the picture. They have been the cause of an amusing instance of British persistency. As late as 1879 the Bishop of Gibraltar was insisting that their church at Nicosia, Saint Nicholas, was in his diocese.

It must be a source of satisfaction to the Knights of Malta, as they gaze on the dome of Saint Peter's from the idyllic quiet of their priory on the Aventine, to remember that their corporation long antedates the church whose servants they now are. The original name of the order was an imposing one: *Order of the Hospitallers of Saint John of Jerusalem*. Pope Clement II in a bull refers to the "Hospitalem domum sancte civitatis Jerusalem, qua a longis retro temporibus Christi pauperum usibus dedicata, tam christianorum quam etiam sarracenorum tempore." Zacharias, father of John the Baptist, was one of the early heads of the hospital whose services to pilgrims in the Holy City, before and after the Christian Era, Pope Clement acknowledged. It was a going concern when the Crusaders besieged the city in 1097. The siege came near being fatal to the brethren of the hospital. Knowing the besiegers to be short of food they hurled bread at them from the battlements instead of rocks as they were required to do. When summoned before the Mussulman governor the remaining loaves had miraculously turned into rocks so, the *pièces à conviction* being lacking, the charge could not be proved! Godfrey de Bouillon showed his gratitude in a practical way, other sovereigns followed suit and soon the order was on its way to wealth and fame.

We shall omit the purely military exploits of the order and come to its role in Mediterranean affairs. After the fall of Saint Jean d'Acre the Hospitallers followed the other orders to Cyprus. Their Grand Master, Foulques de Villaret, was shrewd enough to realize that Cyprus would be the undoing of his order. He therefore made an arrangement with a Genœse pirate, Vignolo de Vignoli, for a joint attack on the island of Rhodes, then in the possession of the Greek Empire. Details of the operation are lacking but by 1310 the order was safely established in that island and a period of even greater prosperity and power awaited it.

The Hospitallers remained in Rhodes from 1310 until expelled by the Turks in 1523. It is during these two centuries that they developed their curious international organization. Internationalism is generally assumed to be a modern idea. As a matter of fact, the only successful application of the system is that furnished by the Knights of Saint John who contrived to build a sovereign state on "made ground" so to speak, on a voluntary amalgamation of several distinct nationalities. Catholic Christianity alone could produce such a result. The Knights of Saint John differed from the Templars in several respects. The Templars never aspired to nor attained sovereign powers, in spite of the fact that they maintained an army and a navy and exercised many of the attributes of sovereignty. Moreover there was always a certain Salvation Army attitude about the rank and file of the Templars that was totally absent in the Hospitallers, who were perfectly willing to assist "down and outers" but not to admit them to membership. Quarterings of nobility were insisted on, a certain affluence was a prerequisite to admission. We have but to stroll down the now deserted "Street of the Knights" in Rhodes, to gaze on the imposing "auberges" or chapter houses, in which the various "tongues" congregated, to realize that we are dealing with aristocrats who, whatever their nationality, spoke the only universal language, bore the only title no court in Christendom can confer, that of a gentleman.

The Age of Chivalry! What a mystical, unreal thing it seems to the modern mind! Born of a profound religious belief, nursed by an impelling sense of duty, it was in the wars of the Cross against the Crescent that chivalry reached the pinnacle of its grandeur. It is in Rhodes that it can be seen in its most impressive form, free from the abuses that at times tarnished its fame. A walk around the moat of the stronghold that long stood as a bulwark of our civilization will make the most matter-of-fact of us wonder whether the modern spirit is not built on the ruins of some ideals that should not be dismissed as Quixotic. Here, for once in history, Christendom united in an effort to preserve a moral heritage whose guiding spirit was not of this world. The path leads us through a series of Mohammedan cemeteries that, in accordance with eastern custom, had been placed immediately outside the city walls. The graves are marked by tottering headstones, each capped with a knob by which the initiated can distinguish soldier, official, scholar, saint who had made his three pilgrimages to Mecca on foot and the unassuming symbol of Moslem womanhood. On all sides the roses that gave Rhodes its name drop petals in silent homage to the departed faithful of a creed that is not devoid of a nobility of purpose of its own. Beyond the moat, tier after tier of defiant crenellations. I search my memory for the correct technical term to fit each feature of medieval military art. What a delight Rhodes would have been to fervent admirers of this romantic period, such as Victor Hugo or Sir Walter Scott!

As you wander along the battlements you will notice from time to time the coat of arms of some Grand Master set high in the wall. They serve to remind us of the international organization of the order. We need not go into the complicated structure of the Hospitallers. Suffice to say that the Knights were grouped according to "tongues" which were eight in number: Allemagne, Aragon, Castille, Angleterre, Auvergne, Provence, France and Italy. This subdivision is surprising in that the two nations whose unity was not achieved until our time, Germany and Italy, are nevertheless united under one "langue," whereas France and Spain, whose unity was a *fait accompli* while the order was still comparatively young, retained a division based on a difference of language that was rapidly disappearing. Germany and England were soon to leave the fold, so the order may be considered an essentially Latin organization. The weakness of the structure lay in the fact that the Knights being vowed to celibacy could form a state but not a nation. They were dependent on recruiting for their continued existence and with the decline of the crusading spirit this became increasingly difficult as years went by.

One feature should be remembered as it was to have a decided effect on modern history. A census of the order taken in 1631 showed that the Italian "tongue" was the most numerous, although the French "tongues," considered jointly, outnumbered the Italians. The House of Savoy has always claimed Rhodes as the cradle of its military fame. The motto of Piedmont still is the acrostic FERT, *Fortitudo Ejus Rhodum Tenuit.* The tricolor of united Italy bears the white cross on a red mantle that the Knights of Rhodes wore over their armor. The eight-pointed Maltese Cross was a ceremonial, not a combatant emblem. No wonder Italia Irredenta would not rest until the island was hers. When Soliman the Magnificent captured Rhodes at last he walled up the gate by which he had entered. In 1912 the Italians opened it, a symbolic gesture quite in accord with the unerring dramatic sense that chracterizes modern Italy.

Unfortunately the Hospitallers were to discover in course of time that spiritual and temporal matters are hard to reconcile. The war against the Infidel, which was far from profitable when waged against Moslem armies, gradually gave way to a war against Turkish trade, a most profitable occupation. A tinge of commercialism occasionally affected the policies of the order. Perhaps we cannot blame them, as the island was not self-supporting. Supplies had to be secured from Asia Minor and Africa. The most serious threat to the security of the order, however, came from the attitude of Europe toward the Knights. It was far from a creditable one. In spite of the fact that the order was waging relentless war against the growing power of Turkey, the Knights were left to fight the battles of Christendom practically unaided. After the fall of Constantinople Mohammed II announced his intention of attacking Rhodes, whose galleys had long been a thorn in the side of Islam. In 1480 the Turks laid siege to Rhodes only to meet with a repulse at the hands of the gallant soldiers of the Cross. In 1522 the Turks, now commanded by Soliman, renewed the attack in earnest. In vain the Knights appealed to the Catholic powers for help. The next year, in spite of the heroic resistance of Villiers de l'Isle Adam, Rhodes was compelled to capitulate. Abandoning their splendid city the order retired to Crete. "Nothing in the world has been so well lost as Rhodes," Charles V exclaimed on hearing the news. It would have been better had he sent reinforcements in time to prevent its loss instead of bestowing belated praise on its defenders.

The loss of their state would have been a staggering blow to any ordinary power, but not to the Knights of Saint John. If any body of men deserved the witticism that they were "too stupid to know when they were beaten" it was this bellicose order. In 1530 we find them in possession of Malta, which Charles V deeded to them. Again they began the tedious process of building impregnable fortifications, ornate churches and comfortable "auberges" for the "langues." Soon the war against the

FRERE JEAN LA VALETTE QUARANTE-HUITIEME GRAND MAITRE anno 1557

Caro Sculp

Jean de la Valette

Infidel was again in full cry. Again the Turks attempted to rid themselves of their persistent foe. In 1565 Malta withstood one of the most memorable sieges in history, in which Dragut, the great Arab admiral, lost his life and Jean de la Valette, who conducted the defense, achieved immortality. The harbor of Valetta has been named in his honor. "Plus quam valor Valette valet," is the motto inscribed on the sword Philip II presented to the Grand Master.

The battle of Lepanto eliminated Turkey as a formidable naval power but did not put an end to the activity of the Knights. Every year saw a "caravan," as the raiding expeditions were called, sail forth on a "corso." Every candidate for the Grand Cross of the order must perform at least three such cruises. No matter what truces the other European states made with the Infidel, "the Religion" stuck to its guns. As a result the order became a recognized training school for naval officers. Suffren, the greatest admiral the Mediterranean ever produced, was a Bailli of the order and divided his allegiance between his native country and his beloved Malta. As late as 1790 sixty-five French naval officers were Knights of Malta, among them one vice-admiral, four commodores and six captains.

A walk through Valetta, however, will convince the visitor that the order had undergone a change. The austerity of the Crusader had given way to *la guerre en dentelles*, now that Lepanto had removed the threat of Turkish sea power. Periwigs and silks are more noticeable in the portraits of the Grand Masters than helmets and armor. The rugged medieval "auberges" of Rhodes have been replaced by rococo palaces. The outward signs of affluence are everywhere visible. The defensive works with which Valetta was overladen after the siege give one the impression of having been constructed to defend acquired wealth. *"Un luxe de précautions inutiles,"* is how Admiral Jurien de la Gravière has described them, and correctly so. When the hour of need came Valetta did not fire a shot in its defense. It took the Master Mind of modern Europe, however, to see that in spite of the prestige the *guerre de course* had given "the Religion," the imposing giant was now merely a façade, a picturesque survival of an ideal devoid of energy. Had the Maltese navy possessed any modern value, Bonaparte, who was always on the lookout for possible naval allies, would not have allowed the Directoire to confiscate the property of the Order. The once formidable navy of the Knights was now as baroque as the paintings of Preti that adorn the churches of Valetta.

What France did need, however, in her struggle with British sea power was the harbor of Valetta. In 1798, after a mere pretense of resistance, Baron Ferdinand Hompesch surrendered to the young French general then on his way to Egypt and retired to Trieste taking with him some relics, the inevitable piece of the True Cross, the hand of John the Baptist that the Sultan Bayezid, with true oriental courtesy, had presented to his devout adversaries in the days of their might, and the memories of a glorious past. Needless to say he did not save any of the order's wealth; the only objects of value to escape the French perquisition were the silver doors of the cathedral which had been painted to resemble wood just before the French landed. Two years later, the French garrison surrendered to a British force commanded by General Pigot. The failure of England to return Malta to the Knights, as stipulated in the Peace of Amiens, was one of the reasons for the renewal of the Anglo-French war.

Did this second expropriation put an end to the hopes of the Order? Most certainly not. The vitality of certain ideas in history is truly amazing. Hompesch put himself under the protection of heretical Russia and resigned his post in favor of Paul I. In 1826, taking advantage of the Greek War of Independence, the Knights suggested to the Allies the recapture of Rhodes for their benefit. In the hopes of enlisting British support an English "tongue" was temporarily reconstituted. It did good work as a hospital unit and still maintains an ophthalmic hospital in Jerusalem.[3] Great Britain, however, had no intention of allowing a romantic revival to interfere with her control of the Mediterranean or of adding another naval force to those already in that sea, especially one whose course was wholly unpredictable. In 1834 the Order had to content itself with a haven in Rome, its priory on the Aventine. Nevertheless, if you will turn to the Almanach de Gotha you will find the "Ordre Souverain et Militaire de Malte" sandwiched in between the Grand Duchy of Luxemburg and the Empire of Manchukuo. I leave the reader to determine which of the three enjoys the most real sovereignty. The statutes originally promulgated by Alphonso of Portugal, but slightly altered, still govern the Order. The proportions, however, are sadly changed. The number of Knights who have taken the full vows is now less than forty. The "Knights of Justice," *i.e.*, those admitted by right of noble birth, number less than 250. The remainder of the 3500 members are "Knights of Devotion." The title of Bailli is still given, *honoris causa*, but never again will the waters of the Mediterranean reflect the brilliant ornamentation of the galleys, to which the Order clung long after they had been discarded by more progressive navies, nor tremble under the strokes of their ponderous oars. The shrill voices calling forth orders in a fantastic mixture of Provençal, Aragonese and Arabic are stilled forever.

A certain amount of swank still surrounds the Order although only two "tongues" now remain, Germany and Italy, the former a reconstituted "tongue." As can be seen, the strength of the Order is now as mythical as that of Hercules, who

---

[3]The "Brandenbourg Bailiwick" maintains a *hospice* in Jerusalem and the Grand Priory of Bohemia maintains another on the road to Bethlehem. The various Reformed branches of the Order have evidently not forgotten its original duties. The Order itself has an office in Rome from which it does considerable relief work.

once inhabited the same Aventine. The "Prince Grand Maître" is Son Altesse Éminentissime Fra Ludovico Chigi della Rovere Albani, etc. (I wonder what the "etc." stands for!) The Order maintains four "Grand Priories," a "Sovereign Council," also ambassadors to Austria, Hungary, France, the Vatican and Roumania. Somewhat Gilbertian, rather suggestive of the Grand Inquisitor, Don Alhambra del Bolero, you will say. Perhaps; but a touch of Sir Arthur Sullivan is not lacking. A goodly number of Christian soldiers, Knights of the Order, marched onward to war not so long ago and upheld the traditions of their predecessors of old!

CHAPTER X

"Ce Jacquet"

FATHER went again to see Madame de Staël. He came back very depressed as he fears she will not last long. She was very excited, talking about Jacques Cœur, from whom she is descended through the Gallatins." Thus reads an entry for the month of April, 1817, in that delightfully frank diary of James Gallatin. It is sandwiched in between the confessions of some youthful escapades that brought down on the culprit stern reproofs from his strait-laced father, Albert Gallatin, and moved his virtuous mother to tears. "To my great pleasure," another entry in October, 1822, informs us, "he proposed that we, he and I, should go to Bourges and see the fine palace of Jacques Cœur. This is a pleasure long postponed." Let us follow the example of the Gallatins, father and son, and journey to the pleasant capital of Aquitaine. The trail will soon lead us back to the Mediterranean.

Examples of "fine palaces" of the early Renaissance, as distinguished from *châteaux*, are not numerous in France. Conditions were too unsettled to permit the bourgeoisie amassing vast fortunes by trade. Our American financier was therefore quite right in concluding that the education of his son required a visit to the combined counting-house and manor erected by the celebrated *Argentier*, or Treasurer, of Charles VII. The building is as unique as the career of its builder. We may wonder, however, whether it ever occurred to the Swiss banker who had put American finances on a sound basis, or to the daughter of another Swiss banker who had put French finances on an unsound basis,

109

that the outstanding feature of the house their common ancestor had built was a certain German coziness that makes it seem more than likely that Jacques Cœur was Jacob Herz gallicized.

An atmosphere of *Gemuetlichkeit* pervades the home of Jacques Cœur, for all the affluence it bespeaks. A *Hansel und Gretel* spirit of toyland is omnipresent. Jacques and his wife smile at us from windows carved on either side of a huge fireplace, gnomes crouch under the weight of the vaulting they are supporting; blackamoors grin at us from balustrades; shepherds and swineherds mounted on donkeys engage in jousts with broomsticks as lances and baskets as bucklers. How much Jacques Cœur's aristocratic friends relished such attempts to antedate Cervantes is another matter. A childish, sentimental conception of art did this bourgeois trader impose on his architect. One touch, however, is prophetic and pathetic. From one of the windows of the façade the figure of his favorite retainer is gazing patiently down the street waiting for his master to return from his journey . . . in vain.

It was a sadly reduced kingdom that Charles VII took over from his feeble-minded father Charles VI. Civil war and the invasion of Henry V of England had resulted in the loss of most of the territory north of the Loire. The young prince must perforce establish his government in the town of Bourges and begin the stupendous task of ridding the country of the British invaders and their allies, the Burgundian rebels. If he succeeded in so doing it was thanks to two of his subjects, Joan of Arc and Jacques Cœur. Their services, though differing widely, had this in common. They were repaid by an ingratitude without parallel in history. Charles' failure to bestir himself when Joan was standing trial at Rouen undoubtedly sealed her doom.

Into the troubled France of the Hundred Years War Jacques Cœur was born about 1395. His father was a wealthy fur merchant of Bourges, so Jacques had an auspicious start for a career of money-making, as old-time New Yorkers will concede. He received a good education. In his subsequent difficulties with the crown he pleaded "benefit of clergy," *i.e.*, the right to be tried by the more merciful ecclesiastical tribunals by reason of his having been granted "letters of tonsure," in those days the equivalent of a degree. In 1422 he married Macée de Léodepart, the daughter of the Provost of Bourges, an excellent match. The first trade at which he worked was that of goldsmith, an occupation then closely allied with banking. It is not surprising therefore to find Jacques Cœur one of the directors of the royal mint at Bourges. Here the first of his unpleasant clashes with royal authority occurred. Charles VII was in dire need of funds with which to wage his war against the British. He accordingly resorted to a very old, or a very new, expedient: the "clipping" of the contents of his currency. When detected he put the blame on the directors of his mint. Jacques Cœur was condemned on December 6, 1429, to pay a fine of one thousand livres. Disgusted by his experience with "managed currency" he decided to abandon banking and engage in oversea trade.

French traders in the Mediterranean were still laboring under heavy handicaps when Jacques Cœur transferred his activities to Montpellier. Aigues-Mortes, the fiat seaport of Louis IX, was rapidly becoming useless owing to the silting of the channel leading to the sea. The trading privileges which that King had granted were accordingly extended to include Montpellier, which at that time was connected with Aigues-Mortes by canal. The new seaport, being situated on the river Lez five miles from the sea, was far from a convenient harbor. Cette was the port through which the trade of Montpellier was usually cleared. Nevertheless Montpellier enjoyed a flourishing trade with Egypt though of late her merchants had suffered from the persecution of the Egyptian rulers. Details are lacking concerning Jacques Cœur's first ventures in commerce. We know they took him to Damascus. An unpleasant life was the lot of Christian traders in Asia Minor at that time. The hatred engendered by the Crusades had resulted in restrictions similar to those of which the Jews were the victims in Europe. On his return journey he met with the usual mishap. His ship was wrecked off Calvi and the piratical Corsicans stripped it of its valuable cargo. His losses do not seem to have dismayed him, however. All his life he was to live up to the motto we find repeated in the ornamentation of his house: *A vaillans Cœurs, rien impossible.*

Jacques Cœur's requirements soon outgrew the capacities of Montpellier. In 1446 we find that letters of citizenship were granted him by Marseilles. As Provence was then ruled by King René of Anjou this made him the subject of a none too friendly state, a fact that does not seem to have prevented him from rising to high office in his native country. The steps in Jacques Cœur's rapid rise to fortune are, unfortunately, impossible to trace. Suffice to say that by 1440 he was so pre-eminently the outstanding financier of the realm that Charles VII made him his treasurer. As such he took part in the triumphal entry into Rouen on November 10, 1449, when his rich apparel vied with those of the other nobles present among whom the captain of industry theoretically belonged, he having been ennobled in 1440. With houses in all the principal cities of France and trading posts throughout the East, also a silk factory in Florence, Jacques Cœur had reached the pinnacle of a fortune whose base, unbeknownst to him, was being steadily undermined. King and courtiers were heavily in his debt. The fate of the Templars was awaiting him. Powerful enemies had decided that the pride of *"ce Jacquet"* must be humbled. Soon they saw their chance.

On February 9, 1449, Agnes Sorel, the King's mistress died. There was nothing mysterious about her death as she died in childbirth. Jacques Cœur was nevertheless accused of poisoning her. His accuser was a lady of fashion to whom he had made repeated loans. The charge was obviously a flimsy one, as the lovely Agnes had given birth to a child who survived her, a situation hard to reconcile with poison, so some equally preposterous charges were invented to bolster up the case. The twenty-year-old accusations of maladministration of the mint were revived. His trading relations with the East were made the basis of a charge of treasonable connection with the Sultan. Charges of illegal exportation of precious metals (a very modern-sounding charge), illegal impressment of seamen and a vague dragnet charge of dishonesty and extortion followed to complete the "framing." Jacques Cœur did not have a chance in the royal courts. In vain did he plead benefit of clergy. A confession was extorted by torture to all charges save one. His tormentors could not wring from him an admission that he had had anything to do with the death of Agnes Sorel. On his deathbed he was to repeat this denial. After dragging through the courts for two years a judgment was rendered against him that was typical of medieval justice. Jacques Cœur was found guilty of most of the charges. The penalty involved was death, but the Holy Father having interceded in his favor the death sentence was remitted and banishment substituted. He was condemned to go through the humiliating ordeal of an *amende honorable*. This was followed by a more lucrative *amende profitable* and therein lies the "joker." The judgment carried fines amounting to 400,000 écus (about 4,500,000 francs present French currency). Until that sum was forthcoming the condemned man was to remain in jail. As all his property had been confiscated he faced the pleasant prospect of life imprisonment instead of banishment. All this in spite of the fact that the charge of poisoning had not been pressed. That accusation was still being held over him.

The best vindication of Jacques Cœur is the loyalty his factors and captains displayed during his hour of need. With an ingenuity that is positively amazing one and all proceeded to secrete the assets of their employer, to place them beyond the reach of the King's henchmen, often at considerable risk to their own safety. A tidy sum was later turned over to Jacques Cœur. His estates and personal effects, however, were put up at auction. Some were bid in by Charles VII and used to establish the successor he had chosen for Agnes. Before her promotion to this dubious honor the new incumbent had led a cleansing if not a clean life. She was a laundress. Macée de Léodepart did not long survive her husband's disgrace.

We now come to the mysterious side of the whole affair. For some reason that is not clear the Holy See and King René took a great interest in the convicted *Argentier*. In 1454, about one year after his conviction, Jacques Cœur managed to escape from prison. A safe chain of hiding places seems to have been arranged for him by powerful protectors. At Beaucaire, the last stop in French territory, his faithful seamen were massed in force. The King's sheriffs who attempted to prevent him from crossing the Rhone were soundly trounced. Once in Tarascon he was on Angevine soil and safe. He proceeded to Marseilles and thence by sea to Pisa. A royal welcome awaited him in Rome. It is difficult to avoid the conclusion that at some time in his career Jacques Cœur had evinced a devotion to the Church that conflicted with his duty to his sovereign. Two of his sons were in holy orders and their rapid promotion is evidence that their father was held in high esteem in Rome. A loan of 100,000 ducats by the Pope to the royal treasury has never been satisfactorily explained. Nicholas V in reporting the matter to his cardinals openly stated that Jacques Cœur had "procured for us some other things contrary to the wishes of said Majesty (Charles VII), on account of which he has suffered unjustly very grave and prolonged persecutions." The Holy Father thereupon proceeded to declare Jacques Cœur "completely innocent of the crime with which they (the French) have accused him." Could it be that the only plausible excuse for the harsh treatment meted out to the royal Treasurer was one that the crown did not dare make public? Now that our sailor is once more free to roam about in his element let us examine his contribution to Mediterranean history.

It was not only a sailor but a diplomat that Nicholas V had added to his forces when he took Jacques Cœur into his employ. His predecessor Eugenius IV had recourse to his knowledge of Oriental statecraft in one very serious matter. The Knights of Saint John could not fight the Turks, the Saracens and the Egyptians combined. Christian diplomacy relied on the mutual distrust existing between the various Moslem states. Jacques Cœur was selected to negotiate a treaty between the Sultan of Egypt and the Knights. His success in this delicate mission undoubtedly enabled the order to remain in Rhodes one hundred years longer. But then, Jacques Cœur had been trading in Egypt long enough to know the mentality of the people with whom he was dealing. This diplomatic success he followed up with another equally difficult, patching up a schism that threatened the church at the time of the election of Nicholas V.

A grief-stricken man was Nicholas V when the exile presented himself before him. The capture of Constantinople by the Turks weighed heavily on his mind. "It is a second death to Homer and Plato," was how he summed up the event. In a few words the Pontiff had probably given the best analysis as to why it was a blow to civilization. The light that Byzantium had shed over Christendom for centuries was extinguished. A practical man, however, was Nicholas V even though his learning was so profound that Æneas Silvius, later Pope Pius II, said of him that "what he does not know is without the range of human knowledge." He knew a fighter when he saw one and accordingly gave him rank in the Papal navy. The Hungarian leader Jean Hunyadi was hard pressed in Belgrad when Calixtus III succeeded Nicholas V. A diversion against Constantinople was all indicated. Unlike some recent attempts along the same lines this one succeeded. Sixteen galleys besides smaller vessels, mounting in all some three hundred cannon and carrying one thousand sailors and five thousand troops, were assembled in the spring of 1456 under the command of Jacques Cœur. Several of his captains whom King René had refused to extradite joined their old master. In June the armada appeared before Constantinople and proceeded to give the Turks such a "strafing" that they recalled their troops from the siege of Belgrad. From Constantinople the expedition went up the Danube; then finding that they could be of no further service to the Hungarians, wended its way to Lemnos, which it captured. The exact manner in which Jacques Cœur met his death is not known. All that we know is that he died in the island of Chios, probably from wounds received in action. He was buried in the church of the Cordeliers, his allies the Genoese according him "the highest honors as though to one of the great of Genoa."

In the museum at Bourges you can see a stained-glass window depicting one of Jacques Cœur's ships. The only flag it flies is the burgee of his house, the only escutcheon on its stern is the coat of arms of its owner, the curious punning device of alternating hearts and cockleshells, the latter the emblem of his patron, Saint James. It was not the oriflamme of France that first announced to the Mediterranean that a new sea power was soon to cleave its waves. That honor belongs to a fearless trader who, after seeing his King and country through one of the worst crises of history, quaffed the cup of ingratitude to its last bitterest dregs. His bones lie forgotten somewhere in a strange, far-off island. Could it be that when he built the pretentious mansion in which he was to know but a few brief years of happiness Jacques Cœur had a presentiment that one day he would pass its imposing portals never to return? Who knows? His faithful retainer, however, is still patiently gazing down the street, waiting for his master to return . . . in vain.

CHAPTER XI

"Don Juan of Austria Has Burst the Battle Line!"

I T WAS a stirring sight that greeted the shepherds who were watching their flocks of goats on Mount Exogi one morning toward the end of September in the year 1571. The water separating the islands of Ithaca and Levkas was swarming with ships whose sails cut "alla trina," or lateen fashion,[1] were glistening in the sun. As they approached the crews could be seen climbing up the slanting yards and slowly gathering the canvas into a neat furl. This done, each ship stretched forth her banks of oars, not unlike the tentacles of a centipede, and began heading for the middle of the narrow channel separating Ithaca from Cephalonia. At first, alarm seized the onlookers. The Turkish fleet was known to be somewhere in the Gulf of Corinth. The last visit was still remembered as a nightmare. On that occasion Ithaca had been so ravaged that the Venetians on taking possession had been compelled to import Cretans to till the soil. These newcomers, who arrived in caravels, were called Karavias, a name as common in Ithaca now as Lopez in Spain.

But to return to the fleet that was now entering the Ithaca Channel. No, they were not Turks. Fully one half were flying the banner of Saint Marc, some of the others that of Spain or her allies and some the holy standard of Saint Peter. Slowly they passed between the small harbor of Polis, where Ulysses had equipped his twelve ships for the Trojan expedition, and the

[1] Literally: "triangularly."

diminutive island of Asteris, where Penelope's suitors had hatched their plot to murder Telemachus for having tried to defend his father's honor; then inclining westward the armada dropped anchor in the Bay of Same, a deep indentation in the coast of Cephalonia.

When last we were considering Venice she had been ousted from her position in Constantinople by the Genoese and Greeks who soon combined forces and began nibbling at Venetian possessions in the Ægean and Ionian seas. Finally in 1379 the Genoese fleet appeared in the Adriatic and captured Chioggia, one of the islands of the lagoons. With great difficulty were they driven off by Admiral Pisano. In order to regain her hegemony of the Mediterranean, Venice was compelled to build a "second to none" navy.

No sooner were the Genoese disposed of than an even more formidable enemy loomed on the horizon. Between 1520 and 1566 Turkey was governed by a sultan whose wisdom and ability made the Ottoman Empire a world power, Soliman, surnamed "the Magnificent." He began his reign by capturing Belgrad from the Hungarians, then turning his attention to the sea he conquered Rhodes. Under the leadership of the Barbary admiral Barbarossa the new Turkish navy scored a decided success over a combined Genoese and Papal fleet commanded by Andrea Doria at Prevesa in 1538. Soliman was now able to conclude an alliance with Francis I. French naval power being weak, the Most Christian King was only too glad to enlist Mohammedan aid in his struggle with Charles V. The prestige of Turkey had reached its zenith. Soliman's successor Selim II, although he did not possess one atom of his father's ability, was animated with an even greater lust for power. His chief claim to distinction, however, was his taste in wines, an accomplishment that earned for him the surname of "the Drunkard." Having on one of his carouses tasted a vintage grown on the island of Cyprus, in spite of the Islamic prohibition, he

HORUSCE en HAREADEN BARBAROSSA
Koninghe van Tunis en Algiers en opper Zee vooghde

I. Lux Fec.

Keyr-ed-Din surnamed Barbarossa and his brother Uruj

decided that he must annex that island, and its vineyards, then in the possession of Venice. Before long the Turks captured Nicosia and were laying siege to Famagosta.

Not since the days of Charles Martel had Christianity been in such peril. Rhodes and Cyprus were obviously only trial balloons. The Turks were aiming at more than the islands of the Ægean. Having reduced a large part of the Balkan peninsula they were undoubtedly aiming at nothing less than the conquest of Italy. The Turk had succeeded the Arab as the exponent of militant Mohammedanism. Fortunately for Christianity the Holy See was then governed by one of the most energetic pontiffs in the history of the Papacy, Pius V. An austere Dominican monk, his pontificate was marked by a zealous persecution of the heretic. Pius, however, had the qualities of his defects. If he spurred Philip II to severe measures in the Netherlands, by the same token he compelled that calculating monarch to forget politics and join Venice in a campaign against the Infidel. The Holy League was the result. It was their fleet the shepherds on Mount Exogi had spied.

The catalog of ships was Homeric in its comprehensiveness. The backbone of the armada was the Venetian contingent of 105 galleys, 10 ships and 6 galeasses. The last-named were by far the most formidable warships constructed until then, measuring 150 feet in length and mounting 30 bronze cannon. The Venetians were under the command of the veteran admiral Sebastian Veniero and numbered no less than 11,200 soldiers, 7000 sailors and 22,000 rowers. The Venetian artillery exceeded 900 guns. A Papal fleet of 12 galleys commanded by Marc' Antonio Colonna was the next most important Italian contingent. Savoy, Malta and Genoa contributed two ships each. Spain was represented by an imposing squadron of 13 galleys and 20 ships. The Two Sicilies, then united under Spanish rule, furnished 13 galleys. Tuscany and various other Italian states added 27 more. The united force reached the grand total of 207 galleys, 30 ships and 6 galeasses, mounting 1815 guns and manned by 20,000 soldiers, 12,000 seamen and 43,000 rowers. This powerful armada had been assembled at Messina during the summer of 1571 and, after touching at Corfu and Goumenitza, had anchored off Same. Its commander-in-chief was no less a person than the half-brother of the King of Spain, Don Juan de Austria.

We are not in the habit of considering the sombre monarch who, after advancing the Catholic Empire to its apogee of might, retired a melancholy and disillusioned old man to the seclusion of a cloister as being capable of any youthful dreams. But even the gods are human in one respect. During one of his voyages around his vast dominions Charles V tarried a while in the city of Regensburg. Barbara Blomberg was endowed with two attributes that are hard to resist, surpassing beauty and a pleasing voice. That the Emperor fell deeply in love is evident from the precise orders he gave in a codicil of his will. "Whatever walk of life he may choose, I command the Infanta to accord my son the honors due his birth." This injunction Philip II complied with, distasteful to him though it may have been.

Although Venice had contributed over one-half of the expedition, out of deference to Philip his brother was given supreme command. The task confronting Don Juan was a difficult one, his appointment being considered favoritism by the Venetians. As a matter of fact the choice was a wise one, as the forethought he displayed in preparing for battle was soon to show. One of Don Juan's first steps was to place Spanish infantry on board the Venetian galleys as they were badly undermanned as regards marines. The move, although a sensible one, was to cause considerable friction. The Spaniards proved insubordinate and quarrelsome. Veniero, who was a "string 'em up" type of martinet, soon had several Spaniards swinging from his yard-arm. Don Juan's indignation can be imagined. As commander-in-chief he was within his rights in claiming that death sentences affecting Spanish subjects should be referred to him for confirmation. This incident which occurred in Goumenitza harbor nearly ended the campaign then and there. Instinctively the Venetian ships gathered around their admiral, the Spaniards and their allies around *La Real*, Don Juan's Catalan flagship. It took all the diplomacy of Marc' Antonio Colonna to prevent an open breach. As it was, Don Juan refused to have any further dealings with Veniero except through the intermediary of Barbarigo, another Venetian admiral.

The humor of the Venetians was not improved by news that reached them on October 3. They had been clamoring for immediate action ever since Messina in the hopes of relieving the pressure on the garrison of Famagosta before it suffered the fate of Nicosia. Don Juan, however, had insisted on awaiting the arrival of his full force before sailing. Now a hideous calamity had overtaken Venice. Famagosta had fallen. On entering the city the Turks claimed to have found some Moslem prisoners who had been rendered insane by long and cruel confinement. As a reprisal the Venetian commander, Bragadino, whose heroic defense entitled him to more considerate treatment, was flayed alive. The unfortunate wretch is said to have lived a whole day in torment during which he saw his skin, stuffed with straw, paraded on an ass through the streets. The grewsome trophy was shipped to Constantinople. There it remained on exhibition until a fearless Venetian, Girolamo Polidoro by name, managed to abstract it and to bring it to Venice, where it was placed in an urn and buried in the church of San Giovanni e Paolo.

It was not until he reached Same that Don Juan established contact with the Turkish fleet. His light galleys discovered the enemy at anchor at Lepanto in the Gulf of Corinth. By way of demonstrating that certain localities are inherently strategic it may not be amiss to point out that Actium, Prevesa and

Lepanto are so close to each other that I have sailed over all three battle grounds in the course of one day. Don Juan accordingly moved his fleet to the harbor of Petala, one of the Kourtsolari Islands northwest of Cape Skropha. His plan was to come around that cape suddenly and fall on the Turks unawares. Both sides, however, had been grievously misinformed by their scouts as to the exact size of their opponent. Ali Pasha, the Turkish admiral, had likewise decided to attack his enemy and was proceeding down the Gulf of Corinth on Sunday, October 7, when he fell in with Don Juan as he was rounding Cape Skropha, a surprise encounter for both sides. Before going into action Don Juan and Veniero exchanged signals. This long-range reconciliation aroused great enthusiasm in the entire fleet and with shouts of "Death to the flayers!" the Christians charged.

On paper the Turks were superior, nearly 300 ships of which 222 were galleys had they mustered, a homogeneous force commanded by an admiral who lacked neither courage nor skill. The Turks were, and still are, magnificent fighters. As seamen they are entitled to respect, as any one who has seen the ease with which a Turkish felucca is handled will concede. Yet they went down at Lepanto to one of the worst defeats in history. The causes of this reversal in form are worth examining. The battle of Prevesa did not furnish a fair test, as the Genoese did not want to see the Turks crushed. They were serving the useful purpose of keeping Venice in check. Hence the hesitating tactics of Andrea Doria at that battle. At Lepanto all were in earnest. The danger to Christianity had at last overcome mutual jealousies.

"All galley actions are alike," Admiral Jurien de la Gravière once remarked. In spite of the introduction of gunpowder the tactics of Mylæ were used at Lepanto. Naval engagements were still a question of ramming and boarding. We are still far from the rigid line-of-battle formation of the eighteenth century which sought above everything to avoid a mêlée. Two remarkable paintings portraying the battle have been preserved; from them we can reconstitute the engagement. In the Sala Regia of the Vatican a fresco by Vasari and Sabatini can be seen and in the Ducal Palace of Venice another can be found, the work of Paolo Veronese and Andrea Vicentino. In both paintings the vessels are in inextricable confusion. Every ship has its sails furled and is relying on its oarsmen to outmaneuver its nearest opponent so as to permit boarding or ramming, preferably the former. Lepanto was one of the last battles in which the marine was called upon for decisive work. The excellence of the Spanish infantry, the foot soldiers commanded by the Infantas, was here apparent. Like the Roman legions at Mylæ they clearly outclassed their opponents.

The antiquated matériel of the Turks was largely responsible for their defeat. At Lepanto the Turks were still using bows and arrows. The Turkish archers were placed in extremely exposed positions, whereas the Christian musketeers fired from behind barbettes. There are, however, some details that the paintings referred to do not bring out. In any action in which ramming plays a part the construction of the hull is an important factor. By the time of Lepanto Europe had completely surpassed the East in technical skill. The Allied vessels were far ahead of the Turkish in solidity of build. In artillery Europe had progressed far beyond Asia. We have seen that the Turks had practically no small arms. In short at Lepanto Europe had established an intellectual hegemony in naval matters that was never questioned until the Russo-Japanese War revealed the latent possibilities of the Far East. The Christian victory at Lepanto was assured before the two fleets ever came within range. It had been won in the arsenals and shipyards of Europe. It was the oft-repeated story of preparedness and mental alertness overcoming routine and inertness. Add a brilliant young commander and you have a Lepanto.

The results of the battle speak for themselves. The Allied losses amounted to fifteen ships sunk and 8000 casualties, among them Barbarigo, whose tact had prevented the Venetian and Spanish contingents from flying at each other before the enemy was reached. The Turkish losses in ships were ninety vessels sunk and 178 captured. Their losses in men have been put as high as 30,000. In view of the fact that only thirty ships escaped that figure does not seem improbable. Twelve thousand Christian galley slaves were liberated and 367 cannon divided among the victors. No wonder Cervantes, who was present at the battle, described it as "the greatest day the ages have seen." He had good cause to remember the day, as he suffered a wound that permanently injured his left hand. He consoled himself, however, with the thought that "he still had his right hand with which to write."

On hearing of the victory Pope Pius exclaimed: "There was a man sent from God whose name was John." What manner of man was the young prince who had changed the current of history? The Germans have always claimed him as their own and with a certain show of reason. He certainly possessed German efficiency and thoroughness. If the League was slow in getting into action it was a carefully drilled fleet that faced the impetuous but individualistic Arab commanders. Unlike a real Spaniard not a trace of religious fanaticism can be attributed to him. He never allowed his Catholicity to interfere with his Christianity. The Turkish admiral, Ali Pasha, lost his life at Lepanto. Don Juan took his two sons and their entire retinue on board the flagship, treated them with the utmost kindness and used his influence to have the lads returned to their family. "My pride commands me to conquer my enemy," he once remarked, "my honor forbids me to humble or hate my enemy." A romantic character was Don Juan, eminently fitted to win the most colorful naval battle of history. Although an aura of fame now surrounds the victor of Lepanto he was not allowed to reap any fruits of victory. On his deathbed he was heard to say: "As I have not a square foot of ground to call my own, I long for the kingdom of heaven."

After the battle he took up his abode in the sombre Castel Nuovo where the Aragonese kings held court after the expulsion of the French from Naples. For a while he planned to revive the Catalan principality of Morea. This idea he discarded for a kingdom in Tunis. He captured that city in 1573 but soon lost it. His royal brother was of no assistance, the Venetians his former allies had made their peace with the Turks. He must perforce do his brother's dirty work in the Netherlands. While endeavoring to pacify that region he died of the plague at Tirlemont in 1578. His age was only thirty-three. During his delirium his mind reverted to Lepanto and he breathed his last clutching the Crucifix he had worn on that day of glory.

It required more than one defeat to cripple so wealthy and powerful a state as Turkey. As one contemporary Turkish chronicler grandiloquently put it "Turkey could make her anchors of silver and her cables of silk if necessary." Moreover, the inherent weakness of all coalitions became apparent immediately after Lepanto. To the great disgust of Venice, the League disbanded without pressing the advantage. The morale of the Turkish navy, however, had been seriously impaired and Ottoman sea power entered on its decline. Gone were the dreams of Mohammed the Conqueror. Italy was never to be added to the realm of Islam. Henceforth it was to be the neighboring continental states, rather than the maritime states, that were to bear the brunt of Turkish arms. Don Juan had therefore done more than "burst a battle line." He had reduced Turkey from a Mediterranean to a Balkan power. Therein lies the real historical importance of the battle.

CHAPTER XII

In Which *Weltpolitik* Makes Its Appearance

THE LITTLE GARDEN on the Prins Hendrik-Kade seemed particularly restful that July evening with its straight paths, neatly strewn with fine gravel, running between rows of boxwood trimmed in the shape of men or animals. Its owner was obviously a seafaring man as he had given the place of honor to a figurehead of a warrior carved out of massive oak by some shipwright. It stood at the farther end of a walk along which a peacock was strutting. Where the paths intersected lay a pool of clear water enclosed by a border of Delft tiles. In the center on a moss-covered rock a marble Triton stood, a peril to navigation against which the toy boat of some child had once more come to grief. The tulips had long since faded but the roses were doing their best to make up for the loss. You have seen similar gardens in the paintings of Gerard Dow. This one was in Amsterdam behind the gabled house of modest proportions in which Michael Adrianzoon de Ruyter had hoped to end his days as comfortably as his infirmities would permit. But three years before, on June 7, 1672, to be precise, had he not earned his rest by defeating the combined fleets of England and France at Southwold? And yet now so serious was the plight of Holland, caught between the upper grindstone of British navalism and the nether grindstone of French militarism, that the College of Admiralty was actually considering calling the sixty-eight-year-old veteran from the retirement of his snug harbor.

The aging admiral was seated in his garden discussing his recent campaign with his son-in-law while the women folk busied with their spinning and sewing were silently praying that peace, which always seemed just below the horizon, might come in time to save the hero of many a hard-fought battle from further exertions his wearied frame could with difficulty endure. The conversation had just turned to the subject of de Witt's fireships when the Admiral's servant approached to inquire whether his master could receive Herr de Weldt, Councillor of the Admiralty, who had come with a message from his colleagues. Slowly the grizzled old seaman regained his house leaving his family in sorrowful apprehension.

Night had fallen when de Ruyter entered his study, an imposing room worthy of the great man whose seclusion it guarded. Walls hung with Flemish tapestries, high-backed chairs covered with damask, a bronze chandelier with six candles, a cabinet in which the Admiral kept his collection of Japanese porcelains and one painting, only one, a portrait of Martin Luther.

"Good evening, Herr de Weldt," he said courteously as he motioned his visitor to a seat at one end of the long table on which maps and papers lay in some confusion.

"Good evening, Admiral. I hope your troublesome gallstones are no longer causing you to suffer."

"I am still suffering, Herr de Weldt, but God's will be done. What has the Admiralty decided concerning the expedition to Sicily?"

"The College is still resolved to send a force to help the Spaniards hold Milazzo. The French, so His Highness the Prince of Orange has been informed, are about to despatch a force to besiege that fortress."

"If the French take Milazzo," the Admiral interposed, "the

whole coast as far as Palermo is theirs. What naval forces have the French in the Levant?"

"Eighteen ships and twelve galleys," was the answer.

"And I am to be given but eighteen vessels?"

"Yes, Admiral."

"Too few! The College will regret sending so small a force."

"But Admiral, you are forgetting the Spanish fleet of forty sail!"

"No, sir. I am not forgetting them. I simply do not count them. If I take command I shall ask leave to disregard them. That is why I consider the forces assigned to me insufficient."

"But Admiral, the expense involved . . ."

"To practice economy," de Ruyter interjected, "when the honor of our flag and the lives of our seamen are involved is a crime."

"You have seen the French routed at Southwold in '72," the Councillor began.

A sharp glare from the Admiral made him pause. De Ruyter was the last man to underestimate his enemy. The French commander at Southwold had merely been seeking sea room in which to maneuver. Had the Duke of York done likewise the result might have been different.

"Yes, sir," interrupted the Admiral, "but today the French are commanded by Duquesne. I would not care to face him with inferior forces."

"Admiral, you surely are not afraid to fight Duquesne with a less numerous fleet!"

"Yes, sir, I am."

An awkward silence followed this blunt remark. Coming from so great a fighter it was disconcerting. We shall presently see de Ruyter's grounds for holding his new adversary in such wholesome respect.

"You will go though, Admiral?" the Councillor finally ventured.

De Heer Michiel Adriaensz Ruyter, Ridder,
Lt Admirael over de Provintie van
Hollandt ende Westvrieslandt.

De Ruyter

"I am always ready to risk my life wherever the Republic is willing to risk its banner," was the prompt reply from the old sea dog.

On July 29, 1675, de Ruyter went. "I do not expect to come back," were the parting words spoken in a low whisper to his son-in-law, the Reverend Bernard Somers.

By what chain of events did a Dutch fleet come to be dispatched to a region so far removed from its normal orbit? What is even more pertinent, how did Holland happen to form an alliance with her hereditary enemy Spain? The answer is that *Weltpolitik* is a quicksand on which no permanent policy can be built. As the sands shift, so must the policies of those who wish to stay on the surface.

The battle of Lepanto marked a turning point in Mediterranean history. Until then we had been concerned with invaders, conquerors, defenders. Now for the first time the Mediterranean became the scene of warfare having its origin far from its confines, a situation that has continued to our time. During the war with England Holland dispatched a fleet under Admiral Van Galen to the coast of Italy. On March 13, 1653, he fought an engagement with a British fleet in which he lost his life. The Dutch were not so lucky in the Mediterranean as they were in the Channel. Another such war was now calling de Ruyter from his quiet retreat on the Prins Hendrik-Kade. The traditional feud between Spain and Holland was now a thing of the past. Both nations had to face the growing ambitions of naval England and territorial France. The openly avowed intention of Louis XIV to advance his frontiers to some point in the Netherlands that would give him the strategic security he craved involved a threat to the might of Spain. To the Dutch it meant much more. The very existence of Holland as an independent state was at stake. When France resolved to strike at Spain by coming to the aid of Messina, which had rebelled against Spanish rule, a situation had arisen that made an alliance between Holland and Spain a logical combination. Dutch co-operation in the Mediterranean was the price of Spanish co-operation in the Low Countries.

The plan of William III was not lacking in sound strategy. What the Stadtholder had failed to grasp, however, was the change in the relative efficiency of the navies involved. The loss of the Armada had started the Spanish navy on a decline ulti-mately leading to a state of decrepitude that quite justified the contemptuous remark of de Ruyter. France, on the other hand, had finally become a naval power. During the reign of Louis XIII the French navy came into being at the urgent request of the Parliament of Provence, who were alarmed at the in-roads on French commerce perpetrated by the Barbary corsairs. Under the reign of Louis XIV a powerful Mediterranean base was built at Toulon on plans drawn by Vauban. It was there that the French expedition to Sicily was assembling. De Ruyter, however, would have to operate far from any adequate base.

There was another disadvantage under which the Dutch navy was laboring that neither de Ruyter nor the Admiralty could overcome. The age of the big line-of-battle ship was approaching. Unfortunately for Holland, the gradual silting up of her harbors had rendered it impossible for her to keep pace with this new development in naval architecture. The shallow draft imposed by nature on Dutch ships not only affected their tonnage and consequently their armament, it also affected their stability and consequently their gunnery and handiness.

But to return to the expedition to Sicily. Who was this new commander whom de Ruyter considered so formidable? Abra-ham Duquesne was born at Dieppe in 1610, the son of a sea cap-tain. Not being of noble birth his advancement in the French navy was entirely due to his merits. His early training had been under the eye of his father and had consisted of the usual blending of trading and raiding that was the common lot of all seamen of the period. By 1637 he had risen to the command of a vessel of the royal navy and had distinguished himself by recapturing the island of Lerins, near Antibes, which the Spaniards had seized two years previously. About the same time his father was killed in an engagement with the same enemy. We do not know how much property he bequeathed his son but we do know that he left him a grudge. Duquesne's hatred of the Spaniards was so violent that we must seek some other reason than filial devotion. The explanation probably lies in the fact that the Duquesne family were rabid Protestants. During the next five years he seized every opportunity of serving against a foe who had killed his father, in a fair fight be it said, and whose faith had been the cause of the persecution of his co-religionaries.

During the minority of Louis XIV the French navy saw little active service, so Duquesne obtained permission to accept a commission of Vice-Admiral that the King of Sweden offered him in 1643. Twice he inflicted stunning defeats upon the Danish fleet besieging Gothenburg. After two years' service he returned to France. The Spaniards had incited the city of Bordeaux to rebel against royal authority. Duquesne was given command of the fleet sent to retake that important harbor. So well did he discharge his mission that the king gave him as a reward the island and château of Indre, near Nantes. In 1659 peace having been declared Duquesne, now a *chef d'escadre*, and a lieutenant-general, was assigned the task of combating the Barbary pirates in the Mediterranean. In 1672 he was present at the battle of Southwold. The failure of the combined French and British fleets on that occasion is in no way attributable to him. The French, as can be seen, had picked the right man to oppose to de Ruyter.

The Dutch fleet got under way promptly. The month of September, 1675, was spent at Cadiz, where de Ruyter's predictions were abundantly verified. In spite of his urging only one vessel could his allies furnish him. By December he was off the Lipari Islands and in a position to intercept Duquesne's fleet and convoy. On January 8 the two fleets met near Stromboli, the volcanic peak half-way between Naples and Palermo. The French had twenty-eight sail to his nineteen. Under ordinary circumstances the fiery Dutchman would have attacked in spite of the disparity in forces. De Ruyter, however, had served in the Danish navy shortly after its disastrous experience with Duquesne. The reputation the terrible Frenchman had left behind him in the Scandinavian countries undoubtedly influenced de Ruyter. He chose the prudent lee gauge. The engagement began at 9.30. At 4.30 de Ruyter broke off, after having inflicted so much damage on the French fleet that they were in no condition to prevent his retiring to Palermo. His only loss was one ship which foundered during the night. His crippled vessels were taken in tow by Sicilian galleys. Considering the odds against him he had good reason to be satisfied even though he had not succeeded in preventing the French expedition from reaching Messina.

It was not until April 22 that the two fleets had sufficiently recovered for another trial of strength. Duquesne now had twenty-nine ships and eleven smaller vessels. De Ruyter had twenty-seven ships, of which ten were belated Spaniards, and twenty-two galleys. The ensuing battle, which was fought off Agosto, near Catania, has been claimed by both sides as a victory. Without analyzing the conflicting claims, this much is certain. It was a disaster for the Dutch, as it cost them the life of de Ruyter. In the thick of the fight a shot struck the quarter deck of the *Eendragt* and carried off the admiral's left foot. To make matters worse, the impact threw him to the deck below, a drop of seven feet, causing a fracture of his right leg. Night separated the contestants, the Dutch retiring to Syracuse, where on April 29 death put an end to the sufferings of that sturdy fighter, "the admiral who had remained a sailor." His gloomy presentiment had been fulfilled. His first and only serious wound in his long career afloat was his last.

His death affected Dutch operations. Soon the French were able to drive their enemy away. The battle of Palermo was decidedly a French victory although Duquesne had been superseded by an admiral of noble birth, the Duke de Vivonne. The Dutch expedition had, however, produced the desired result. It stiffened the resistance of the loyalist party so that, in spite of help from within, French intervention in Sicily had been a failure. In March, 1678, the French fleet in turn departed, leaving the Spaniards in possession of the island and the French partisans to their fate.

Posthumous honors were freely accorded de Ruyter. The King of Spain created him a duke and it was with a ducal mantle covering his coffin that he was borne up the channel where, with gallant courtesy, the French forts saluted their late enemy. His tomb you can see in the Niewe Kerk in Amsterdam.

What reward did his hard-hitting opponent reap? On his return to France Duquesne called to pay his respect to Louis XIV. "You are a Protestant, Monsieur Duquesne?" the *Grand Monarque* inquired. "Yes, Sire," was the ready answer, "but my services are good Catholics." No wonder Colbert described Duquesne as having "an inconvenient humor." In vain did Boussuet essay his eloquence on the testy Huguenot, in vain did Colbert plead with him. "The infinite difficulties which you raise on all occasions and on all subjects," he warned him, "greatly grieve the King." Although his promotion was at stake Duquesne persisted in his ungracious attitude. A Puritan is a Puritan regardless of nationality. The title of Marquis and an estate at Bouchot were granted him but not the one thing he wanted, the rank of Vice-Admiral in the French navy. He had to content himself with Colbert's assurance that "nothing can be added to the glory you have acquired," a most ambiguous remark. The Edict of Nantes was soon to be revoked. Protestant admirals were not wanted. Although Duquesne was excepted from the decree of banishment he saw his family and friends driven into exile. He did not long survive the blow. His death occurred in Paris in 1688.

The Dutch expedition to Sicily under de Ruyter, although the most imposing, was not the last appearance of Holland in the Mediterranean. In the War of the Spanish Succession Holland was leagued with England and Austria in an unsuccessful attempt to prevent Philip V, a grandson of Louis XIV, from retaining the crown his other grandfather, Charles II of Spain, had bequeathed him. To have the Austrians in the Spanish Netherlands was better than having the Bourbons there, as far as the Dutch were concerned. Holland, as can be seen, had once more shifted her position on the quicksands of *Weltpolitik* with the greatest of ease. Six Dutch ships assisted in the capture of Gibraltar in 1704, after which Holland, except for an occasional punitive expedition against the Barbary corsairs, withdrew from further participation in Mediterranean affairs, which is tantamount to saying that she ceased to be a world power. *Weltpolitik*, however, remained.

CHAPTER XIII

In Which Major Strategy Makes Its Appearance

"EGYPT is the most important country in the world," Napoleon is said to have remarked at Saint Helena, a somewhat enigmatic statement in view of the fact that the voyages of discovery, by opening new trade routes, had greatly diminished the importance of the Mediterranean as an artery of commerce, a situation the piercing of the Suez Canal has only partly overcome. Venice, of course, was the chief sufferer from this development, as she was in no position, geographically or politically, to engage in any large-scale oversea program. America and India were beyond her reach. Moreover, the Atlantic navies born of the Spanish and Portuguese discoveries had brought into being a new type of vessel, the broadside ship. The Venetian galleys were the product of navigation in narrow seas. For threading their way around headlands, between islands, in and out of small harbors they were invaluable, but the "military rowboats" inherited from antiquity could not be pitted against the incipient battleship. Tactically as well as commercially the tide was running against Venice.

In the broad oceans the first result of the voyages of discovery was a keen rivalry between Spain and Portugal. Pope Alexander VI, to whom the respective claims were submitted for arbitration, settled the matter as between the first two claimants without, however, bringing peace any nearer. The late comers, Holland, France and England, who were in no way bound by the award, soon came to blows, the struggle finally narrowing down to a long duel between France and England. Hence the alacrity with which the British seized Gibraltar in 1704. From the outset British policy was a long-range one. Not the war being waged but the wars that were to follow determined England's decisions. Although the capture of Gibraltar had been a joint operation, the British admiral, Sir George Rooke, unceremoniously hauled down the Austrian colors the Prince of Hesse-Darmstadt had raised and took possession of "the Rock" in the name of Queen Anne. The capture of Minorca in 1708 followed and the Peace of Utrecht confirmed both occupations. France and England had locked horns.

The new order in the western Mediterranean weighed heavily on French naval effort. Besides holding what in the days of sail was the key to the straits, England had acquired a base from which she could watch the Toulon squadron, rendering its junction with the Brest fleet doubly difficult. It is not surprising, therefore, that one of the first moves France made during the Seven Years War was to lay siege to Port Mahon. An expedition under the Duc de Richelieu was landed on Minorca. La Galissonnière's fleet blocked Byng's attempt to relieve the island. The court-martial that followed the defeat of the British admiral is one of the most controversial episodes of Mediterranean history. A slave to his "Fighting Instructions," he lost sight of his main mission, which was at any cost to interrupt the French communications. Instead of so doing he retired to Gibraltar after an engagement in which, though worsted, he was not put *hors de combat*. In spite of a plea for clemency by the court that tried him he was made the scapegoat of a failure that was more damaging to the British ministry than to British arms. He was shot on the deck of the *Monarch*, a miscarriage of justice that enabled Voltaire to indulge in a sardonic bit of humor.

"As they were talking they arrived at Portsmouth. The water

ADMIRAL BYNG.

MINORCA

We have lately been told —   They met after Noon,
Of two Admirals bold, —   Which I think was too soon;
Who engag'd in a terrible Fight: As they both r*n away before Night.

The SHOOTING of ADMIRAL BYNG. on board the MONARQUE.

front was lined with crowds of people who were intently watching a rather stout man kneeling with bandaged eyes on the quarterdeck of one of the ships of the fleet. Four soldiers stationed opposite this man fired three bullets each into his skull as peacefully as humanly possible; after which the assembled multitude departed well satisfied.

" 'What is all this,' Candide asked, 'and why have they just killed this stout man with so much ceremony?'

" 'He is an admiral,' Candide was told.

" 'And why kill this admiral?'

" 'Because,' Candide was informed, 'he did not kill enough people. He fought a battle with a French admiral and he is accused of not having been close enough to his opponent.'

" 'But,' said Candide, 'the French admiral was equally far off from the British admiral.'

" 'That is undeniable,' was the reply, 'but in this country it is advisable to kill an admiral now and then to encourage the others!' "

With the encouragement thus given to British commanders in mind we can understand why the Seven Years War proved a major disaster for France. Majorca was restored to England but what was more important Canada was irretrievably lost and the work of Dupleix and La Bourdonnais in India was undone.

It would seem at first blush as if the importance oversea colonies had assumed would tend to lessen the importance of the Mediterranean strategically as well as commercially. Such, however, was far from being the case although a considerable time lag occurred before it was generally recognized that the eastern end of the sea was quite as important as the Straits of Gibraltar. Keen intellects were not lacking to point out the growing strategic value of Egypt but unfortunately for France their advice was not heeded until the disintegration of French naval strength had rendered impossible the one strategic move that might have turned the scales in favor of France. The occupation of Egypt was a brilliant conception of major strategy, one that France, owing to her proximity, was in a much better position than England to undertake. The voyages of discovery had increased rather than lessened the strategic importance of the Mediterranean and had brought Egypt to the fore for reasons not connected with her wealth.

We have seen that during Jacques Cœur's time Provence carried on a profitable trade with Alexandria. The impetus that enterprising Frenchman gave trade in the Levant continued unabated after his death until in 1724 the Marquis de Bonneval, the French Ambassador at the Porte, was able to report that it had attained the figure of 4,400,000 piastres annually,[1] of which over one-quarter was attributed to Cairo, Alexandria and Rosetta. The astonishing feature of this Egyptian business was that it was carried on by a mere handful of French residents, about fifty.

The idea of a French colony in Egypt and the construction of a canal to the Red Sea had been frequently discussed. As far back as 1586 the report of a Turkish survey was forwarded to Paris by the French ambassador. Richelieu seems to have coupled the idea of a canal with a chain of French settlements in India and Australia. Regularly the French consuls renewed their recommendations but the exigencies of the European situation prevented action. So far the matter had been viewed from the commercial point of view. In the hopes of diverting Louis XIV from his dream of subjugating the lesser German states that versatile German, Leibniz, elaborated a scheme whereby France would occupy Egypt, build a canal and thereby be in a position so to threaten Dutch possessions in India as to force a satisfactory settlement of the entire international situation. Major strategy was invented by a scientist and not by a soldier. Armed with a letter of recommendation from his

[1] The piastre was the equivalent of about twenty-five centimes gold.

sovereign, the Elector of Mainz, Leibniz submitted his memorandum to the ministers of Louis XIV, who could only see in it another crusade. Holy wars had "ceased to be the fashion" Pomponne informed the amateur strategist. Leibniz's report met the fate of most such documents. It was buried in the government archives. In 1803 General Mortier, then in command of the army occupying Hanover, came across a copy in the town library and sent it to Bonaparte. Whether this belated endorsement of a campaign that had by then ended in a pathetic failure was any consolation to the general who had planned it we do not know.

In 1738 d'Argenson again took the matter under advisement. During the reign of Louis XV the possibility of a partition of Turkey made the first of its many appearances in European chancelleries. Choiseul seems to have revived the interest in Egypt by suggesting that France take that country as her share of the spoils. The disgrace of that minister and the refusal of Turkey to partition once more relegated the Egyptian project to a state of innocuous desuetude.

With the accession of Louis XVI Egypt was once more given careful consideration. English intrigue in the Levant was undermining the prestige of France and the favored position of the French trader was in danger of being lost. The outbreak of the War of American Independence gave France an exceptional opportunity to settle old scores with England both in the East and in the West. Hyder-Ali had started a formidable insurrection against British rule in India. The victories of Suffren had revived French hopes of regaining the lost *comptoires*. England, not Holland, was now the enemy. The new King began by sending a confidential agent to inspect the lay of the land and to make a detailed report. The choice of Baron Tott was a wise one. His report was a comprehensive document in which every phase of the Egyptian situation was gone into with German thoroughness. Once more, however, action was deferred, probably for fear of opening up the troublesome Turkish question.

When Talleyrand took charge of the foreign relations of the new republic he therefore found a mass of information awaiting his perusal. What was more important, he found the leader whose enthusiasm resulted in action, Napoleon Bonaparte. The fascination the Orient exercised over Napoleon's imagination at all times has frequently been attributed to a spirit of mysticism. Be that as it may, in advocating the occupation of Egypt Bonaparte was but giving an illustration of what Carlyle has called his "ineradicable feeling for reality." Unless and until France could establish a naval superiority in the channel an invasion of England was out of the question. Unless and until France by successful land operations could secure control of the seacoast of Europe England could not be excluded from the continental markets. The only remaining way of humbling England was to menace India. The report Bonaparte made to the Directoire under date of February 23, 1798, after a hurried tour of inspection of the arsenals of Flanders, speaks volumes for the realism with which at that time he viewed the strategical problems of France. The Egyptian campaign was the result of that report.

The story of the French invasion of Egypt and Syria is one of the most romantic chapters of Mediterranean history. The expedition got off to a good start. During the early months of 1798 an imposing armada of 13 ships-of-the-line, 14 frigates, 72 corvettes and 400 transports was quietly assembled at Toulon, Marseilles, Genoa and Civita Vecchia without their concentration arousing British suspicions. The troops to be conveyed amounted to 35,000 men. The generals were the pick of the new republican army, Kléber, Desaix, Murat, Davoust, Lannes, Marmont; also Bonaparte's brother-in-law Leclerc and that extraordinary mulatto, General Alexandre Dumas. Admiral Brueys cleverly gave the British the slip and suddenly appeared before Malta. Thanks to Bonaparte's forethought a "commercial mission" had so undermined the discipline of "the Religion" that the French knights refused to fight their fellow-countrymen. An insurrection among the Maltese did the rest. As there was good ground for believing that the Czar Paul I was contemplating taking over the island no time was lost in forestalling that move. The knights were shipped to Trieste, as we have seen. "Upon my word, General, it is lucky there was some one to open the gates for us!" was General Caffarelli's comment as he surveyed the "luxe de précautions inutiles" the French had acquired without fighting. On July 2, 1798, the expedition was before Alexandria. The troops were landed and with a bold rush entered the city.

It was no ordinary army republican France had landed on the historic soil of Egypt. On the voyage to Alexandria the young commander-in-chief delved deep into a library of 125 volumes he had taken on board consisting of historical works, classical poets and books of travel. By the time he landed Bonaparte had acquired a familiarity with every aspect of the ancient country he hoped to bring into the French fold. In many respects the expedition was a scientific one. Caffarelli was an astronomer of repute, Monge and Berthollet were impressed into service as archæologists, although the former was a mathematician and the latter a chemist. "True conquests, the only ones which cost no regrets, are those achieved over ignorance," Bonaparte had recently told the Genoese. These words seem to have inspired the French in their relations with the Arab and Copt populations of Egypt. That the French *savants* made an honest endeavor to start the Egyptian people on the road of progress is undeniable. The *Institut du Caire* they founded was the cornerstone on which the intellectual awakening of Egypt was built. Unfortunately the French collided with an antipathy against which many similar attempts have come to grief, Moslem fanaticism. In spite of a consistently conciliatory attitude

toward Mohammedanism, in which the prevailing anti-clerical-
ism of the French republicans played an important part, the
invaders had to fight to maintain themselves in Egypt.

On July 3 Bonaparte set out from Alexandria to complete
the occupation of the country. The Battle of the Pyramids
ensued. The Mamelukes gave an impressive demonstration
of the fact that a *fantasia* cannot overcome a human mowing
machine. "Soldats, du haut de ces pyramides quarante siècles
vous regardent!" At Saint Helena Napoleon admitted to Gour-
gaud that his speech on that occasion had been "un peu charlatan," but it fired his tired and thirsty troops to such a pitch
of enthusiasm that the Mamelukes were easily defeated. The
French entered Cairo. Here Bonaparte sent orders to Brueys
to sail for Corfu or Toulon, preferably the former. It was for
precisely some such situation that he had acquired the Ionian
Islands at Campo Formio. In view of the oft-repeated assertion that the great military strategist never grasped the principles of maritime strategy it should be noted that he realized
the importance of a "fleet in being" on this occasion better than
the admiral in command. To Brueys, however, leaving Egypt
before a final victory seemed desertion. Disregarding orders
he anchored in Aboukir Roads hoping thereby to be in a position to protect the rear of the army. As Bonaparte had sensed,
he could have done so better by threatening enemy communications from a secure base. The disposition of the French
vessels was faulty in that it allowed room for an enterprising
commander to slip in between them and the shore and thus
take them between two fires. That is exactly what Nelson did
on August 1, 1798. It was a massacre, not a battle. Brueys was
killed. Casabianca and his young son perished in the flames
of his ship, as most American schoolboys will remember. Among
the losses we must mention the treasure Bonaparte had seized at
Malta, all of which was lost when the *Orient* blew up. Ville-
neuve managed to escape with two frigates. Firmly convinced

Painted by G. Arnold, A.R.A.

The Battle of the Nile

that "Bonaparte had gone to the devil," Nelson proceeded to do likewise, figuratively speaking. He went to Lady Hamilton.

The French were now cut off from France. Nothing daunted, however, the French scientists began to develop the resources of the country. Soon the new colony was self-supporting. Agriculture was fostered, the apportionment of taxes so improved that money was available for improvements. A mint and a commercial company were started, a camel corps recruited to police the desert and Desaix despatched to Upper Egypt there to establish contact with the anti-Turkish Abyssinians. Yet in spite of the benefits the French were undoubtedly conferring on Egypt, serious rioting occurred which had to be sternly repressed.

Having organized his administration Bonaparte now proceeded to invade Syria, Turkey having declared war. Jaffa was taken on March 6, 1799, after a gallant defense by its garrison. Here a new and terrible enemy made its appearance, the pest. In vain did the French hasten their march to Saint Jean d'Acre, the plague dogged their footsteps. At Acre Bonaparte found the British awaiting him. The fleet Sir Sidney Smith commanded had a few days previously captured the French vessels that were transporting the siege artillery. These guns were now turned against the invaders by the British seamen who had been landed to reinforce the Turkish garrison. The French had to settle down and lay siege to the citadel their distant forebears had defended against many an assault. The Turkish army sent to relieve the siege was defeated at Mont Thabor (April 17, 1799), a battle that gave a foretaste of the victories the Emperor was to win. Thirty thousand Turks routed by four thousand Frenchmen, thanks to a masterly concentration. Bonaparte spent the night after the battle at the convent of Nazareth where the Prior showed him the pillar the Angel Gabriel had broken at the moment of the Annunciation. The outburst of hilarity among the general's staff that followed this manifestation of primitive piety was soon quelled by a scowl from the future author of the Concordat.

For nine weary weeks the siege of Saint Jean d'Acre dragged on. In all forty separate assaults were repulsed by the defenders and twenty-six sallies by the besiegers. The French troops finally refused to charge again over the putrefying bodies of their slain comrades. After losing five thousand men, including four generals, among them Caffarelli, the French were compelled to retreat (May 17, 1799). With great difficulty were the sick and wounded evacuated from Jaffa. The legend that they were disposed of by an overdose of opium is, of course, unfounded. Sir Sidney Smith, be it said to his credit, did all in his power to relieve their sufferings.

In spite of attempts to gloss matters over in official despatches, the Syrian expedition had been a ghastly fiasco. On reaching Cairo more trouble was in store for Bonaparte. First he had to repel a Turkish attack on Aboukir, one of his greatest victories. *"Vous êtes grand comme le monde, Général!"* Kléber exclaimed after the Turks had been hurled back into the sea. Then came the news that a powerful coalition had been formed in Europe; the French armies in Italy and on the Rhine had been defeated. Here Bonaparte took the most criticized step in his career. Leaving Kléber in command, he re-embarked on the night of August 22 taking with him Berthier, Marmont, Duroc, Bessières, Lavalette; also Lannes and Murat, both of whom had been wounded. Monge, Berthollet and Bourienne, his secretary, completed the list of homeward-bound. Admiral Ganteaume managed to avoid the British patrols. The party landed at Fréjus on October 9, where Bonaparte was given an ovation. "We prefer the plague to the Austrians," the townsfolk cried as they insisted that the quarantine regulations be suspended. Rushing to Paris he found the Directoire tottering on the brink and a new lover sneaking out of his house in the Rue de la Victoire.

What happened to the French expeditionary force? For two years did the French maintain themselves against British and Turkish attacks. The gallant Kléber fell a victim of an assassin's knife. The British naval preponderance in the Mediterranean prevented any assistance reaching the hard-pressed French troops. Finally General Menou, who commanded at Alexandria, and General Belliard who was holding Cairo, agreed to evacuate. About 24,000 men were repatriated in September 1801.

The historical importance of the French expedition to Egypt far transcends any question presented by the conflict between revolutionary France and conservative England. Bonaparte had demonstrated that a small army of resolute men in control of the country which by its location dominated the shortest route to India could compel Great Britain to forsake the broad oceans over which her fleets roamed at will and concentrate on a restricted but intricate area. The possibility of a renewed attack on Egypt influenced British naval policy during the entire Napoleonic period, as Nelson's movements during the Trafalgar campaign clearly reveal. The French plan was not a diversion; it was more than a mere colonial venture. It was a bold flight of major strategy which, if successful, would have compelled England to release the strangle hold she held on French naval effort. If Gibraltar prevented the French Mediterranean fleet from co-ordinating its movements with those of the Atlantic fleet, France could exert an irresistible counter pressure from Egypt that would draw a large British force away from the defense of the British Isles. The maritime control of the channel, which Napoleon so ardently wanted for a few brief hours, might well have been his had France been able to hold on in Egypt. No truer words did Napoleon ever utter than when he ruefully exclaimed in his declining years: *"J'ai manqué à ma fortune à Saint Jean d'Acre!"*

CHAPTER XIV

In Which a Very Young Nation Takes Part in a Very Old Conflict

THE STARS AND STRIPES proudly floating over a Moorish fortress! Surely of all the extraordinary sights the Mediterranean has witnessed this is the most extraordinary. The events leading up to it are, however, nearly as strange.

The repulse the Saracens had suffered before Constantinople deflected their offensive from the European to the African coast of the Mediterranean. Meeting with little resistance, Belisarius having created a vacuum, they soon reached the Atlantic (711) and began their invasion of Spain. The year 721 saw them ready to invade Aquitaine. The moribund Kingdom of Toulouse called upon the Franks for help. The victory of Charles Martel turned the tide. Recovering from their setback, the Saracens proceeded to consolidate their position in Spain. It was not until the beginning of the ninth century that they cast about for new conquests. Sicily was the objective chosen. It took them one hundred and forty years to subdue that island. Palermo was captured in 831 but the last stronghold of the Eastern Empire, Rametta, did not fall until 965. The conquest of Sicily marked the high water of Saracen power. Since their first appearance before Constantinople they had overrun the southern Mediterranean coast from Palestine to the Pillars of Hercules, occupied all of Spain except for a narrow strip along the Bay of Biscay and seized all the major islands of the western Mediterranean, Sicily, Sardinia, Corsica and the Balearic Isles.

Christianity and Islam had locked horns in the Mediterranean. The reconquest of the lost territory is the longest war waged in the history of that sea. It began with a clash between the Moors of Spain and an entirely new opponent, the first invaders to enter the Inland Sea from beyond the Pillars. In 844 the Norsemen first appeared off the coast of Galicia attacking Gijon and Corunna, then rounding Cape Finisterre they attacked Lisbon, Cadiz, Seville and Cordoba, thereby establishing contact with the Moslems. They even extended their raid to Arzilla on the western coast of Morocco, passing by the Straits of Gibraltar. It was not until 859 that they entered the Mediterranean. Starting from their base on the Seine they sailed to the mouth of the Guadalquivir, where they were defeated by a Moorish fleet. Reaching the Straits once more they burned the mosque at Algeciras then plundered the northern coast of Morocco and the Balearic Isles. Continuing eastward they took up winter quarters on the island of Camargue and ascended the Rhone as far as Valence. On their return journey they again landed near Gibraltar but another defeat by a Moorish fleet sent them home. The astonishing feature of these wanderings was that they were performed in boats so small as to be able to penetrate miles inland along shallow rivers. So far the Norsemen had limited themselves to piracy and had not aimed at occupying any territory, much less fighting the battles of the Faith.

It was the Normans, as the Norse settlers in France were called, who first colonized the Mediterranean. In 1026 a colony of Norman mercenaries was founded at Aversa, near Capua, which under the leadership of Robert de Hauteville, surnamed *Guiscard* or Wiseacre, grew into the Duchies of Apulia and Calabria. Soon the Normans were ready to cross the Straits of Messina. In 1061 Robert's brother Roger began the conquest of Sicily. It took him nearly thirty years to wrest the island from the Saracens, a considerably shorter period of time than the Saracens had required to dispose of the Greek garrisons. Under Roger II Calabria, Apulia and Sicily were united under one crown and the Kingdom of the Two Sicilies was thereby founded.

The loss of Sicily was a serious blow to the Saracens. It was not the only disaster to befall them. In 930 the Tuscans expelled them from Corsica and in 1022 Pisa and Genoa drove them from Sardinia. Finally in 1229 the Catalans and Aragonese captured the Balearic Isles. The lack of real sea power was telling heavily against the Saracens. They had, to be sure, more than held their own in the few engagements they had fought with the first Norsemen. That, however, was raider against raider. In a conflict with organized sea power such as the Italians and the Catalans were beginning to develop they were outmatched. With their northern bases gone the Saracen corsairs were compelled to transfer their headquarters to the Barbary coast. Soon they were to receive an unexpected and important reinforcement. The conquest of Granada was driving large numbers of Moslems from Spain into the narrow strip of territory bordering northern Africa. As the country was unable to support them the sea became their only recourse. Barbary piracy was now to begin in earnest.

As can be readily seen, the Saracens had good cause to hate all Christians without distinction. The Crusades had sent all Christendom swarming over their possessions in Asia Minor. "The Religions" were recruiting in practically every country of Europe the Knights whose galleys were waging relentless war against the Saracen cruisers. Such distant nations as Britain, Denmark and Norway had sent their kings to the Holy Land to battle "the Infidel." No wonder the Saracens could not conceive of a Christian who was not an enemy. To make matters worse the Christians were now preparing to invade Africa.

Dragut attacking Malta

In 1509 Ferdinand the Catholic seized Oran, Bougie and Algiers. On his death in 1516 the Algerines revolted and called to their aid the celebrated corsair Barbarossa. Under his leadership the Saracens soon recovered their lost cities and began the systematic raiding of the Two Sicilies and the Balearic Isles that has remained legendary. Travellers along the Amalfi coast can still see the picturesque watch towers built to resist the African rovers, the so-called "Saracen Towers," and in Capri the castle Barbarossa captured still bears his name.

An amusing story is told about this raider. Soliman the Magnificent had made him Viceroy of Algiers as a reward for his services. Obviously the honor required some acknowledgment, so, knowing his master's tastes, he staged a nocturnal raid on the Castle of Fondi, near Gaëta, in the hopes of capturing Julia Gonzaga, Duchess of Trajetto. The lovely widow, however, managed to escape accompanied by one knight whom she promptly executed on her return home. As Julia's costume was that of Lady Godiva when she hurriedly mounted her steed the reader can surmise the charge.

Barbarossa, however, was more than a corsair. His professional skill was such that he was given command of the Turkish fleet that defeated Andrea Doria at Prevesa. Mention should also be made of one of his captains, Dragut, who lost his life while conducting the famous siege of Malta in which Jean de la Valette distinguished himself. It was not the first time the two had met. Both had at various times in their careers been captured and compelled to wield an oar until ransomed. On one occasion la Valette, while inspecting some Genoese galleys, recognized his old opponent chained to a rower's bench. "Usanza de guerra, Señor Dragut," said the Grand Master. "Y mudanza de fortuna," countered the captive. Barbarossa, assisted by la Valette, ultimately ransomed his captain, who at once, nothing daunted, took to the sea again. The bitterness with which the long naval war between the Barbary States and

Christendom was waged has probably never been equalled in history. Charles V made an earnest effort to crush his piratical opponents. He succeeded in gaining possession of Tunis in 1535, on which occasion he outdid his Mohammedan foes by slaughtering over 20,000 men, women and children and selling 10,000 into slavery. Six years later he attempted to repeat the performance at Algiers with an army led by the Duke of Alva and a fleet commanded by Andrea Doria, only to meet with a sanguinary repulse that nearly ended in a major disaster.

The battle of Lepanto, as we have seen, started the Turkish navy on its downward path but had no effect on the activities of the Barbary navies. The *guerre de course* they waged well into the eighteenth century undoubtedly constituted a diversion which enabled Turkish armies to operate successfully in eastern Europe. Skillfully playing upon the mutual jealousies of the Christian powers their corsairs extended their activities to the Atlantic. In 1631 one of their captains, Murad Reis, sacked Reykavik in Iceland and Baltimore in Ireland and returned safely to Algiers with a goodly cargo of captives to be sold into slavery.[1] Another carried off the wife and daughter of the governor of the Canaries. In the course of three centuries the total number of prisoners taken by the Algerines is said to have reached the staggering total of 600,000. Algiers often had as many as 30,000 prisoners on hand, Cervantes having been one of them. Between 1674 and 1680 three hundred and fifty British vessels were captured. During Cromwell's rule the fines collected from members of Parliament who arrived late for prayers were placed in a fund to be used for the ransoming of British captives. The Mediterranean, however, was the main cruising ground of these rovers. As late as 1798 Tunisian

---

[1]Daniele Varè in his amusing book of recollections, *The Laughing Diplomat*, states that during the first World War the Icelandic fishermen hesitated to venture far to sea for fear of "the Turks" and were only reassured by hearing that "Venice" had entered the war. *"Se non è vero, è ben trovato!"*

corsairs carried off the entire population of the island of San Pietro, near Cagliari. A religious order, the Mathurins, was founded for the express purpose of ransoming and caring for Christian captives. Piracy had become a business with a heavy investment of capital, much as "rum-running" was with us in America. In the latter part of the seventeenth century the privately owned Algerine corsairs numbered more than one hundred. To keep them busy war must be waged continually against some nation or other, else the unemployed crews would become a menace to the state. Christians were not above sharing in so profitable a business. Barbarossa himself was born a Roumeliot Christian and Murad Reis was an enterprising Dutchman who had "taken to the turban" and had married a Moslem wife, a fact that did not prevent him from visiting his first wife at Veere and bringing his daughter back for a visit to Salé, of which he was governor for a while.

As might be expected, England, France and Holland made countless attempts to bring the corsairs to terms by bombarding their strongholds. The service record of every admiral of the period contains at least one citation of service against some Barbary state. Two factors, however, made permanent results impossible of attainment. The first was the connivance of the European powers at attacks directed against their particular commercial rival. The British complained that if there were no Algiers it would be worth Holland's while to build one, a remark Benjamin Franklin was in turn to apply to England. The second impediment to success was that the problem called for a joint land and sea offensive. Naval bombardments, to quote Thomas Jefferson, were "much like breaking glass windows with guineas." On one occasion Duquesne gave Algiers a thorough "strafing." When the Dey heard what the expedition had cost France he exclaimed that for half that sum he would have burned the city himself! Duquesne was driven off, however, by a new type of projectile, the mangled bodies of the French residents, among them the Consul and the Apostolic Vicar. The recollection of Charles V and his unfortunate experience made European nations hesitate to land an army. It was cheaper to buy protection and get the benefit of the damage done to the trade of other countries. As a result of this policy Algiers in 1799 had seven kings and two republics paying tribute. One of the republics was the United States.

The situation was really very simple viewed from the Barbary standpoint. As soon as British protection was withdrawn from American ships they became fair quarry for the Barbary cruisers. Several American vessels were captured shortly after our peace with England but pending the adjustment of treaties with the various Barbary States their crews were not too badly treated. Early in 1786 John Adams had an interview with the Tripolitan Ambassador in London, Abdurrahman, who inquired with great interest about the resources of the new nation. "It is a very great country," he remarked and then added ominously, "but Tripoli is at war with it." Adams expressed some surprise. "Turkey, Tripoli, Tunis, Algiers and Morocco," the ambassador continued, "are the sovereigns of the Mediterranean and no nation can navigate that sea without a treaty from them."

The story of our negotiations with the Barbary States is not pleasant reading. The only consolation to be found is the fact that European nations, in a better position than ourselves to resist, were complying with demands nearly as humiliating. As Adams wrote to John Jay in 1794, "as long as France, England, Holland, the Emperor, etc., will submit to be tributaries to these robbers, to what purpose should we make war upon them?" Jefferson, to his credit be it said, was in favor of more drastic action. While in Paris he sounded out the ambassadors of the powers with a view to forming an international police to rid the seas of these aggressors. Portugal, Naples, Sicily, Venice, Malta, Denmark and Sweden seemed favorably inclined to this embryo League of Nations but, as might have been foreseen, the major powers held aloof, so the plan was still-born. In 1787 Jefferson endeavored to enlist the services of the Mathurins to ransom the American captives but the suppression of the religious orders by Revolutionary France rendered that solution impossible. Finally in 1792 the Senate passed the first appropriation to purchase the liberation of the American prisoners and to secure the future safety of American merchantmen. By 1797 nearly one million dollars had been paid to Algiers alone. The terms of the treaty were galling in the extreme. They included the delivery of a frigate loaded to the gunwales with stores.

Fortunately Congress soon realized that force might have to be used and on March 27, 1794, authorized the construction of the first of the famous Humphreys frigates. Work on these vessels was interrupted while the treaties were being negotiated but was resumed again in 1796. The United States Navy had come into being. It was high time. In 1800 Bainbridge, while commanding the *George Washington*, the first American warship to enter the Mediterranean, called at Algiers with our tribute only to find that he was expected to continue his journey to Constantinople with a cargo of slaves the Dey was sending to the Sultan. During the voyage he was required to fly the Algerine flag, the crowning insult. His visit to Constantinople created quite a commotion, the Sultan never having heard of the new nation whose warship had entered the Golden Horn. The very generosity of the tribute paid to Algiers was the cause of the outbreak of hostilities with Tripoli. Shortly after the conclusion of the treaty with the Dey, similar though less onerous ones were concluded with the Bey of Tunis and the Bashaw of Tripoli. The Bashaw now repudiated his agreement and demanded $250,000 down and $20,000 annually. Not meeting with a prompt acceptance the Tripolitans cut down the flagstaff on the American Consulate (May 10, 1801), the usual mode of declaring war in the Barbary States. Our consul, James L. Cathcart, withdrew to Leghorn leaving the Danish consul, Nicholas Nissen, whose services to our prisoners of war should always be gratefully remembered, in charge of our interests. A Tripolitan squadron commanded by a renegade Scotchman, Peter Lisle, sailed for the Atlantic to prey on American shipping. The United States had been drawn into a conflict that antedated the discovery of America by over seven hundred years. Our first attempt to keep out of war had been as unsuccessful as our recent one, possibly for the same reason, our hesitancy forcibly to resist the first infringement of our rights as a neutral.

The performance of the United States Navy in the War with Tripoli need not be retold. Glorious as were the actions of our seamen they nevertheless demonstrated one fact that is frequently overlooked. Naval warfare unsupported by land operations seldom accomplishes definite results. If we were able to bring the Tripolitan War to a victorious conclusion it was partly due to a resourceful amateur soldier and diplomat, William Eaton.

A picturesque character was William Eaton, the kind that can flourish only in the untrammeled atmosphere of the New World. A Connecticut Yankee born on a farm near Woodstock in 1764, his first experience in matters military was in the Revolutionary Army. Running away from home he enlisted at the age of sixteen and was mustered out a sergeant. Of a studious turn of mind, he next worked his way through Dartmouth College and in 1792, two years after his graduation, secured a commission as captain in the Army. After seven years of stormy service he was appointed consul to Tunis and in December 1798 sailed for his post, "the Well-guarded City, the Abode of Felicity." After presenting his credentials to the Bey, whom he described as "a huge shaggy beast sitting on his rump," he discovered that his new abode was anything but felicitous, the cupidity of that potentate having been thoroughly aroused by the unending stream of "presents" the United States was showering on the neighboring Dey of Algiers, whom Eaton described as "an elevated brute." The pusillanimous attitude of our government so disgusted Eaton that he was on the point of resigning from the service when the war with Tripoli broke out. How to further the action of our navy was now Eaton's concern. The blockade was getting us nowhere. Eaton, however, soon hit upon a scheme that was little short of genius, and incidentally sound strategy.

The Bashaw of Tripoli, Yussuf, had succeeded his father by the usual oriental method of making away with his brothers. Hasan, the eldest, was promptly murdered. Hamet, the next in line of succession, managed to escape to Tunis, where he was living at the time of Eaton's arrival. He seems to have been a peaceful, retiring soul, not the type to undertake the conquest of a throne. Eaton, however, had energy and courage enough for two. He struck up a friendship with Hamet and endeavored to instill in him a desire for revenge. "Now see here, Hamet, I'm your friend," to quote his own account of the adventure, "and I'm going to put you back on your throne if you will only say the word." At the same time he expounded his plan to James Madison. "We need but cash and a few marines!" Among Eaton's claims to distinction we must give first place to the fact that he was the first to sense the possibilities that lay in the judicious use of cash and a few marines.

After considerable haranguing Hamet finally "said the word" and Eaton left for a much-needed vacation in Italy. On his return he found that Hamet had changed his mind. Brother Yussuf had gotten wind of the plan and had bought Hamet off by promising him the governorship of Derne. All that Hamet needed was a pass from Eaton to go through the American blockade. Eaton, however, soon got Hamet back in line by telling him that all his brother wanted was to get him where he could conveniently cut his throat. In the meantime Eaton had gone into debt to the tune of $23,000 fomenting the insurrection that was to put Hamet on the throne of his father and thereby accomplish what we had vainly been striving for with blockades and bombardments. To complicate matters still further the Bey of Tunis had suddenly been persuaded by his good cousin of Tripoli that in harboring Hamet he was guilty of an unfriendly act. The Bey accordingly cut off the allowance he had been giving the rightful heir. Eaton thereupon shipped his protégé to Malta and decided to go back to Washington to get his accounts passed on by the State Department and to press his plan for creating a backfire in Tripoli. Commodore Morris called at Tunis on March 10, 1803, to fetch Eaton and was promptly arrested for the latter's debts, an incident that did not increase Eaton's popularity with the Navy.

On reaching the United States Eaton presented his accounts and his plan of action and then went home to spend the summer with his family while the State Department mulled over his accounts and the Navy Department picked flaws in his plan. In January he returned to Washington. Congress was still considering both accounts and plan. While matters were thus hanging fire astonishing news reached Washington. Soon Decatur's name was on everybody's lips. Nelson had pronounced his burning of the *Philadelphia* in Tripoli harbor one of the outstanding feats of the age. Our Navy was demonstrating its ability to conduct sustained operations far from home. The oft-quoted remark attributed to Charles Cotesworth Pinckney, "Millions for defense but not one cent for tribute," although intended for French demands, was now being applied to Barbary piracy, thereby putting Europe to shame. In short, the United States had become a naval power over night. What was more astonishing, Eaton was apparently not the wild schemer he was supposed to be. Hamet had landed at Derne and had inflicted a defeat on Brother Yussuf. President Jefferson thereupon decided to send Hamet some much-needed supplies and a few pieces of artillery, also $40,000 in cash. Eaton was appointed Navy Agent to the Barbary States. Unfortunately, before he could get started for his new post disquieting news reached Washington. Hamet had been defeated and compelled to retire to Alexandria. Derne had been recaptured. Instead of realizing that had assistance been given Hamet promptly he might now be in Tripoli, Jefferson lost heart and countermanded his shipments. Eaton was nevertheless despatched on an ill-defined mission to Hamet. He had no illusion on the role he was to play, it was second fiddle to the Navy. If successful he would be recognized, if unsuccessful he would be diavowed.

In June 1804 Eaton sailed with Commodore Barron who had been sent to relieve Preble. It was not until December 8 that he finally reached Cairo and attempted to get in touch with Hamet, who, with a few adherents, had taken part in one of the periodical uprisings of the Mamelukes and was somewhere in Upper Egypt. The only reinforcements he brought were nine Americans, six of whom were marines. The marines were "few," as can be seen. Fortunately he brought some cash.

Kipling once described the American as one who "turns a keen untroubled face home to the instant need of things." Eaton was to have ample opportunity of living up to that definition. In view of the responsibilities he was about to assume it is not surprising that the sights of Egypt left him cold. He found the crocodiles inferior to our alligators and as for the pyramids they "disgusted" him as monuments of "the superstition, pride and folly of their founders." The first matter to arrange was to secure a pass from the Turkish viceroy for Hamet and his release by the Mamelukes. After some difficulty this was accomplished and on February 5, 1805, Eaton and Hamet met and arranged their fantastic Anabasis, the four-hundred-mile trek across the Desert of Barca to Derne. How did Eaton account for the lack of visible American support? Probably by emphasizing the assistance the fleet would furnish. On March 8 the advance began. The Hametian forces consisted of one hundred and seven camels, a troop of Arab horse, ninety of Hamet's personal escort, thirty-eight Greeks with two officers, two American naval officers, an English surgeon picked up in Alexandria, a non-commissioned officer and the six marines, Hamet and last but not least "General Eaton"; about four hundred persons all told.

Before twenty-four hours had elapsed the camel drivers struck. On March 18 they struck again. Failing to secure their exorbitant demands they deserted in a body. Fifty, however, returned the next day and the march was resumed. On the twenty-second the expedition came upon three Arab tribes who had never seen a Christian. Eaton persuaded them to join him, thereby securing ninety camels and some much-needed food. From now on, however, he had to drag an Arab village along with him. On the twenty-sixth a courier arrived from Derne with the news that Yussuf's army was marching on that city and would probably arrive there before Eaton. Now camel drivers and Arabs began deserting. On April 8 a serious incident occurred. Hamet had sent ahead to see whether the American squadron was off the coast, having apparently grown suspicious that perhaps Eaton had overstated the co-operation the fleet would render, wherein he was nearer the truth than Eaton cared to admit, as we shall learn. Both men lost their tempers and an ugly row seemed imminent when news was brought in that the American squadron was at Bomba. "We have a difficult undertaking," the American Xenophon calmly noted in his journal.

Finally on the fifteenth the expedition reached Bomba. Not a ship in sight! Eaton had spent his last sequin and eaten his last grain of rice. The next morning the *Hornet* and the *Argus*, having seen his campfires, returned to port. Eaton gave a sigh of relief. On the twenty-third the march was resumed and on the twenty-seventh the force was before Derne. So were the *Argus*, the *Hornet* and the *Nautilus*. The American vessels began a spirited bombardment of the fortifications. Eaton boldly put himself at the head of the Greeks and the six marines and charged. By four o'clock for the first and only time in history the American flag was flying over an African citadel. Eaton had lost only fourteen men but had himself been wounded. While recuperating in Derne news reached him that Yussuf's army was approaching. On May 13 the Tripolitans attacked. It took Eaton until June 10 to drive them off. Now, on to Tripoli!

But wait! On the eleventh the *Constellation* was seen entering the harbor. She bore dispatches. Peace, and none too honorable a peace, had been signed with Yussuf on June 4. The war was over and Eaton was told to disband his army. In spite of his success his government had let him down, thereby losing a unique opportunity of teaching the world at large and the Barbary States in particular that the young American republic was not to be trifled with. If Barron had been able to conclude peace it was because Yussuf was panic-stricken at the prospect of facing Eaton and his rapidly growing army. What blockades and bombardments had failed to accomplish an invasion had brought about.

How could Eaton break the news to Hamet, Hamet who had trusted him, who had believed him when he said the United States would see him through. Hamet, however, took matters with Moslem fatalism. All he now asked was safety for himself and his followers from the fury of his brother. The instant need of things was pressing. If the Arabs got an inkling of the situation Eaton's life was not worth the small change he had left in his purse. So the army was drilled as if the march on Tripoli were to be resumed. Then in the dead of night, "with silence and alacrity, but with astonishment," to quote Eaton's journal, the Greeks, Hamet and fifteen of his suite were rowed with muffled oars to the American squadron. Suddenly the sleeping city awoke. A frantic rush to the water front. Eaton Pasha and his *Americanos,* where are they? Gone! Dogs of unbelievers, they have abandoned us! Curses and imprecations rent the air. Then a mad dash for the hills, camels and pack animals mingling with screaming women and howling children. Eaton sorrowfully watched the spectacle from the last boat. "This moment we drop them from ours into the enemy's hands," he noted, "for no other crime than too much confidence in us!"

The epilogue is quickly told. A munificent allowance of two hundred dollars a month was awarded Hamet. For a while he lived in Syracuse, then, as a result of our intercession, he was given the governship of Derne. Eaton's prediction, however, was soon verified. Two months later he fled for his life to Egypt where he shortly died in poverty. He seems to have borne Eaton no ill will, as he presented him with a sword, subsequently adopted by our Marine Corps as a model for its commissioned officers, and corresponded with him until his death.

As for Eaton it was not until 1807 that his accounts were finally passed, but by then his testimony at the trial of Aaron Burr had put the government under heavy obligations to him. His services in Tripoli apparently had not. Massachusetts gave the "Hero of Derne" 10,000 acres which he sold for fifty cents an acre. He died in 1811, the typical old retired army officer who over his tipple in the tavern perorates on his services, which in his case were indeed hard to exaggerate, and on the ingratitude of republics, which is also hard to exaggerate.

And here we shall leave the Barbary States for a while. One feature of Eaton's adventure, however, we should remember. Eaton had pricked a bubble. He had proven that European armies need no longer fear the fate of Charles V if they landed on African soil. The Barbary navies, to be sure, still had a nuisance value. In 1815 we were compelled to send a squadron to bring the Algerines to terms. As late as 1825 Denmark, Portugal and Naples were paying tribute. But the days of Barbarossa, Dragut and Murad Reis were past. The spirit that had taken Tarik ben Said across the Pillars of Hercules had long since spent its force. It remained for the self-confident navy of a new nation and the ingenuity of a Yankee consul, however, to open the first breach in the ancient but tottering structure of Barbary power.

CHAPTER XV

The Parthenopean Republic

THE H.M.S. *Seahorse* dropped anchor in the Bay of Naples on July 8, 1799. Although the fighting was over and all that remained to be done was to expedite the executions, His Sicilian Majesty Ferdinand IV was unwilling to risk his august person ashore and accordingly transferred himself and his suite to the more comfortable quarters of H.M.S. *Foudroyant*. The next morning the British officers on looking over the rail beheld a strange apparition. The body of a man half protruding from the water was moving steadily toward the vessel. His eyes were open, his hair flying in the breeze. Word was sent to the King. When he came on deck and recognized the features of the dead man he became panic stricken. "Carraciolo!" he exclaimed. "What does he want?" An awkward silence followed. Finally a priest spoke up. "Sire, I think he has come to demand Christian burial." "Let him have it," the King stammered as he turned to go below again. The body was recovered and secretly buried. The weights that had been attached to the feet of the admiral when his corpse was lowered from the yardarm of the Neapolitan frigate *Minerva* had not been sufficient to keep his decomposing body from rising to the surface, they merely kept it upright.[1] It was not until 1873 that his tomb was discovered in the church of Santa Maria delle Grazie e Catena. In 1881 an inscription was

[1]The incident has been used by James Fenimore Cooper in his novel *Wing-and-Wing*.

placed over it stating that his death had been due to "the spite of an ungenerous foe," a scathing but fully deserved indictment of an act that will always remain a stain on the name of Lord Nelson.

Great popular movements are seldom isolated occurrences. No amount of censorship can prevent the spread of ideas. In spite of the excesses, the violence, the mob rule that unfortunately have tarnished the achievements of the French Revolution, the French republicans found in adjoining nations an element which had of its own volition indoctrinated itself with the '89 spirit and was anxious to repeat the experiment in their respective countries. The element in question prided itself on being philosophic. Today we should probably dub it the intelligentsia. The bond of union, of course, was a revolt against institutions, feudal in origin, that had long outlived their usefulness. A crop of "sister republics" rapidly sprang into being under the protection of the French armies that were carrying the counter-offensive of republican France across her own borders. No sooner had the danger of invasion been conjured than the French tide began breaking through the dikes of monarchical Europe. Italy was one of the first countries to be invaded.

What were the French objectives? Bonaparte stated one of them very frankly to his army about to descend on the rich plains of Lombardy. France was bankrupt, her armies starving and in rags. Her prosperous neighbors must supply her needs. The desire to set up republican governments that would be in sympathy with the new regime in France was another powerful incentive to an expansionist policy. These two motives were the ostensible ones. Their popular appeal was enough to keep the nation at a proper pitch of enthusiasm but the idea that ultimately developed into the *Grand Empire* was in the minds of the Directoire statesmen at an early date. France was aiming at putting French goods into the markets of which Great Britain then had a practical monopoly. Failing to defeat England afloat, every continental port was to be barred against British trade.

We need not trace the steps of France's penetration of Italy. It was anything but pacific. By 1797 the Ligurian Republic was in control of Genoa. Lombardy soon succumbed and the Cisalpine Republic, capital Milan, added another rich client state to the rapidly growing French system. Two years later Piedmont was annexed and a republic soon thereafter displaced the Pontifical government in Rome. Would Naples have escaped the fate of the northern Italian states had the Neapolitan Bourbons refrained from antagonizing the Directoire? Possibly. The French were not anxious at that time to venture so far south but Ferdinand brought matters to a head by an ill-advised expedition to Rome. The Roman Republic never enjoyed the degree of popular support that the other sister republics had enlisted. The mass of the Roman citizens remained loyal to the Papacy and insurrections continually endangered the French hold on the Eternal City. Taking advantage of an uprising Ferdinand advanced on Rome in November 1798. The French army commanded by General Championnet withdrew, allowing Ferdinand to enter the city. A short but inglorious occupation followed, sullied by the usual reprisals on the French and their adherents. Then suddenly Championnet gathered his forces that had been scattered throughout the Papal States and fell upon the Neapolitan army. Ferdinand was soon in headlong flight. Without waiting for instructions from his government Championnet now invaded the Neapolitan kingdom. Ferdinand had drawn the French lightning by his own foolhardiness.

Of all the converts to French republican ideas no band was more sincere than the small but ardent intellectual group that was anxiously awaiting the arrival of the French army in Naples. Its make-up was the usual one: a few idealistic young nobles, a larger body of radical students and a solid block of professional men and scholars. One of the leaders was a young nobleman, Ettore Carafa, who had spent the winter of 1787 in Paris with his tutor. Having witnessed the first flowering of the revolutionary movement he enjoyed a great prestige with the republicans of his native city, by whom he was regarded as an oracle. At his own expense he had two thousand copies of the *Rights of Man* printed and distributed. Two copies were actually smuggled into the apartments of Queen Maria Carolina. As might be expected, this exploit had its repercussion in wholesale arrests and soon the prisons of Naples were overflowing with suspects.

The court was strongly anti-French and for very good reason. Queen Maria Carolina was the sister of Marie Antoinette. After the execution of the French Queen, Ferdinand refused to receive the new French ambassador. A French fleet was accordingly despatched to Naples in 1793 and the Neapolitan government given the alternative of receiving the French representative or preparing for immediate war. Being in no position to resist the French squadron Ferdinand yielded, to the great delight of the partisans of the new ideas who flocked to Admiral La Touche's flagship, the *Languedoc*, and entertained the French officers at a banquet given in the Villa Roccaromana in Posillipo. After the inevitable distribution of Phrygian bonnets and tricolor cockades the French departed, whereupon the "Jacobins of Posillipo" soon found themselves in the dungeons of Saint Elmo fortress. Obviously, without active French help the intellectuals could not aspire to any status other than that of conspirators. So conspirators they became. "Repubblica o Morte," was the name of one secret society, "Libertà o Morte," the name of another. The choice of the latter word in both titles was an apt one, as we shall see. As they numbered but a scant two hundred members each their influence was limited to propaganda, in which respect they aped some of the worst features of their French prototypes. In 1794, for instance, Ettore

Carafa's father died leaving him his titles and estates. Ettore at once proclaimed his republican principles by refusing the decoration the King tendered him and by smearing the armorial bearings on his ancestors' tombs with black paint. As a result he soon found himself in prison together with several other hotheads, three of whom were chosen at random and hanged in the piazza of the Castel Nuovo. This triple execution was the occasion for a riot in which scores of persons were injured. It took the French ambassador, Garat, four years to secure the release of the surviving prisoners, but then his prestige at court was nil. With characteristic lack of tact the French Republic had named as their envoy the man who had read to Marie Antoinette her sentence of death.

A brief period of calm now settled upon the troubled city. It was, however, soon broken by startling news. Nelson had destroyed the French fleet in Aboukir Bay and was on his way to Naples. In spite of the cordial welcome he was accorded by the court and the people his estimate of the country was neither flattering nor accurate. "A country of fiddlers, whores and scoundrels," was his verdict. In his blunt sailor fashion he nevertheless volunteered the advice which had brought about the French invasion: "Either to advance, trusting in God and His blessing in a just cause, to die with *l'épée à la main,* or to remain quiet and be kicked out of his kingdoms." Ferdinand advanced, as we have seen, yet he was being kicked out of one of his kingdoms. On December 21, in the dead of night, Nelson received the royal family on board the *Vanguard* and ferried them across to Palermo. The Hamiltons were among the fugitives. In spite of his hatred of everything French Nelson was about to give a demonstration of a *ménage à trois* that no French novelist has outdone.

The lack of spirit displayed by the King in thus abandoning his realm before it was seriously threatened soon communicated itself to the army which had retired to the fortified town of

Capua. On January 11, 1799, Pignatelli, who had been left in charge as regent, concluded a two months' truce with Championnet whereby Capua and its stores were surrendered to the French and an indemnity of ten million francs promised. General Mack, whom the Austrians had loaned to Ferdinand for the purpose of driving Championnet out of Central Italy, put himself under French protection and handed his sword to the French commander as he entered Capua. "Keep it, General," said Championnet, probably with his tongue in his cheek, "my government does not allow me to accept goods of English manufacture."

While the Neapolitan army was thus retiring before the invaders, the Neapolitan navy was faring even worse. After the departure of Nelson, the Allied naval command devolved upon the ranking officer of the Portuguese squadron in the harbor, a Britisher by the name of Campbell. Although the French were still some distance from the city Commodore Campbell, without waiting for the outcome of the peace negotiations, ordered the destruction of such Neapolitan vessels as had not accompanied Ferdinand to Palermo. Nelson later brought Campbell before a court-martial, but the charges were dropped at the express request of Queen Maria Carolina, who seems throughout this entire period to have usurped the prerogatives of her husband. Always an Austrian at heart, she displayed a deep-rooted distrust of the Neapolitan officers, whom she believed tainted with "Jacobinism," and a contemptuous hatred of the Neapolitan people. "The cowardice and ill-will of the navy forced us to destroy vessels," she wrote her brother the Emperor, "in order not to leave them in the hands of the enemy, a loss of more than four million ducats." As Campbell's record is otherwise an honorable one it is only fair to assume that, taking the Queen at her word, he concluded that the Neapolitan crews could not be trusted. On January 8 the infuriated populace saw the result of years of effort go up in smoke. With difficulty did the Town Council, who alone seem to have kept their wits and courage, dissuade the regent from destroying the arsenal and the food supplies, a course that would have been in accord with Maria Carolina's parting instructions: "Nothing should be left the Neapolitans but their eyes with which to weep."

Matters stood thus when on January 14 the French commissioners drove into the city to collect the first installment of the war indemnity. They soon made a hasty exit. Naples was in a ferment. The much-despised *lazzari* were about to give a demonstration of loyalty that is astounding, considering how little the Bourbons had done to deserve it. The home-coming troops were promptly disarmed by the people, who forthwith stormed the Castel Nuovo, the Carmine, the Castel del Ovo and Saint Elmo. Pignatelli and the other government officials who had signed the armistice barely escaped with their lives and the half million ducats remaining in the treasury. By his persistent refusal to co-operate with the Town Council he had left the city at the mercy of the unruly element. It was under these trying conditions that the republicans, or "patriots," as they preferred to be called, decided that the time for action had arrived and sent word to Championnet, who was marching on the city, that they would attack the *lazzari* from the rear as soon as he appeared before the Porta Capuana. The young officer, Eleuterio Ruggiero, who carried this message that saved Naples from a massacre, was later beheaded by the royalists. In the meantime the "aristocrats" tricked the *lazzari* out of two key positions, Saint Elmo and the Castel del Ovo, to which they had been admitted in order to strengthen the garrison. The *lazzari* vented their anger on an innocent victim. Ascanio Filomarino, Duca della Torre, was a typical liberal, a scholar and "vesuvianisto" of note, also a poet. The mob broke into his palace. When they left a few hours later the duke and his brother were lying dead amid the wreckage of their scientific instruments, books and paintings. The Terror had raised its ugly head. "I believe the people were abundantly right," was Maria Carolina's only comment. One of the first acts of Championnet on entering the city was to shoot the ringleader.

In the meantime, however, the *lazzari*, with that instinctive hatred of the foreigner that is one of the characteristics of mob psychology, prepared to defy the French. Their first step was to liberate six thousand criminals. For three days they fought with tragic desperation. Hemmed in, front and rear, they stubbornly defended every house, every alley between the Porta Capuana and Chiaja. When on the twenty-third the French finally captured the Carmine and the Castel Nuovo ten thousand casualties had fallen in the Via de Toledo and adjoining streets. In spite of many excesses, such as the sack of the royal palace, we must turn to the Peninsula War for anything equalling the misguided but magnificent heroism of the Neapolitan populace. "The Lazzaroni, those astonishing men, they are heroes," was Championnet's tribute.

Jean Antoine Étienne Championnet, the young general who who had captured Naples, was the type of the early French revolutionary commander, idealistic, spontaneous and firmly convinced of the truth of the political gospel his nation was preaching. One of his first thoughts nevertheless was to pay his respects to San Gennaro, the patron saint of Naples. As a result of his tact and conciliatory attitude order was soon restored and the difficult task of installing a republican government begun, a task in which his fluency in Italian stood him in good stead. The name chosen for the new Utopia was a picturesque one, the Parthenopean Republic, named in honor of the Siren who, heartbroken over her failure to lure Ulysses, threw herself into the sea, her body drifting to the Bay of Naples. The wily Greek, as we know, had taken the precaution of stopping his sailors' ears with wax besides having himself lashed to the mast of his ship.

Championnet's choice for president of the provisional government was less happy. Carlo Laubert was a former monk who had taught chemistry until his liberal opinions forced him to flee to France. There he became a convert to republicanism, shed his cowl and took a wife. Now he had returned to Naples as head chemist of Championnet's army, resplendent in a uniform with tricolor sash and plume. The other members of the government were also men of education. Pasquale Baffi was a professor of Greek, Mario Pagano a professor of criminal law. Francesco Conforti, a priest, was professor of ecclesiastical law. Domenico Cirillo was a professor of botany, Ignazio Ciaja was a poet. The new regime, as can be seen, had all the earmarks of a "brain trust." Disregarding urgent practical matters the body proceeded to draw a constitution, debating article by article. Occasionally they interrupted their labors to harangue the crowd. The impression they produced is best illustrated by the fact that the *lazzari* were convinced that the word "citizen" was a title akin to "excellency" by which the upper classes were usually addressed. As no republic was complete without a Monitor, a bluestocking by the name of Eleanor Pimentel, released from prison by the general jail delivery, undertook to publish one. The first issue which appeared on February 2 was dated: "14 Piovoso, Anno VII della Libertà, I della Repubblica Napoletana una ed indivisibile." The Neapolitan Liberals had swallowed hook, line and sinker!

While the patriots were abolishing feudalism and titles of nobility and legislating on every conceivable subject, including puppet shows, Championnet was insisting on his war indemnity. Soon one of the inevitable Civil Commissioners of the Directoire, Faitpoult by name, appeared. He declared all the royal palaces, collections, the porcelain factory of Capodimonte forfeited to France; also all the antiquities discovered and yet to be discovered in Pompeii and Herculaneum. As the greater part of these cities still lies buried Faitpoult was taking a long-range view of the archæological requirements of the Louvre, to put it mildly. Championnet, be it said to his credit, gave Faitpoult twenty-four hours to leave town. Needless to say he was soon recalled himself as a result. He managed, however, to justify his conduct and was given another command in northern Italy, where he died a few months later. "A man of gentle and courteous manners, full of moderation and humanity," is how the Austrian Chargé d'Affaires described him. Before considering his successor let us turn to the fugitives in Palermo.

We shall pass over the stormy journey during which one of the royal princes, a lad of six, died. Once safely in his Sicilian dominions Ferdinand began casting about for some means of regaining his Neapolitan ones. What forces did he have at his disposal? There was Nelson's fleet to begin with. Unfortunately the situation required an army as well. That Ferdinand was unable to supply. Fortunately a churchman was at hand to furnish the energy and resourcefulness the Bourbon government lacked. Fabrizio Ruffo was a member of the princely family of Ruffo-Scilla. His mother was a Colonna. A man of education and an able economist, his distinguishing characteristic was a versatility that ranged from such strange subjects for a cleric as canals and pigeon breeding to cavalry maneuvers. Although a cardinal he was something of a reformer and hence none too popular at Rome nor at court. He was shrewd enough to realize two things, however. First: that the patriots would soon run foul of the rural populations, whose tenacity in clinging to customs, honeycombed with abuses though they were, was proverbial, and, second, that Calabrian brigandage would prove a very acceptable substitute for the vanished Neapolitan army. All he asked for was *carte blanche*, which was granted him, *faute de mieux*.

On February 7 Ruffo accordingly landed in Calabria with eight companions. He was "travelling light" but the least of his impedimenta were scruples, which were totally lacking. Within a week he had 350 followers, mostly tenants from his estates, and the "Christian Army of the Holy Faith" was in process of formation. In a country where the poorest peasant had a crucifix and a blunderbuss hanging on the wall recruiting was easy for a cardinal. By the end of the month he had over 15,000 men. The only contingent the King supplied was a consignment of one thousand convicts. The British navy did provide some light artillery and gunners which did such good work that one of the Sanfedisti leaders, Vitella by name, sent to Captain Troubridge, R.N., a token of his appreciation in the shape of the head of Don Carlo Granozio, supposedly a republican official, whom he had killed as he was trying to escape from Ponte Cagnaro. "A jolly fellow!" the Britisher noted on the margin of the flowery letter that accompanied this trophy. But the jolliest part of the incident is that Granozio turned out to be a perfectly good royalist. It was merely an unfortunate case of mistaken identity (or of personal revenge) which was rectified by granting a pension of twenty-five ducats a month to the widow. Prompted by the hope of plunder and the promise of pardon for past offenses the brigand chiefs of Calabria, Apulia and the Abruzzi flocked to the standards of the Santa Fede, among them Fra Diavolo, of operatic fame. Vainly did the patriots and their French allies strive to stem the tide. Ettore Carafa, who had contrived to escape from prison and had joined the French army, defended Pescara heroically. With its fall the road to Naples was open.

While matters were thus going against the republic in the field the situation in Naples was anything but reassuring. One counter-revolutionary plot, the conspiracy of the Baccher brothers, was nipped in the bud thanks to the indiscretions of a young noblewoman, Luisa Sanfelice, the mistress of Gerardo

Baccher.[2] The relations between the republic and General Macdonald, who had succeeded Championnet, were strained from the start, partly due to the exactions of Faitpoult, who had returned to Naples in Macdonald's train. It was therefore with a sigh of relief that the patriots saw the bulk of the French army retire to Caserta, ostensibly because the republic was now "established," in reality because Macdonald was convinced that he could not hold Naples against the Sanfedisti now reinforced by a Russian and a Turkish contingent and a British squadron commanded by Captain Foote.

And now we come to the most controversial episode of the entire period. Francesco Carraciolo was the only experienced officer of the Neapolitan navy. He had been through the hard school of the Knights of Malta and was a Bailli of the Order. He had moreover served in the British navy under Rodney and had been present at the siege of Toulon. His services against the Barbary corsairs should have entitled him to the confidence of his sovereigns. Maria Carolina's insistence upon taking passage on the *Vanguard* must have wounded him as deeply as the cowardice of the King must have disgusted him. He accompanied the fugitives with his vessel, the *Sannita*, then, finding that his services were not wanted, he applied for leave to return to Naples and attend to some urgent personal matters. That he endeavored to keep aloof from the insurrection is evident from the fact that Macdonald had the greatest difficulty in persuading him to take command of the few gunboats that had escaped destruction by Campbell. What finally decided him to abandon his neutral position? Even Nelson admitted that he was not "a Jacobin." The plain truth is that as a brave and patriotic officer he could not stand idly by while the British, who had occupied Procida, were waging war on his fellow countrymen. His skillful handling of the meager

[2]The tragic life of this frivolous but harmless creature has been delightfully told by Vincent Sheean in his novel *Sanfelice*.

forces at his command was deeply resented by Nelson and probably sealed him doom.

The closing scenes of the tragedy are not pleasant reading. I shall spare the reader the harrowing details of the atrocities committed by Sanfedisti and *lazzari,* although they adorn a set of Capodimonte that was subsequently presented to Cardinal Ruffo. What cannot be glossed over, however, is the cynical violation of the capitulation entered into by Ruffo, the Russian and Turkish commanders and the commandants of the republican forces in the Castel Nuovo and the Castel del Ovo, a capitulation that was approved by General Méjean commanding the French garrison of Saint Elmo and by Captain Foote. The terms provided, among other things, that "every individual shall be at liberty to embark or to remain at Naples unmolested." The fury of Maria Carolina on reading the agreement is best illustrated by the notations she made in the margin of the document. They cover more space than the articles themselves. The snarling rage of a tigress whose prey is about to escape her. Nelson! Lady Hamilton! They alone can give her the blood of her enemies. The British navy was about to be prostituted by two worthless women.

The unsavory story of Nelson's infatuation for the adventuress who had climbed from the gutter to the position of Ambassadress and confidante of a queen, only to relapse into the mediocrity and poverty from which she sprang, is too well known to require retelling. Apologists of Nelson, however, are entirely too prone to lay the blame for his ruthlessness on the fair shoulders of the Welsh Circe. It is unfortunate but true that Nelson did not need the urging of his mistress to make him pitiless on those who had espoused French ideas. Hurrying to Naples he at once declared the capitulations null and void except in so far as they affected the French troops. Faced by the protests of his allies he relented and agreed not to prevent the embarkation of the republicans for Toulon. Did this agreement prevent him from seizing them as soon as they weighed anchor? A pretty point, as the equity lawyers would say, but not one we should expect a British admiral to raise. In vain did Ruffo plead with him not to stain his honor, in vain did the Russian and the Turkish commanders urge the sanctity of treaties. Foreigners have such queer notions of honor. It was upon Carraciolo, however, that Nelson's fury was mainly directed. He made it his business to track him to his hiding place and to bring him in chains before a packed court sitting on board the *Vanguard*. "Nothing was promised by a British officer which was not carried into effect," Nelson subsequently stated. Nothing, except the promise implied in the words "an officer and a gentleman."

"We are restoring happiness to the kingdom of Naples and doing good to millions," was Nelson's conception of the part he and the Hamiltons were playing. The Bourbon methods which Nelson was facilitating were simple. The scaffold was erected *en permanence* in the Piazza del Mercato. Day after day for over a year the flower of the Neapolitan ·people mounted the steps to where the headsman or the hangman awaited them. The spectacle became so common that it soon failed to draw the usual crowd. All who had taken a prominent part in the ill-starred Parthenopean Republic paid the death penalty. More than eight thousand jail sentences, besides confiscations and decrees of banishment were imposed for minor participations. No wonder Captain Troubridge wrote: "I curse the day I ever served the Neapolitan government." Eleanor Pimentel and Luisa Sanfelice were among those executed.

The vindictiveness displayed by Nelson is at first blush difficult to fathom. It cannot be attributed to any righteous indignation at revolutionary violence. The Parthenopean Republic had been exceptionally free from the excesses that usually accompany revolutionary movements. By allying itself with France, however, the republic had committed an unpardonable sin. It had taken sides in the bitter struggle being waged between "the Carthaginians of the North Sea," to quote Heine's definition, and the growing continental power of France. Into this gruelling fight to a finish the dreamers and theorists of the Parthenopean Republic had been drawn, only to be crushed between the upper and nether grindstones.

It is some consolation to know that the victims of Bourbon reaction did not die wholly in vain. Their example inspired their successors. In the Piazza dei Martiri stands a shaft to the memory of those who perished in the four revolutions that Naples had to undergo before ridding herself of a misrule probably unequalled in history. At its base four lions are crouching. One of them, mortally wounded, still clutches the fasces of the Parthenopean Republic.

CHAPTER XVI

"Il Re Gioachino"

THE COMMANDANT of the garrison at Ajaccio drew a sigh of relief as he dimly perceived a flotilla of six boats quietly slip out of the harbor shortly after midnight on September 28, 1815. The royal authority was none too solidly established on the island and the presence of the brother-in-law of "the usurper" had caused him considerable anxiety. As a mere gesture intended to clear His Most Christian Majesty of any charge of connivance the citadel of Cauro fired one shot at the parting guests and then let the five gondolas and the felucca pass out to sea. A gondola in Corsican parlance is a small decked ship between fifteen and twenty tons burden rigged with one lateen sail. The felucca is the familiar coasting vessel of the eastern Mediterranean, lateen-rigged with a jib. A rather unimpressive armada for the former Grand Admiral of the Empire, nevertheless it was the only one Murat had ever actually commanded, his branch of the service having been the cavalry. But recently he had astonished friend and foe alike by leading charge after charge with only a riding whip in his hand. Whatever killing he had to do he preferred to do vicariously. The admiring Cossacks made way for the strange horseman arrayed in a uniform so fantastic that on seeing it for the first time Napoleon voiced his disapproval with one of those cutting remarks he knew so well how to make. "Take off that costume, you look like a circus rider!" Two hundred and ninety-eight persons all told were crowded on the six small vessels. With this diminutive force Murat had resolved to attempt to recapture his lost kingdom of Naples. "I shall either succeed or I shall end my misfortunes with my life. I have faced death many thousand times fighting for my country. May I not do so once more for myself?"

"My misfortunes!" Yes, Murat was a desperately unhappy man. His dominant characteristic, aside from a reckless bravery, was an inordinate vanity. Having achieved his ambition, a royal crown, there was no sacrifice of principle he was not prepared to make to keep it. His reign had been one long series of differences with Napoleon. At first they were limited to attempts to emancipate himself from Napoleonic tutelage. In vain did Caroline endeavor to persuade her husband that his only chance of maintaining himself on the throne was by a close co-operation with her brother. Here she was faced by Murat's boundless conceit. The court at Naples promptly fell into two coteries, that of the Queen and that of the King. If Caroline headed a French faction, Murat was flirting with an entirely novel political group, the Italians. *Singeries* (monkeyshines), the Emperor called his brother-in-law's obvious bids for popularity. He might have expected them, as his own brothers were indulging in the same short-sighted policy. They were annoying tricks, however, as they were rendering the application of the continental blockade difficult. As for the contingents and the revenue Murat was supposed to furnish the Empire, the shoe was on the other foot.

Murat's ambitions were soon to cause an open breach. The new King of Naples was determined to exchange his title for that of King of the Two Sicilies. While on a visit to Paris in March 1810 Murat wrung from his brother-in-law permission to try an expedition to Sicily and for that purpose to use the French garrisons stationed in his kingdom. After all, his vigorous attack on Capri which resulted in the expulsion of Sir Hudson Lowe, an ominous name for us who know the

Joachim Murat, King of Naples

sequel, deserved some recognition. The French and Neapolitan armies were therefore concentrated in lower Calabria, so near and yet so far from Sicily. As a fiasco Murat's Sicilian venture has few equals. The British fleet refused to be misled by any feint. Murat finally managed to slip one detachment across the Straits of Messina and waited for the British to rush their vessels to the threatened point. The British commander, however, never took his eye off Murat and the main force. The detachment that had been landed in Sicily was compelled to return to the mainland, minus one regiment, the *Royale Corse,* which had started on its way to Messina and was promptly surrounded and captured.

Mutual recriminations between the French and the Neapolitans naturally followed. Murat accused the French generals of never having intended anything more than a feint. The French countered with a charge that the proposed landing was foolhardy in view of the British command of the sea. Both were probably right. What the Emperor wanted was to prevent the British from withdrawing any troops from Sicily for service in Spain or any vessels for an attack on Corfu. Murat, whose main aim now was to save his face, announced grandiloquently that having demonstrated that the enemy could not prevent him from landing in Sicily the expedition would be postponed and the forces disbanded for the present. That was all the British were waiting to hear before shipping their Sicilian garrison to Portugal. The Emperor's rage can be imagined. "You act without any sort of prudence!" he wrote Murat.

What little prudence Murat possessed he now threw to the winds. By allying himself with the patriotic party at Naples, which as we have seen was considerable, he fondly believed that he could survive any change of fortune that might befall the Cæsar who had put him on his throne. In other words, Murat was ready to kick from under him the rungs of the ladder by which he had climbed. His bravery during the Russian campaign must be put to his credit. His haste in leaving the army and returning to Naples is less creditable. His conduct after Leipzig is absolutely indefensible. Yielding to the persuasion of de Neipperg he entered into a secret treaty with Austria. Whatever may have been his lack of scruples, Murat had enough common sense to realize that this alliance could not be long-lived. He therefore made another about-face and turned conspirator, an easy step to take as central and northern Italy abounded in secret patriotic societies. Then, suddenly, on March 15, 1815, he came out with a startling *pronunciamento*. Calling upon the people of Italy to unite he proclaimed himself their Liberator and marched north with an army of 40,000 men. For once the Austrian army was equal to the occasion. As a strategist Murat had always been a nullity. A series of defeats culminating in a disaster at Tolentino soon drove him back to Naples, where he found a British squadron preparing to bombard his forts. Leaving Caroline to make such terms with the Austrians and the Anglo-Sicilians as she could Murat, with a few followers but without any gaudy uniform, fled to Ischia and thence to Cannes which port he reached on May 25 after narrowly escaping the British cruisers. Caroline meanwhile was a prisoner and on her way to Trieste, although Murat believed that she had voluntarily taken refuge with his enemies, a thought that distressed him greatly.

Napoleon, then in the throes of the Hundred Days, accorded his brother-in-law a far kindlier welcome than his disloyalty bordering on treason warranted. Permission was granted the fugitive to settle near Toulon. His defection in 1814 had made a difference to France of sixty thousand men and was one of the causes of the collapse of the Empire. Now by raising the standard of revolt in Italy he had seriously compromised Napoleon's plans for a recognition of his rule over a France restricted to her natural geographical boundaries. That there was no connection between Murat's insurrection and Napoleonic strategy was more than any statesman in Europe was prepared to admit. Yet such was the case. Murat's offer to serve was naturally declined, although Napoleon later had cause to regret the absence of his brilliant cavalry leader. The mishandling of the French cavalry at Waterloo, which was one of the reasons for the French defeat, would probably have been avoided had Murat, whose instinctive grasp of battle tactics has never been excelled, commanded that arm.

How Murat persuaded himself that he was being unjustly treated is hard to fathom. It was probably one of the symptoms of self-delusions from which he had been suffering for some time past. After Waterloo his position again became perilous. The "White Terror" was in full swing. An angry mob brutally murdered Marshal Brune at Avignon. Rallying a few Napoleonic die-hards, Murat once more embarked on a small coasting vessel hoping to connect with a Swedish vessel that was to take him to Corsica. A storm nearly swamped their small craft. Fortunately they fell in with the Toulon-Bastia packet, whose captain, being unaware of the identity of the travellers he was rescuing, agreed to take them to Bastia.

On August 23 Murat reached Bastia but it was merely a case of out of the frying pan into the fire. The island was pretty evenly divided between royalists and bonapartists but Bastia, as luck would have it, was decidedly Bourbon in its sympathies. Murat's companions were promptly arrested. With difficulty did he escape to the neighboring town of Vescovato, where an old Corsican officer with Napoleonic leanings, General Franceschetti, was ready to assist him. There must have been some real qualities in the man to enable him to secure support when his fortunes were at their lowest ebb. He was without funds, as his cash was on the Swedish ship he had missed. It was some time before he recovered it. His courage never failed him however. Indignantly refusing the asylum which the Emperor of Austria generously offered him in spite of his breach of faith,

Murat surrounded himself with a band of partisans who, electrified by his personality, consented to accompany him on the wild expedition that was to revive the revolutionary tradition on Italian soil. How Murat contrived to persuade any sane man that his following in Italy extended beyond a small intelligentsia will ever remain a mystery. Suffice to say he did. The authorities of the island were, as can be seen, in a tough spot. If they allowed Murat to remain civil war was sure to result. Can they be blamed for giving the turbulent adventurer enough rope to hang himself?

But to return to the filibusters. After leaving Ajaccio the six vessels passed through the Straits of Bonifacio where they were fired on by the fort at La Maddalena whose garrison mistook them for pirates. Stopping at the uninhabited island of Tavolara Murat held a review of his forces and distributed forty uniforms he had procured at Ajaccio. Murat always had a weakness for uniforms. Arms were sadly lacking but he did have a liberal supply of printed proclamations to the people of Italy. The expedition then sailed east until Vesuvius was sighted. They had made a landfall considerably farther north than intended so the course was turned to the south. By this time the ardor of some of the Corsicans had considerably cooled. It began to dawn on the leaders that Murat was merely drifting and intended, as usual, to "make his plans in the presence of the enemy." Desertions ensued and by the time the gulf of Policastro was reached Murat was reduced to the felucca and the royal gondola.

Here Murat took a wise decision. He decided to call off his "return from Elba" and to accept the Austrian proposal. All compromising papers were cast overboard. Taking stock he found that he did not have enough provisions to reach Trieste, his new destination. He must perforce make some purchases and, if possible, secure a more seaworthy vessel before venturing into the Otranto channel. The town of Pizzo lay conveniently at hand. The captain of the gondola was a Maltese by the name of Baron Barbara. For some time past his conduct had seemed suspicious. He always found some good reason for not making the port Murat had chosen. Frederic Masson, who has delved deep into the history of the period, accuses him of having deliberately led Murat into a trap. Be that as it may, when Barbara before going ashore to make the purchases asked for the passport Metternich had sent together with the offer of asylum, Murat demurred. If a Neopolitan cruiser should happen along while Barbara was ashore Murat would be in an awkward position. Without the passport, Barbara protested, he could not secure provisions, leave alone charter a vessel. "Very well, sir," said Murat, "I shall go ashore myself."

Calling his remaining officers together Murat thanked them for their loyalty and bade them return to Corsica on the felucca. At the same time he tendered them one thousand francs, all he could spare. The scene was a painful one. Murat was visibly affected. At this stage of the proceedings General Franceschetti spoke up and protested against abandoning the project. "With the sentiments Your Majesty inspires, what need have we for arms and armies? Your presence alone, Sire, is the terror of your enemies and the hope of your faithful subjects. Your expedition will be the most brilliant period of your history! How beautiful it is, Sire, to accomplish great things with slender means. That is reserved for heroes only. Let us land and long live Gioachino!"

Poor Murat! Franceschetti had touched the secret springs of all his actions, his courage and his vanity. Instead of landing with the intention of securing supplies Murat landed with the hope of conquering a kingdom, the Kingdom of Italy. Only one man had enough sense to speak in opposition. It was his valet, Charles. "Do not disembark, Sire," he warned. "If you disembark you are lost. You have never been willing to listen to your faithful servants." Unfortunately it now required more than an old servant to hold his master in check. At the head of twenty-seven men Murat landed and proceeded from the beach to the town of Pizzo. On his way he was met by a captain of gendarmerie, Trentacapilli, an unfortunate coincidence, if coincidence it was. A few years previously Murat had put a crimp into the principal industry of the town, banditry. On that occasion three of Trentacapilli's brothers had graced the gallows. In vain did Murat exclaim "Do you not know your king?" In vain did his followers shout "Viva il Re Gioachino!" The spectators remained hostile. Two young men approached Murat and advised him to make for Monteleone, where he would find adherents. In the meantime an armed mob had gathered and was barring his passage. Murat turned and endeavored to regain his boat in the offing. Shots flashed. Three Corsicans fell, several were wounded. Then a mad rush. One woman actually struck Murat in the face screaming, "You talk of liberty and you had four of my sons shot!" Murat's golden epaulets were torn from his shoulders. He was a prisoner in the hands of his most implacable enemies, the Sanfedisti, or their successors.

The sequel is well known. Murat was brought before a military court of seven officers sitting in the Castello of Pizzo. Did he by any chance remember a similar court eleven years before that had sent the young Duc d'Enghien to his death in the moat of Vincennes? Although Murat denied any participation in that monumental blunder, as military governor of Paris he carried the sentence into effect. It was probably but small consolation to Murat to know that the Bourbons were about to commit a similar blunder. He met his fate as might have been expected. After confessing to the parish priest whom he had helped in happier days and writing a pathetic farewell to Caroline he faced the firing squad. The last order the fearless soldier gave was the one that sent him to an unmarked grave in a miserable Calabrian town. The date was October 13, 1815.

I shall spare the reader the ghastly tale of reaction and reprisals that followed the collapse of the Murat conspiracy. It has been calmly but scathingly told by Gladstone, when serving his apprenticeship in statecraft. It was a repetition of the horrors committed after the fall of the Parthenopean Republic with this added evil. It lasted forty-five years.

"You cannot trifle with a throne," was Napoleon's comment when four months later he heard of his brother-in-law's death. "He tried with two hundred men to recapture a kingdom he had lost at the head of eighty thousand." A severe verdict but undoubtedly a sound one. One fact, however, Napoleon could not have foreseen. Murat, although a foreigner, had started one of the great national movements of history, the Italian Risorgimento. To the Italians Murat means infinitely more than he does to his fellow-countrymen. Perhaps therein lies his surest claim to immortality.

CHAPTER XVII

"General Veeron"

THERE WERE no two ways about it, said Captain Scott of the brig *Hercules* to himself as he weighed anchor at Genoa on July 13, 1823, he had shipped a boatload of madmen. Take the Noble Lord who had chartered his vessel; any man who for no good reason would leave so lovely looking a creature as the Italian countess (Guiccioli) with whom he had been living in the Casa Saluzzo must be mad. And his friend, Captain Trelawny, a nice travelling companion for a British Peer! What was the aristocracy coming to! It was an open secret that he had deserted from the Navy in India. Recently he had burned the body of that poet who was drowned off Viareggio instead of giving him Christian burial as might be expected from a fellow-countryman. 'Tis a wonder he did not make the widow commit suttee! As for the foreigners they were queerer than most of their ilk. There was young Pietro Gamba, the brother of the countess; you might think that he and my lord were brothers-in-law! Then there was a young Italian medico, Doctor Francesco Bruno. He was so frightened every time he saw the *Lordo Inglese* and his two fierce-looking dogs, "Moretto" the bulldog and "Lion" the Newfoundland, that he would be quite useless in an emergency. (Bruno subsequently admitted that at first he was afraid that he as well as his physic would literally be thrown to the dogs if he made a mistake.) Then there was a Greek, Schilizzi by name, a relative of Alexander Mavrocordato and consequently one of those insurgents who were urging His

Lordship to embark on his wild expedition. To complete the picture the skipper noted in the ship's papers two Italian retainers, Tita Falcieri, a gondolier, and Lega Zambelli, His Lordship's "intendant," Captain Trelawny's negro groom with five horses (who at once started kicking down the partitions of their stalls), several crates of ducks and geese and 10,000 Spanish dollars.

The only one of his passengers who seemed sensible was His Lordship's valet, Fletcher, a typical "gentleman's gentleman." They had one bond in common, a liking for an occasional tipple. One evening a few days out the skipper and Fletcher were comparing notes over a glass of grog.

"What is your master going to such a wild country for? My mate was at Corfu and he says an officer of the garrison crossed over to Albania to shoot and was shot by the natives; they thought the brass buttons on his jacket were gold. What may the country be like?"

"Bless you," answered Fletcher, who had been to Greece before with his master, "there is very little country; it is all rocks and robbers. They live in holes in the rocks and come out like foxes; they have long guns, pistols and knives. We were obliged to have a guard of soldiers to go from one place to another."

"How did you live?" asked the skipper.

"Like dogs, on goat's flesh and rice, sitting on the ground in a hovel, all eating out of one dirty dish, tearing the flesh to pieces with our fingers; no knives, no forks and only two or three horn spoons. They drink a stuff they call wine but it tastes more of turps than grapes and is carried about in stinking goatskins and every one drinks from the same bowl. Then they have coffee, which is pounded, and they drink it, dregs and all, without sugar. They are all smoking when not sleeping; they sleep on the floor in their clothes and shoes; they never undress or wash, except the ends of their fingers and are covered with lice and fleas. The Turks are the only respectable people in the country. If they go, Greece will be like Bedlam broke loose. It's a land of flies, and lice, and fleas, and thieves. What my lord is going there for the Lord only knows."

Just then it dawned upon Fletcher that His Lordship had overheard the entire conversation so he added: "And my master can't deny what I said is true!"

The master's comment to Trelawny was illuminating. "To those who look at things with hog's eyes and can see nothing else, what Fletcher says may be true; but I did not notice it!" That is exactly it. What Lord Byron did for the cause of Greek independence was to make Englishmen see it as he saw it, through the rosy lens of his own romanticism, and not notice the many shortcomings of the Greek people, shortcomings be it said that were the natural outcome of centuries of oppression.

The Greek War of Independence got off to a bad start as far as securing British support was concerned. It savored too much of a Russian maneuver. It was the work of a secret society, the Hetairia of Odessa, which enjoyed Russian protection. In March 1821, the society organized a general uprising that embraced both the eastern and the western Greeks. The first move was an ill-advised attack on Constantinople via Moldo-Wallachia and Thrace by a Phanariot Greek, Alexander Ypsilanti, aided by a motley assortment of Philhellenes. The Prime Minister of the Czar at that time was Capo d'Istria, himself a Greek. In spite of his warnings of certain failure Ypsilanti invaded Moldo-Wallachia expecting all Christians to rise. The rule of the Phanariot Greeks, among whom the Hospodars of Moldo-Wallachia were formerly chosen, had left so unpleasant a memory that the Roumanian and Slavic populations refused to stir. Ypsilanti, nevertheless occupied Bucharest without much difficulty. Soon, however, the Turkish Pashas recovered from their surprise and defeated the Greek volunteers at Dragatschina on June 19. Ypsilanti escaped to Austrian territory where he was promptly interned. The eastern uprising had been a flat failure and the chancelleries of Europe drew a sigh of relief. Their relief was to be short-lived.

In Greece proper the Hetairia had done a thorough job. About the time of the invasion of Moldo-Wallachia the Turkish governor of Tripolitza found that he was faced with a serious situation. Every church and monastery in Morea had suddenly become an arsenal. He therefore issued a proclamation demanding the surrender of all arms and invited the heads of the religious communities to a conference. Some of the clergy obeyed; not so Archbishop Germanos of Patras. Taking refuge in the convent of Saint Laura, near Kalavryta, he raised the standard of revolt, a black flag with the figure of the Virgin which you can still see in the convent, and marched on Patras. That he was amply supplied with ammunition can be inferred from the fact that a few years ago the hanging monastery of Megaspelæon, likewise near Kalavryta, was wrecked by an explosion of gunpowder that had been stored there in the cellar ever since the War of Independence.[1] The revolt spread rapidly. By the end of the year the Turks had been driven out of the entire country south of the Thessalian border. The Acropolis of Athens and the towns of Lepanto, Nauplia, Coron, Modon and Patras alone held out.

So far, so good. When it came to organizing a government the real difficulties began. The Hetairia put forth a candidate in the person of Demetrius Ypsilanti, a brother of Alexander. As his conception was a Byzantine Greece his candidacy did not meet with much support from the Athenian partisans. Greece was soon split up into three factions. In western Greece Mavrocordato and his lieutenant, the Souliot Marco Botzaris, held sway; in eastern Greece a certain Negris was in control and in southern Greece, thanks to Ypsilanti, the factions were hopelessly at odds. As a matter of fact the real power lay in the

[1] The writer had spent a night in the monastery a few weeks before!

military chieftains. In January 1822 an assembly met at
Epidavros. In the meantime the Turks were planning a counter-
attack. This threat had the effect of making the factions unite
under the nominal rule of Mavrocordato. His first campaign
was marked by a defeat at Peta at the hands of Reshid Pasha
while Botzaris failed to relieve Souli. The two insurgent forces
thereupon retired to Missolonghi followed by the Turks who
proceeded to lay siege to the town. The Greeks fortunately had
from the first, thanks to the energy of Admiral Miaoulis, gained
control of the sea. Arming the Greek merchant fleet of 175
vessels Miaoulis soon drove the Turkish fleet to cover. A Greek
squadron appeared before Missolonghi, whereupon Reshid
Pasha withdrew in disgust. Another attempt by a Turkish army
30,000 strong to invade Morea was equally unsuccessful. The
Greek fleet again interrupted communications by sea while the
bands of Colocotronis harassed the Turks on land. On the whole
the year 1822 was decidedly favorable to Greek arms. Peta had
been avenged.

The Greek uprising had been characterized by considerable
persecution of Turkish settlers. The inhabitants of Tripolitza
were exterminated on the capture of that city by Colocotronis.
Reprisals naturally followed. On Easter Day 1822 the Patriarch of Constantinople was seized as he was leaving mass and
hanged in his vestments. The island of Chios, which was supposed to be the center of Greek propaganda, was sacked and
23,000 of the inhabitants massacred. These incidents of course
created a stir throughout Christendom. Delacroix's dramatic
painting "The Massacre of Chios" made a sensation, although
Baron Gros objected that the picture should be called "The
Massacre of Painting"; but then Gros was hardly a romanticist.
It was not until January 1823 that a committee was formed
in England to assist the Greek insurgents. Its meetings were
held at the Crown and Anchor Inn, by which name the London
committee was generally known. Public opinion in England

was difficult to arouse. The distrust of Russia persisted. Moreover the Greek insurrection was hurting British trade. The success of the Greeks through their own efforts gradually allayed British fears as regards Russia but it was the adherence of Lord Byron that raised the Greek question above the level of business and party politics and endowed it with the quality of a thrilling and emotional human adventure.

Such briefly was the situation in Greece when Byron was elected a member of the Crown and Anchor and appointed their representative in Greece, in which capacity he displayed an unselfish devotion coupled with shrewd common sense for which he is seldom given credit. He began by making a correct analysis of the Greek needs. They were: mountain artillery, medical supplies, ammunition. The two latter he was able to procure at Leghorn whither the *Hercules* proceeded. After they were taken on board the expedition continued down the coast, past Stromboli, through the Straits of Messina and into the Ionian Sea. The next decision Byron took again demonstrated his common sense. Before joining any of the parties that were contending for the control of Greece he decided to spend some time in one of the Ionian Isles, then under British rule. Cephalonia was the island chosen, largely owing to the fact that the British resident, Colonel Charles Napier, had an intimate knowledge of affairs and, unlike most British officials, was favorable to the Greek cause.

It cannot be said that Byron embarked on his odyssey with any enthusiasm. Moreover, he seemed to have a presentiment that he would lose his life in Greece. "Mind you, Trelawny," he said toward the end of his journey, "don't you repeat the ceremony you went through with Shelley. No one wants my ashes." "You will be claimed for Westminster Abbey!" replied Trelawny. "No," answered Byron, "they don't want me—nor would I have my bones mingle with that motley throng. There is a rocky island off Maina—it is the Pirate's Isle. No one knows it. I'll show it to you on the way to Morea. There is the spot I should like my bones to lie!" In spite of his gloomy forebodings Byron proved a delightful travelling companion. He fenced with Gamba, boxed with Trelawny. When becalmed he went swimming. On one occasion he opened the crates to let the ducks and geese stretch their legs, then sent the dogs overboard to retrieve them. The birds that fell to the bulldog probably remembered it. Most of the time he spent reading. At Leghorn he had received a mysterious package from Germany. It proved to be a long letter from Goethe enclosing some poetry dedicated to the hero that was to be.

On the evening of August 2 the *Hercules* entered the passage between Cephalonia and Zante. In the distance the pale blue hills of Morea, like huge waves suddenly transfixed as they were striving to join the deeper blue of the sea before them; on either side the graceful outline of the two islands. The next day the brig dropped anchor in the deep bay of Argostoli. Colonel Napier was absent on a tour of inspection so Byron remained on board. He seems to have been dubious as to the reception he would receive from the officers of the British garrison. Byron greatly overestimated the scandalizing properties of his poems. The British officers were quite able to stand Don Juan, in fact most of them could quote it by the yard and were anxious to meet the author. On Napier's return the mess tendered Byron a dinner at which he made a little speech that was well received. The ice was broken, so Byron proceeded to explore his surroundings pending an answer to the message he had despatched to Marco Botzaris at Missolonghi.

His first thought was to visit the neighboring island of Ithaca. A week's excursion was accordingly organized. It was to be Byron's last venture in classicism. The party consisted of Byron and his three servants, Trelawny, Gamba, Doctor Bruno and a Mr. Hamilton Browne, a former official of the Ionian govern-

ment who had joined the expedition at Leghorn. After crossing
Cephalonia under a scorching sun the little harbor of Santa
Eufemia was reached. Declining the offer of the British magis-
trate to spend the night in his house Byron and his party piled
into a four-oared boat and singing and shouting rowed their
way across the narrow strait, landing on the isthmus that divides
Ithaca into two distinct parts. Byron wanted to spend the night
in some cave. Gamba with practical common sense decided that
Byron's health was not equal to any such exposure and started
with Browne to search for quarters. After an hour he came upon
a cottage hidden among some trees. It belonged to a former
resident of Trieste who had seen better days and was reduced to
living on a patch of ground among classical surroundings, to
be sure, but far from luxurious. He invited the party to spend
the night. The only food he could furnish was the inevitable
fare of figs, grapes and wine that abound in Greece. He made
up for this frugality, however, by giving his guests a pedantic
lecture in the most approved Herr Professor style on the
Homeric background of the island. Byron, than whom few men
were better versed in classical lore, stood it as long as he could.
"I hate antiquarian twaddle," he muttered to Trelawny between his teeth. Finally, casting manners to the winds, he arose
and limped out into the starlit night. Before him lay the passage
through which Don Juan of Austria had led his fleet into Same
Bay. Somewhere on the hill to the north was the site of Ulysses'
house, where Penelope had woven the shroud of Laertes, hoping against hope that the wanderer would return ere it was too
late. In the morning he must climb up there. He should be able
to find the spot, as Homer has described the view. From three
angles the sea is visible. He might also get another glimpse of
Levkas, "where burning Sappho loved and sung." Back of him
Byron sensed the dark mass of Korax rock which was still oozing
black water as in the days when Ulysses' faithful retainer

Eumæos drove his swine to the fountain of Arethusa. What a pity, thought Byron, he could not tarry awhile, get his notes in order and write another canto to Childe Harold.

After a week the party returned to Cephalonia and stopped at the monastery of Hagios Phanentes where the monks celebrated a mass in his honor. Whoever has attended one of these rites and has had a jingling censer swung before him innumerable times knows the feeling of self-consciousness the ceremony arouses. "Will no one release me from the presence of these pestilential idiots?" Byron exclaimed. "They drive me mad!" Seizing a lamp he rushed out of the chapel. The astonished Abbot gazed at the empty choir stall, then putting his finger to his forehead to indicate that the English Lord must be mad, he finished his mass.

Once back at Argostoli disquieting news drifted in. The two Greek leaders upon whom Byron had relied to assist him were Mavrocordato and Marco Botzaris. The former had had a falling out with Colocotronis and was hiding in the island of Hydra. The latter had been killed at Missolonghi. The Greek navy was on strike, the shipowners because their charter money was not forthcoming, the crews because their pay was in arrears. As a result the Turkish fleet was once more at sea and blockading the coast of Morea from Navarino to the Gulf of Corinth. Captain Scott was getting nervous about the *Hercules*. The prospect of a British loan had thrown the golden apple of discord among the Greek leaders. Every petty chief who had a following of twenty men was besieging Byron for money and munitions which as likely as not he would use in waging civil war. On top of all this Trelawny was becoming restless, fearing that Byron would relax and write poetry instead of making history, wherein he was mistaken. Byron had a heavy responsibility thrust upon him. He can therefore hardly be accused of irresolution when he decided to part company with the *Hercules* and wait until the situation clarified itself before deciding in favor of any of the contending parties. In the meantime he proposed to make himself comfortable, so hired a pleasantly situated villa at Metaxata, near Argostoli, which you can still see. This was more than Trelawny could bear. He was burning to join an Ithacan chieftain, then operating in Morea, who had assumed the modest name of Odysseus. His headquarters were in a cave on Mount Parnassus and corresponded pretty closely to Fletcher's description of "rocks and robbers." Trelawny ultimately joined this Robin Hood to the extent of becoming his brother-in-law, a purely Madam Butterfly arrangement, as he promptly abandoned Tersitza when he was ready to return to England. Byron saw him depart on the *Hercules* with genuine regret.

While at Metaxata Byron came into frequent contact with Colonel Napier, who was as ardent a Philhellene as he himself was. In fact Napier was anxious to leave the British service and take command of the Greek volunteers. Byron quickly recognized Napier's ability and warmly recommended him to the London committee. Had his recommendation been adopted the Greek War of Independence would probably have been considerably shortened. Napier was later to make his mark in India. Byron would have liked to remain indefinitely in such congenial surroundings. He even contemplated at one time buying some small island. His idyll was, however, brought to a sudden close. Pending receipt of funds from the British loan the Greek provisional government approached Byron, whose generosity knew no bounds when Greece was concerned, with a view of securing enough money to get the Greek fleet into action without delay. Byron advanced the four thousand pounds required and soon the Greek cruisers had relieved the blockade of Missolonghi long enough to permit the landing of Mavrocordato and Colonel Leicester Stanhope, the military adviser the Crown and Anchor had selected. Both at once sent urgent appeals to Byron to take part in the campaign that had as its objective the old Athenian fortress of Naupactos, the Venetian Lepanto. If in addition the two forts of Kastro Roumelias and Kastro Moreas could be captured the Greeks would control the Gulf of Corinth. These two historic strongholds, which the Venetians not inaptly named "the little Dardanelles," were situated at the narrowest part of the gulf, just west of Lepanto and east of Patras. Besides the romantic appeal of the adventure, Byron at once grasped the strategical importance of the move. Within twelve hours of receiving the call Byron was on his way. Two small boats flying the Ionian flag were hired. In the larger one, called a bombard, Byron embarked Gamba and most of his party. The smaller boat, an open one of the type called a *mystico*, he reserved for himself. After stopping at Zante to procure specie the two vessels headed for Missolonghi. Byron had prepared his own apotheosis.

There are few grander spectacles in all Greece than the coast of Acarnania and Ætolia. In the background, successive tiers of bare mountains, each slightly paler in coloring than the preceding one, reaching upward until they blend with the cumulus clouds whose shadows, clearly outlined on the slopes stretching to the sea, cover the foreground with fantastic and slowly moving dark patches. The scene has the sweep and expanse of a country wherein gods alone may dwell. As we draw nearer the mountains recede. Mountains require perspective to be impressive. So do human events. Of the works of man, not a trace is visible from afar. A string of low-lying islands along the coast now appear. At the far end of the lagoon they enclose we discern a few white structures: Missolonghi. The two rivers Phidari and Archiloos, have made the surrounding country a marsh. The lagoon today barely holds enough water to float a skiff. The few travellers who visit the town usually enter from the land. Although badly damaged by the three sieges it underwent during the War of Independence, Missolonghi has been rebuilt on the original lines and therefore is today much as it was in 1824. It is the typical small town of the mainland which contrasts so unfavorably with the trim little settlements of the Greek islands. Rows of tile-covered houses interspersed with occasional buildings that are more pretentious, hence less picturesque, in that they have the flat roof familiar to the Levant, without the charm of Arab architecture; streets across which stepping stones, Pompeian fashion, protrude from the slime on which some lice-ridden chickens have recently left their four-pronged impress. And yet in so miserable a setting one of the dramas of history was enacted.

The crossing from Zante was a hectic one. In spite of the Ionian flag the bombard was captured and taken into Patras. Gamba kept his head, appealed to the British consul, lied beautifully about his destination and as a result was released after three days. He arrived at Missolonghi on January 4. No sign of Byron! He too had a narrow escape. On the night of the twenty-ninth the *mystico* was proceeding along when a frigate was perceived signalling with oil flares. Thinking it was one of the Greek ships sent to look for him Byron headed for her. The frigate, which turned out to be Turkish, mistook the *mystico* for one of the fireboats the Greeks had been using with such telling effect of late. Both vessels thereupon changed courses and lost sight of each other in the darkness. The next morning, another alarm. A Turkish vessel was bearing down upon them. Byron steered for the rocks off Cape Scropha where the Turk could not follow him, then slid along the coast to Dragomestri. There he despatched a messenger to Mavrocordato, saw a glorious sunrise on January 1 and composed one of his worst poems: "Song to the Souliotes." The Greek ships at once put to sea and escorted Byron to the entry of the lagoon. After donning a scarlet uniform he had borrowed from an officer at Argostoli Byron entered a little one-oared craft called a monoxylon and was sculled across the three miles separating Missolonghi from the gulf. It was at 11 A.M. of January 5, 1824, that Byron, amid salvos of artillery and discharges of musketry, landed among the crowd who were frantically acclaiming "General Veeron."

Colonel Stanhope had already engaged the best house in town as their joint headquarters. Although a few thousand drachmais would have bought the house and preserved it as a shrine, not a trace of it remains today. From all accounts it was apparently fairly large, three stories high, with numerous outbuildings. One of Byron's first acts was to engage a bodyguard of Souliots. It was probably the only blunder he committed during the entire expedition. Byron's poetic sense could not resist the lure of these ruffians, who looked so like bedraggled ballet dancers and behaved like such unmitigated brigands. At Metaxata he had taken one body of Souliots into his service. They proved so unruly that he was glad to ship them off to the mainland. Now, at Colonel Stanhope's suggestion to be sure, he was to repeat his mistake. The ground floor was accordingly given over to a noisy and quarrelsome tribe of mountaineers who made night hideous by intoning some genuine Souli songs and in daytime drove Tita and Fletcher to distraction by infesting the house with the stench of their rancid cooking. The climax came a few weeks later when one of the Souliots shot the officer of the guard who had tried to prevent him from entering the magazine which he wanted to show to a nephew of Marco Botzaris. It cost Byron 3000 dollars to pay off the Souliots and send them back to their mountains. For a while it looked as if the disgruntled tribesmen would join the Turks and raid Missolonghi. This threat was to have a disastrous effect on the projected operations.

Byron consistently endeavored to temper the brutality with which the war was being waged. Early in January a Greek privateer brought in a Turkish prize. Byron asked that the one surviving Turkish sailor be delivered to him, as he wanted to send him to the governor of Patras in recognition of his kindness to Gamba. Hardly was the Turk in Byron's house than two

Greek sailors stormed in and demanded that the prisoner be turned over to them. Byron had to threaten to shoot the intruders. He then, very properly, insisted that the two men be compelled to apologize. This they grudgingly did but the incident undoubtedly affected the zeal of the Greek navy. The Turks were once more able to blockade Missolonghi.

If only he had Napier to help him keep order! He at least had a simple formula for winning the war. All he required was "two European regiments, money in hand to pay them and a portable gallows." Instead he had one of the most curious military misfits on record. Stanhope was more interested in spreading his notions of education, Lancastrian School System he called it, than in organizing the Greek army. He began by founding a periodical in the Greek language called *The Greek Chronicle*. The editor was a Swiss by the name of Doctor Meyer. This disciple of William Tell began the task of preparing the Greeks for republican government by attacking all monarchies, especially Austria. At the risk of appearing reactionary, the last thing Byron really was, he had to suppress several issues of the paper, probably an unnecessary precaution as so few Greeks could read that only forty Greek subscribers were obtained.

Stanhope, however, soon tired of Missolonghi and left for Athens to join Trelawny and his friend Odysseus. Pending his marriage with Tersitza, Trelawny had purchased the harem of a far-seeing Turk who was selling out and retiring to Constantinople. Let us hope he got the fifteen ladies cheap as Gamba, who later saw them, describes them as *brutti mostri*, "ugly monsters." One was black. How to get Byron and his money was what was puzzling the trio. Trelawny tried to appeal to Byron's classical sense by inviting him to come and help capture "the pass of Thermophilly" (sic). Byron, however, had other plans. He still was striving for his original objective, Lepanto. He now had hopes of capturing that stronghold, as the Crown and Anchor had at last heeded his recommendation concerning artillery and had sent out a shipload of explosives and an officer who they assured him was an experienced artificer and well versed in the manufacture of "Congreve rockets," the famous liquid fire that had done so much damage to the French, supposedly, in the Napoleonic Wars. The officer in question turned out to be a civilian clerk in the Woolwich Arsenal, William Parry by name. What little experience he possessed had been acquired as a petty officer in the navy. Parry was incompetence and ignorance personified and a tipler to boot. He quarrelled with most of the officers of the artillery corps. The Germans refused to serve under him. To add to Byron's troubles an earthquake rocked Missolonghi and damaged the fortifications.

One by one Byron had seen his hopes dashed. And yet he kept his courage. After Stanhope's departure Byron practically assumed command of the insurgent forces at Missolonghi. Stanhope, Trelawny, together with Odysseus and Colocotronis had set up a rival command at Athens. Byron obstinately refused to withdraw his support from Mavrocordato and it was his insistence that the western government be recognized that saved the whole Greek insurrection from degenerating into a brawl. His most severe test, however, was yet to come.

Again it was the Souliots who were to upset Byron's plans. After their discharge the mountaineers retired toward Arta but still engaged in foraging expeditions in the lagoon. It was not long before they clashed with some boatmen from Missolonghi and once more marched on the city. At the same time the Turkish fleet appeared off Missolonghi, not a mere coincidence obviously. In the presence of this very real danger Byron behaved splendidly. It was to be his last public appearance. Death had already marked him. At the head of his brigade he rode out to meet the invaders on April 6. First came his escort in their fustanellas, then his mounted staff which included Gamba and Bruno, then Byron dressed in a green jacket with black frogs (a present from Trelawny which you can still see in Newstead

Abbey) waving a small riding whip in his gloved hand, his face pale and drawn, his curls blowing in the wind below his blue foraging cap. The celebrated helmet he had made in Genoa never left its bandbox. Perhaps Byron thought it too heroic to fit him. If so, he was too modest. Byron's resolute attitude made the Souliot chiefs pause. A truce was patched up but all thought of action against the common enemy had to be abandoned. That the Souliots and the eastern Greeks were in accord to shelve the foreigner Byron and the Phanariot Mavrocordato was evident. As far as Byron could judge his mission had been a complete failure. He had not united the Greek factions, his artillery had been a disappointment, his fleet had abandoned him, his volunteers were at odds with each other and worst of all his health was giving way under the strain.

He died on April 19. His body was shipped back to England, all but his lungs which Missolonghi claimed and buried in the Heeron. To the Greeks the breath rather than the heartbeat, is the life-giving function. The apparent cause of his death: malarial fever. The real cause: unwillingness to live. And yet, unbeknownst to him, he had accomplished exactly what he had set out to do.

> For freedom's battle once begun,
> Bequeathed from bleeding sire to son,
> Though baffled oft, is ever won.

Disgusted with the inefficiency of his generals the Sultan Mohammed II called on Egypt for help. In February 1825 Ibrahim Pasha landed at Modon. The brilliant campaign he conducted is one of the most curious episodes of Mediterranean history. It was Egypt's first interference in European affairs since Actium. The fighting qualities of the Egyptian troops were such that we may well wonder what might have happened had Egypt taken a hand in Mediterranean politics sooner. In Morea Ibrahim Pasha was uniformly successful. Missolonghi underwent a third siege, one that ranks with Saragossa and other last-ditch resistances. When the Turks finally penetrated into the town the garrison of the Marco Botzaris bastion blew up the powder magazine, burying captors and defenders in the ruins, also many of the civilian population that had taken refuge in the fort. Eighteen hundred Souliots, who now that Byron was gone had returned to the fold, managed to fight their way through to Salona. The siege furnished Eugène Delacroix the theme of another effective picture, "Greece mourning on the ruins of Missolonghi." Mavrocordato, in despair, was on the point of ceding Morea to Great Britain. Odysseus, who opposed the move, was assassinated by the peace party. The very completeness of the Turco-Egyptian victory, however, was Turkey's undoing. The aura Byron had cast over the struggle had assured Greek success in spite of defeats. Would Europe let the cause for which Byron had died fail? Navarino was the answer. Romanticism had won its only political victory by espousing the only genuinely romantic war the Mediterranean ever witnessed. Byron dead was more formidable than Byron alive. And yet, to the average Greek today, Byron is merely another soldier, "General Veeron."

CHAPTER XVIII

"As-tu vu la casquette du Père Bugeaud?"

N O ONE who has seen French infantry swing by keeping step to the clear notes of their *clairons* can fail to feel a thrill. What are they playing? It is the march of France's African armies, the song all French children sing when they "play soldier."

> *As-tu vu la casquette, la casquette,*
> *As-tu vu la casquette du Père Bugeaud?*
> *Elle est faite, la casquette, la casquette,*
> *Elle est faite avec du poil de chameau!*

If France retains her position as a world power it will be largely due to the strategic strength of her North African possessions. It is somewhat ironical therefore to be compelled to state that the French occupation of Algiers, an event that was to have so far-reaching an effect on Mediterranean history, was brought about by a chance occurrence. France will owe her salvation to no preconceived plan of empire. To be sure, in 1808 Napoleon had thought of putting a stop to Barbary piracy and had a reconnaissance made of Algiers and the surrounding country which formed the basis of the expedition of 1830. No further action, however, was taken until a trivial incident brought about momentous and unexpected results.

During the Revolutionary Wars two Algerine Jews had

furnished wheat to the French government for which full payment had apparently never been made. The two merchants in
question thereupon proceeded to borrow all they could in
France, giving their claim as security. Later they sold their
claim to Hussein, the Dey of Algiers. All attempts by that potentate to collect the full amount of the contract were fruitless,
the French government insisting, quite properly, on deducting
the amounts due French subjects. Finally, during one stormy
interview at a public reception, the Dey lost his temper and
struck the French Consul, Deval, with a "chasse-mouche."
Charles X responded with a blockade of Algiers and soon thereafter declared war. France thereby embarked on an enterprise
that was to influence her subsequent history more than any
other single event and was to give a new trend to her entire
Mediterranean policy. France was about to become an African
power.[1]

The ensuing naval operations followed the familiar course
of all previous actions of this sort. It was a repetition of Thomas
Jefferson's famous dictum about "breaking glass windows with
guineas." After two years of ineffectual gestures the Bourbon
government at last decided upon more drastic measures. It was
to be the last act of the dying monarchy, one that more than
offset whatever incompetence the Restoration may have displayed in other respects. Moreover, the decision required real
courage, as Great Britain threatened to intervene. The French
countered with a threat to reoccupy Antwerp, whereupon the
Foreign Office subsided. An army of over 38,000 men was
assembled at Toulon under the command of General Bourmont. The force put at his disposal was considerably in excess

[1]The extent to which France became an African power is apparent from
the following figures. At the close of the first World War France had at the
front 545,000 colonial troops of whom 86 per cent were African and 200,000
workmen of whom 180,000 were African. The number of African troops
could now be greatly increased. The problem is to fit them into modern mech-
anized warfare.

of the six marines given to Eaton, as we can see. The naval contingent amounted to 600 vessels of all types commanded by Admiral Duperré. On June 14, 1830, a landing was effected at Sidi Ferruch, a beach a few miles west of Algiers. Strangely enough the Algerines did not oppose the landing although they subsequently put up a stiff resistance. It took two engagements to get within range of Algiers. On July 4 the French had reached a position where their siege guns threatened the town. Although thoroughly accustomed to naval bombardments a land attack was more than the Algerines could stand. On the following day the city capitulated.

Judging by the size of the expedition Charles X had launched against Algiers a permanent occupation was intended. No sooner had Bourmont, who had been rewarded with a marshal's baton, secured the city than he moved on Mers-el-Kebir, Bone and Blida. Then, suddenly, astonishing news reached the French army. The July Revolution had driven Charles X from the throne. Louis Philippe had been proclaimed King of the French. On July 12 General Clausel arrived with orders to relieve Bourmont, who, owing to his royalist tendencies and his more than equivocal conduct during the Hundred Days, had been unpopular with the army in spite of the efficiency with which he had planned and executed the campaign. On the seventeenth the Tricolor flag replaced the Lilies and Bourmont sorrowfully took the road to exile. Although Hussein and his numerous family had been transported to Italy on a French cruiser, Duperré refused to take Bourmont to Spain. The marshal was compelled to charter a small Austrian brig. The only treasure he took with him, in spite of legends to the contrary, was a small metal box which he insisted on carrying himself. Thinking it must contain something of value the skipper warned him to conceal it during the voyage. "Do not worry," said the marshal, "it will tempt no one." It contained the heart of his son killed in action.

The French conquest of northern Africa is one of the most

remarkable instances of persistency in history. It was during the July Monarchy, however, that the great effort necessary to bring Algeria under French rule was made. It was the outstanding achievement of Louis Philippe and his sons whose courage and ability have set a record few princes in history have equalled. The hostility of Great Britain, far from discouraging further expansion, spurred the new government to increased activity. A British move on Bougie was promptly forestalled. In 1833 the city was captured but only after a siege of three months. Arab resistance was increasing rather than diminishing.

The Arab resistance soon centred around one man, the Emir Abd-el-Kader, one of the most remarkable men the Arab people ever produced. A descendant of the Prophet, he was born at Mascara in 1807 or 1808. At an early age his father took him on a pilgrimage to Mecca and to visit the tomb of his ancestor and namesake, el Jalili, in Bagdad. In 1827 while in Egypt he came under the influence of another great Moslem, Mehemet Ali. Returning to his native country shortly after the French landing he at once proclaimed himself Emir of Mascara and came forth as the champion of Islam. For fifteen years he was to employ a resourcefulness in combating the invaders that baffled the French until, taking a leaf out of his book, they adopted his methods. In reading the story of his campaigns the reader is struck by the similarity of his tactics with those of another Algerian, Jugurtha, King of Numidia, who defied the efforts of Quintus Metullus and Marius from 111 B.C. to 106. Sallust has given us a good description of Jugurtha's system of warfare. Extreme mobility, the cutting off of isolated garrisons by sudden raids, a continual harassing of the columns sent against him, "neither giving battle nor allowing them rest." (Necque proelium facere, nec otium pati.) These tactics Abd-el-Kader practiced with even greater success than his Numidian prototype for one reason that should be clearly understood, as therein lay the strength and the weakness of the Emir's power.

The sense of nationality is completely foreign to the Arab mentality. Their religion is the bond of union between the various tribes. All who do not share their religion are lumped together and hated accordingly. We have already seen that the Barbary corsairs waged war indiscriminately against all Christians. In the case of the nomadic tribes that were rallying to the Emir's standard the trait was all the more marked as they had kept aloof from Turkish influence. The Emir's kingdom was "in his hat," so to speak. It consisted of an enormous movable village in which the indigenous Berbers, or Kabyles as they are called in Algeria, mingled with the Arabs who, as we know, were an Asiatic people. While this conglomeration moved about from oasis to oasis at a safe distance from the coast his mounted warriors, usually Arabs the Kabyles being mountaineers, executed raids, or *razzias*, on the settlements near the sea. If Abd-el-Kader's camp could be dispersed the Emir would be a man without a country but so carefully were the movements of the Smalah, to use the Arab term, screened that its very existence was for a long time disbelieved.

The French penetration of Algeria meanwhile was making heavy weather. As the armies advanced inland they naturally lost the support of the fleet. Matters came to a head in the spring of 1836 when 3000 French troops who had attempted to relieve the garrison of Tlemcen found themselves in turn besieged by Abd-el-Kader at the mouth of the river Tafna, near the Moroccan border. Once more the fleet came to the rescue of their brothers-in-arms. The French vessels, however, brought more than mere reinforcements. They brought the incarnation of an idea in the person of General Bugeaud. No sooner had he landed than he called his officers together and informed his astonished listeners that everything they had been in the habit of doing was wrong. Heavy artillery was useless against an enemy that had no artillery whatever. The weight under which the infantry was staggering must be cut in half. No wagon trains were to slow up future movements; instead eighty mules were to accompany every thousand men. "I have had some success fighting guerillas in Aragon when I served under Marshal Suchet. I shall be even more successful against the Arabs by using the same methods," he confidently promised the men who after six years' fighting thought they knew something about African warfare. "Has any one anything to say? If so I shall answer him." The officers looked at each other and then at the stern, pock-marked face of the veteran of the Peninsula War whose piercing blue eyes produced "the effect of a cold shower," to quote General Canrobert. No one spoke. "Very well, gentlemen. That is all." A new era of African warfare had begun.

The new arrival who was thus scrapping some treasured traditions was Thomas-Robert Bugeaud de la Piconnerie. He was born on October 15, 1784, at Limoges the youngest of fourteen children, a number that probably did not seem an exaggeration to his father who had been one of twenty-four children. Obviously Thomas could not expect much in the way of a patrimony so his family destined him for the church. The Revolution scattered the family. Thomas and his sister Phillis lived as best they could in the ancestral castle, La Durantie, parts of which had been built during the Hundred Years War. Unless Thomas had been lucky with his rod or gun roast chestnuts would be the only food on the supper table. A miserably unhappy childhood rendered worse by the temper of his father, now a widower. In 1804 young Bugeaud enlisted as a private and was present at Austerlitz. By Iéna he had secured a commission. From then on his promotion was rapid. He was among the first troops sent to Spain, where he attracted the attention of Suchet. Unlike most Napoleonic soldiers Bugeaud never showed any enthusiasm for his profession. His letters to his sister dwell upon the horrors of war rather than upon the victories he had witnessed. His attitude was much like that of another great and successful soldier, General Grant.

The first Restoration found him in command of the 14th Infantry. He retained his command during the Hundred Days and won one of the last victories of the Napoleonic era at Saint Pierre d'Albigny, in Savoy, where with 1780 men he turned back 10,000 Austrians. Needless to say the second Restoration shelved him. For the next fifteen years Bugeaud, having married a wealthy heiress of the Dordogne, devoted himself to scientific farming. After the advent of Louis Philippe he became an ardent Orleanist and took an active part in politics. Reintegrated in the service he was given charge of the confinement of the Duchesse de Berry in the fortress of Blayes. The Duchess, who was a granddaughter of Ferdinand IV of Naples and Maria Carolina, had endeavored to rouse the Vendée to rebellion. I use the word "confinement" advisedly, as the turbulent royalist princess, while awaiting deportation to Palmero, gave birth to an unexpected infant, the fruit of a secret marriage to Count Lucchesi-Palli. Shortly thereafter Bugeaud assisted in suppressing the riots of 1834. These services hardly increased his popularity with either royalists or republicans and as a result his life was for some time a stormy one, with innumerable duels three of which proved fatal to his opponent.

Bugeaud's appointment to the command in Africa although a political one was a wise one. Having revised the army so as to give it the desired mobility, Bugeaud proceeded to out-razzia the Arabs. Instead of waiting to be attacked the French columns began harassing their enemies, carrying off their cattle, raiding their camps, in short completely turning the tables. Soon some of the tribes, yielding to old rivalries, joined forces with "the French sultan."

Among the many colorful leaders the African armies developed we must mention one who was eminently fitted to assist Bugeaud in his new tactics, Colonel Yusuf. His real name was unknown even to himself, Yusuf merely being Arabic for Joseph, and for a very good reason. As a child he had been cap-

tured by Tunisian corsairs while on a journey from Elba to
Leghorn, where his mother was about to put him in school. His
mother was sold into slavery and disappeared from view. The
boy was more fortunate. An agent of the Bey of Tunis noticed
him in the slave market and purchased him for his master.
Yusuf soon won that ruler's favor, was given a good education
and in time became an officer in the beylical cavalry. A youthful
escapade, however, completely altered the course of his des-
tiny. He fell in love with one of the numerous daughters of the
Bey and was rash enough to penetrate into the harem one night,
there to be discovered by a watchful eunuch. Yusuf escaped, lay
in wait for the spoilsport whom he promptly despatched, then
sent one of his victim's eyes and an ear to his inamorata concealed in a bouquet, a touching bit of Arab symbolism intended
to convey that his beloved need not fear any more spying or
eavesdropping from *that* eunuch. It was not long, however,
before Yusuf was wanted by the police. Here a bright idea
struck Yusuf. He was the son of a French official at Napoleon's
court in Elba, supposedly. He appealed to the French consul,
de Lesseps, the father of the canal builder. De Lesseps smuggled him out of the country to Algiers, which the French army
had just captured. Employed first as an interpreter he soon was
commissioned to recruit a corps of native cavalry, a body that
formed the nucleus of the famous *Spahis*. And this leads us back
to Abd-el-Kader.

Bugeaud's plan of operations was put into effect in 1836 as we
have seen. Flying columns were sent scouring the country in
pursuit of any tribe that had committeed any act of hostility.
The columns were skillfully disposed so that in fleeing from one
the Arab horsemen would fall upon another. Still no signs of
the phantom Smalah. Arab exaggeration, some said. Not so
Yusuf. From his intimate knowledge of the Arab people he
remained convinced that somewhere beyond the hills the Smalah
was moving about stealthily. Finally in February of 1843,

while questioning a prisoner, he discovered the approximate
location of the illusive camp. He at once reported his information to the Duc d'Aumale, who was nominally in command. A
flying squadron was organized. It consisted of two battalions of
infantry, one of zouaves, nine squadron of cavalry made up of
Chasseurs d'Afrique and Yusuf's *Spahis*, besides a few gen-
darmes and some friendly native chiefs with several hundred
"goums." The French contingent numbered only 1300 foot and
700 horse approximately.

On May 10 the column left Boghar and headed due south.
Food for twenty days was carried on pack animals. No sooner
had the column started than telltale smoke signals on the
neighboring hills gave the alarm. With difficulty were these
sentinels dispersed. On the fourteenth the native scouts picked
up the trail. The Smalah was apparently heading west. The
march was resumed with the cavalry formed in two parallel
columns, the zouaves mounted on mules to hasten their progress. On the morning of the sixteenth after marching twenty-
nine hours the Duke, seeing that his men had run out of water,
decided to abandon the chase and head for Ain Taguine, the
nearest stream. Dame Fortune, however, was once more smil-
ing on youth, the Duke being just twenty-one. The French had
been following a cleverly laid false trail. By going to Ain
Taguine they were to stumble on the Smalah.

Now that pursuit had been abandoned the marching order
was somewhat relaxed. The Arab contingents, however, were
very careful to stay near their French allies. Did they know
that the trail had been a false one and that the Smalah was
probably heading for the same water hole? Tired and thirsty
the column was stumbling along when one of the native chiefs
who had ridden ahead arrived at a gallop. General Fleury,
who later was to distinguish himself by organizing Louis Napoleon's *coup d'état*, then a young officer, has given us a graphic
description of the event.

"Fly while you still can," the Arab exclaimed. "They are just beyond that hill. If they see you all is lost. Sixty thousand of them. They will kill you with clubs like so many goats. Not one of you will escape!"

"Calm yourself," said Yusuf, "and tell us what you have seen."

Word was sent to the Duke, who with the infantry was escorting the convoy, to make haste and cautiously Yusuf, Fleury and the Arab crept to the top of a knoll. There before them lay the Smalah! The Arab had not exaggerated. Between sixty and seventy thousand people, men, women and children, thousands of camels, horses, mules, donkeys, goats, sheep and cattle were going into camp; a whole city of tents was in the process of erection. Every Arab craft was represented, especially the armorers whose stores of weapons glistened in the sun. In the center stood the white tents of the Emir's harem. During his captivity Abd-el-Kader stated that if a man lost his family in the Smalah it frequently took him two days to find them again.

A hurried council of war was held but only one opinion expressed. Attack! The three hundred *Spahis* led by Yusuf broke into a charge. Owing to the similarity of dress they were at first mistaken for the red bodyguard of the Emir returning from a raid. The women began intoning the shrill *you-you-you* with which they were wont to welcome their masters. Then suddenly they caught sight of the French cavalry, seven hundred strong, charging in perfect alignment, a feat the Arabs never would or could learn. The panic was indescribable. It was as if an ant-hill had been overturned. In Versailles you can see Horace Vernet's stirring picture of the scene. In the foreground camels with their cone-shaped palanquins are scrambling to their feet, animals of all kinds, including tame deer, are rushing about madly, a strikingly handsome Kabyle woman is dragging a child to safety. In the background the Emir's wives, clad in white, are kneeling with arms outstretched toward the oncoming French cavalry. Before the zouaves could come up it was all over. Six thousand prisoners were taken. After distributing a large number of sheep to their Arab allies and keeping a goodly number for themselves the French army turned in forty thousand head to be sold at five francs apiece. The rest of the booty was in proportion. At Chantilly the Emir's tent is preserved. It is in the carriage house of the Duke's palatial stables.

The Emir, however, had not been caught. He was off watching another French column at the time. "Had I been there," he later said, "we should have fought for our wives and children and you would have had a day of it!" Abd-el-Kader was now a man without a country, except that his family had escaped with the connivance of the Arab contingents who recognized them and allowed them to pass. *Ectoub!* "It is written!" was the only comment the descendant of the Prophet made. But the French were not through with him by any means although the victory won by the son of "the French Sultan" profoundly affected the Arabs of Algeria. Passing into Moroccan territory Abd-el-Kader induced the Sultan to proclaim a Holy War against the Christians. An army of 50,000 men was assembled in August 1844 on the plains of Isly under the command of Moulay Mohammed, the son of the Sultan. To oppose this rabble Bugeaud had at his disposal 10,000 men. For several days the two armies watched each other on either side of the stream that divided the plain. Again a bold attack by the French was to bring an overwhelming victory. On the thirteenth, under pretext of foraging, Bugeaud led his forces to the bank of the river toward dusk. Not a fire, not a lamp, not even a cigarette was lit. At 2 A.M. on the fourteenth the French forded the river. At the break of day they charged. It was a repetition of the Smalah episode. The French losses were 27 killed and less than 100 wounded.

The Sultan sued for peace. Owing to British hostility the French reluctantly concluded the Treaty of Tafna, thereby delaying until 1907 the absorption of Morocco.

Bugeaud's task was done. The volunteer who had won his corporal's stripes at Austerlitz was now a marshal and Duc de l'Isly. To his troops he remained *le Père la Victoire*. The Emir, however, was still at large. For three years he continued a hopeless struggle. Finally on December 23, 1847, he appeared before the Duc d'Aumale and, in accordance with Arab custom, delivered his charger, a superb stallion who had many times saved his life, in token of surrender.

Before discussing the historical significance of the events we have described it may be of interest to relate briefly the subsequent careers of the principal participants. After his surrender Abd-el-Kader and his suite were transported to France and confined, first in the Château of Pau and later in the Château of Amboise. When he became President of the Second Republic one of Louis Napoleon's first acts was to liberate the Emir. He retired to Damascus. In 1860 he saved the Christian population of that city from massacre at the hands of the Druses, a courageous act that goes a long way toward redeeming the one unworthy deed of his life, the massacre of his French prisoners at La Deira in 1846. Napoleon III presented him with the Grand Cordon of the Legion of Honor and doubled his pension, bringing it up to the sum of 150,000 francs a year. He died on May 23, 1883. The great Moslem toward the end of his life became a sincere admirer of the French, to whom he looked for the ultimate regeneration of his people.

Bugeaud remained in Algeria until May, 1847. His services in developing the agricultural possibilities of the land he had conquered were quite on a par with his military achievements. The astonishing feature of his career is perhaps the fact that he was one of the few French officers to realize that the methods he had inaugurated in Africa were wholly inapplicable to European conditions. His sound advice, repeatedly given, unfortunately was not accorded the consideration it deserved. The criticism that the Algerian campaigns had unfitted the French army for continental warfare is probably well founded. No part of the blame for this state of affairs, however, can be laid at the door of the French Scipio. When the revolution of 1848 broke out Louis Philippe turned to his old marshal. Had he been given a free hand he undoubtedly would have routed the Parisian mob as he had the Arab hordes at Isly. Louis Philippe, being unwilling to shed the blood of his subjects, abdicated. Calling for a cab and taking his umbrella he went forth to face the exile he had known in his youth. His generals hastily discarded their uniforms and left the Tuileries after him. Not so Bugeaud. In full uniform he faced the surging mob. Cries of "à mort" rent the air. "*Mes enfants,* if you wish to kill a marshal of France you may do so." The groans changed to cheers as the victor of Isly passed unhurt through the crowd. He was again returned to parliament and died of the cholera in Paris on June 8, 1849.

The Duc d'Aumale's latter years are well known. He succeeded Bugeaud as Governor General for a few brief months and then followed his father into exile. His offer to serve his country in 1870 was declined. After the fall of the Second Empire he returned to France and presided over the court martial that tried Bazaine. His answer to the marshal who was trying to justify his surrender of Metz on the ground that "there was no government" remains a classic. "Il y avait la France, Monsieur le Maréchal!" Boulanger deprived the duke of his rank and on his vigorous protest brought about his second exile. He was, however, soon permitted to return and died in 1897 while on a visit to Sicily, the Duchess having been a Neapolitan Bourbon.

And now for Yusuf. His career continued on picturesque lines. During the Crimea the organizer of the *Spahis* was employed to raise a similar corps in Turkey, the *Bachi Bazouks*. Their services were disappointing. On his return to Algeria he served under MacMahon in the campaign of Kabylia. The two men, however, had little in common. Moreover a new spirit had come over Algeria into which Yusuf hardly fitted. When MacMahon became Governor General he insisted that Yusuf be transferred to France. He was accordingly given command of a division at Montpellier. Transplanted to foreign soil he soon withered like an exotic tree and died at Cannes in 1866. His widow, who was the daughter of a French general, brought his body back to Mustapha Supérieur and buried him, Arab fashion, in a *kouba* on the grounds of his Moorish villa, where of an evening he had loved to sit smoking his nargile and gaze on the city and bay of Algiers spread out before him. She outlived her husband by twenty-five years and was one of the personalities of the colony. Those who had the privilege of knowing her remember her as an interesting old lady who delighted in telling stories of her early married life and her recollections of the princes and soldiers who gave France the province that was to make her the really great colonial power of Europe.

A glorious, glamorous adventure, as romantic as the era with which it was coeval. What I have endeavored to bring out at this point, however, is the African tradition with its somewhat theatrical atmosphere, strange uniforms and stranger wearers. In the course of the past one hundred years a colorful and thrilling legend has taken a firm hold on the Gallic mentality. It is part and parcel of the French people regardless of party. The administrative problem facing France is nevertheless a very real one. Will Abd-el-Kader's dream come true? *Qui sait?* One thing, however, is certain. The experiment France is trying is one no other nation could even attempt. To the Frenchman there are no "natives." They are Kabyles, Arabs, Berbers, Algerians, Tunisians, Moroccans, to be treated and respected accordingly. In an age seething with unrest French northern Africa has been comparatively free from disturbance, the loyalty of its inhabitants exemplary.

The mysterious inaccessibility of Islam! No one who has not spent the month of the Ramadan in the old Arab towns of the Barbary Coast has felt its full force. From sunrise to sundown the faithful fast and pray but the night brings a weird relaxation. From the flat roofs of the houses strange music arises. A *chalumeau* is repeating a fascinating cantilena through endless modulations, some very sophisticated, all as bewitching as the piping of a snake charmer. Savage chants now join in accompanied by drums and cymbals. Deep-toned Arab fiddles send their pleadings through the star-lit night. Hour after hour, like an unearthly sabbath, the Song of Islam mounts higher and higher and then suddenly like a cock's crow the raucous tone of the long Moorish trumpet, shaped like an Alpine horn. Silence, unbroken save by the call of the muezzin repeated from tower to tower. A vague feeling of apprehension seizes the European. We are surrounded by a world that refuses to accept us. With the first streak of dawn a faint but limpid note relieves the tension. It is the *diane* being sounded by the bugles of the French garrison. The day breaks. The bustle of the city begins, slowly at first. Some farmers clamoring for admission at the town gate, a clatter of donkey's hoofs on the cobblestones of the narrow, crooked streets, some wealthy Arab, preceded by his runner as he rides to the mosque. And then the confident, exultant sound of the *clairons* leading the regiment out for morning drill! What are they playing?

"As-tu vu la casquette du Père Bugeaud?"

CHAPTER XIX

"I Mille"

THE VILLA SPINOLA at Quarto was an ideal site for a conspiracy. On the rugged coast to the east of Genoa a series of rocky promontories jut out to sea. The growth of the city has now suburbanized the surroundings but three quarters of a century ago Quarto was a pleasant region of country estates. The Villa Spinola, in those days, was separated from the water by only the width of a country road skirting the Gulf of Genoa. Moreover, it was protected from inquisitive eyes by a high wall and further isolated by groves of pines. A tiny bay, barely large enough to allow small boats to beach, lay close to the wall. A narrow path led from the shore to the garden gate. Mysterious, remote, just the spot for a tryst . . . or a *coup d'état*.[1]

On the evening of May 2, 1860, two men who had already made history, and were to make more, were engaged in earnest conversation in the living room of the villa.

"You are the only one who urges me to start for Sicily. All the others seek to dissuade me."

"I do so, General, because I know this undertaking will bring the greatest blessing to our country and much glory to you. I have only one fear and that is because of the sea."

"I will answer for the sea," said the general.

"Then I will answer for the land!"

[1] The Villa Spinola has recently been converted into a Garibaldian museum.

The general who had so glibly assured his visitor that he could run the blockade was Giuseppe Garibaldi. Subsequent events proved him to have been abundantly right. His categorical assertion, however, was proof of an uncanny intuition, in view of the fact that he had several foreign navies to contend with. The Sardinian he was warranted in disregarding. The problem confronting Cavour at that time was a delicate one. In order to save his face before the European chancelleries he must go through the motions of stopping Garibaldi. The simplest way obviously was to arrest Garibaldi. That was out of the question. He accordingly gave orders to Admiral Persano to cruise off Southern Sardinia but without using his engines. Never in history did fuel economy play a greater part. Then the great minister awaited developments. An expedition in aid of the Sicilian insurrection could, at a pinch, be justified. An attack on the Papal States, however, could not. If Garibaldi would only use discretion for once! Discretion unfortunately did not fit into the Liberator's methods. When news reached Cavour that Garibaldi was heading for Papal territory he was "on the spot." He therefore wired Persano: "The Ministry has decided on Cagliari," that name being the code word for "Stop Garibaldi." Persano, however, proceeded to read between the lines. "The Ministry" did not necessarily mean Cavour or Victor Emmanuel. He promptly answered "Ho capito" and kept on under sail, thereby allowing Garibaldi to continue unmolested to Sicily. On such slender threads do the crucial events of history sometimes hang! On May 18 the official *Gazette* was able to state: "The government has disapproved the expedition and attempted to prevent its departure by such means as prudence and the laws would permit." Having seen how Cavour accomplished the difficult feat of saving his face, let us return to Garibaldi's visitor. He was one day to be a prime minister himself. At the time we are considering he was just one of the organizers of the little band of dare-devil patriots whom history has immortalized by the name of "I Mille." His name was Francesco Crispi.

A Sicilian by birth, Crispi was a practising attorney in Naples when the revolution of '48 broke out in Palermo. Hurrying to the island he took a prominent part in that short-lived uprising, so much so that he was excluded from the amnesty of 1849. In 1860 he returned to Sicily, disguised as an Argentinian tourist, and toured the country organizing revolutionary committees as he went. His adherents soon grew too numerous for secrecy. On April 4 the plot was discovered. A depot of arms had been assembled at Palermo in a building hired from the friendly monks of the Gancia convent. Thither the conspirators flocked, prepared to sell their lives dearly. The Neapolitan troops blew down the door and the usual massacre followed.

Crispi had by this time left for Piedmont in the hopes of enlisting the support of Garibaldi. The question uppermost in the mind of Garibaldi was whether help could be gotten to the Sicilian rebels in time to save the movement. Reliable information was difficult to obtain. Crispi turned the scales at the critical time by exhibiting ciphered despatches from one of his agents to the effect that the insurrection was still holding out in the mountains. Whether or not this message was a fabrication of Crispi's will never be known. Alexandre Dumas, the elder, who was then cruising in the Mediterranean on his yacht the *Emma*, visited Genoa while the expedition was being discussed. He was in an exceptionally good position to ascertain the facts as he was on intimate terms with Vecchi, Garibaldi's host at the Villa Spinola. He is emphatic in saying that Crispi "made his own news." Whether aprocryphal or genuine, one thing is certain. Crispi's information turned out to be the truth even though it may have started as a pious fraud.

While the leaders were conspiring in the aristocratic seclusion of the Villa Spinola the nucleus of the expedition was being assembled on an old hulk, the *San Paolo,* that lay rotting near the eastern harbor light. The authorities were meanwhile keeping a sharp lookout . . . to the *west* of the harbor. On May 5, at 11 P.M., up the ladder came an officer who calmly took command. His name was Nino Bixio. Like Garibaldi he had served in the Sardinian navy; then, to the disgust of his family, he shipped on a merchantman to "see the world." For a while he served on an American "windjammer." His adventures had included a run-in with cannibals, so Bourbons held no terrors for him. Transferring his men into small boats he rowed over to two steamers of the Rubattino Line, the *Piemonte* and the *Lombardo,* and proceeded to get up steam. Of course the whole affair had been prearranged, not with the company but with the manager of the line, an unsung patriot by the name of Fauché, who thereby lost his position and ended his days in the civic hospital of Venice.

The volunteers had by this time received their marching orders. Quietly and in small groups they made their way to appointed places of embarkation. No demonstration or flag waving. The realization of the magnitude of the undertaking had produced a sobering effect. With uncovered heads the crowd that had assembled watched them shove off and disappear into the darkness. When the last boatload had left, Garibaldi and his staff bade farewell to their host and joined their comrades. *The Thousand,* to be precise they numbered 1089, were on their way to overthrow one of the oldest dynasties of Europe, one that had it been endowed with vision might have accomplished what the House of Savoy was about to do, unite Italy, a task Murat had vainly attempted.

Who were *I Mille?* They were recruited from every walk of life, from every province of Italy. Four were Hungarians. Most were unarmed, a few had Piedmontese uniforms. The expedition, however, had the two ingredients Eaton had recommended, "cash and a few marines." Unlike most ventures of

the kind funds were the least of Garibaldi's troubles. Owing to
the popular appeal of the leader money had been pouring into
the coffers of the Garibaldian treasurer, Doctor Bertani. Some
of it came from America. Including 90,000 lire cash, which
Garibaldi took with him, a sum just short of 322,000 lire had
been spent in fitting out the expedition. As marines he had
thirty-five Genoese carabineers, the only regular troops in his
command although many of his volunteers had seen service as
members of his famous corps of "francs tireurs," the Alpine
Chasseurs.

Just as the two Rubattino steamers were about to start a
boat belonging to the harbor police came alongside. She was
promptly made fast and detained until the vessel sailed. Another neat bit of "face-saving." The *Lombardo* was having
trouble getting up steam so the *Piemonte* took her in tow. Day
was breaking and a French gunboat at anchor in the outer roads
had to be eluded. Fortunately the Frenchmen did not know
of the projected invasion of the Papal States, so trouble was
avoided. Once outside of the harbor the volunteers who had
been tossing about in small boats for several hours climbed on
board. Coal and a consignment of 1000 muskets were shipped
and at 6.30 A.M. of the sixth the *Lombardo* started for the
Straits of Piombino, leaving the *Piemonte* to pick up the
ammunition which was to have been brought out by some
smugglers Bixio had hired. These light-fingered gentry, however, found a more profitable use for their cargo, so after
waiting a while, the *Piemonte,* supposing that the *Lombardo*
had picked up the ammunition, put out to sea.

A series of petty annoyances now began. The *Piemonte* was
short of oil. A boat had to be sent ashore at Recco to procure
some. The *Lombardo* proved an indifferent sailor, seven knots
being her best speed. A fresh breeze sprang up. Soon the cry
of "man overboard" brought to their feet all who were not
prostrated. The man proved to be slightly demented, having cast

himself into the sea while in the rowboat a few hours previously. After the rescue Garibaldi signalled Bixio to bring the *Lombardo* alongside the *Piemonte*. Here the awful truth dawned upon the two navigators. Neither had any ammunition on board!

A council of war was held at which it was discovered that the consignment of revolvers had also been stolen by Bixio's smugglers. The revolvers could be dispensed with but the ammunition, that was serious. The only thing to do was to wheedle some from the commandant of the garrison at Orbetello, Lieutenant-Colonel Giorgina. Whom to send on that difficult mission was the question. By common accord the choice fell upon Colonel Türr, a Hungarian who had long since abandoned the hated Austrian service. Dumas assures us he was "as eloquent as Cicero and as persuasive as Talleyrand," both of which qualities he would require. But where was Türr? He was finally discovered flat on his back in a secluded corner of the *Piemonte*. The only response that could be gotten from him was a plaintive wail: "I know why that poor devil threw himself into the sea. If I should do so, be good enough to ask the General not to have me pulled out. It is my last wish and the request of a dying man is sacred!"

The expedition duly reached Talamone where a small force of 230 men under command of Zambianchi was detached. So far the strategy of Garibaldi had been 100 per cent perfect. The Zambianchi diversion was the first questionable measure. It came near bringing on an intervention by both France and Piedmont. Zambianchi, whose record during the Roman Republic of 1849 had been unsavory, did not enjoy the confidence or the respect of his men. The force employed was too small to accomplish any result and the apathy of the population did the rest. The Zambianchi raid could not possibly have misled the Neapolitan government into supposing that an attack from the north was imminent unless a more serious offensive had been launched, in which event European intervention in support of the Pontifical government would surely have ensued. It is difficult to avoid the conclusion that the affair was a sop to the anti-clerical Mazzinian element, hence a blunder. After a few days of futile forays the force passed into Tuscan territory and was disarmed. While at Talamone Garibaldi organized his army, practised landing operations and sent Türr in a *calessina* to take a drive along the coast during which he called on the commandant of Orbetello. From the fragmentary accounts of the interview any service man can reconstitute the scene.

Enter Türr, the A.D.C. He presents a letter of introduction from Lieutenant-General Garibaldi couched in such flowery language that with it Türr was willing "to claim Proserpina from Pluto." Salutes, mutual compliments, and then down to business.

"Of course, Colonel, you know the mission that has been entrusted to us."

The Colonel did not, but could make a pretty good guess as to what Garibaldi was up to.

"The General's plans for the invasion of Sicily have been carefully worked out. We have a picked force, sufficient arms, two good (?) steamers, in fact, everything in perfect order and then, would you believe it, some silly ass at the War Office (you know how they are, Colonel) misrouted our ammunition. I am sorry to trouble you, but I must request you to allow us to draw on the government stores in your keeping."

The Colonel pleaded that he should have authority from the War Office. Türr countered by pointing out that by the time that could be obtained the opportunity would be lost. The Colonel, like Persano, "had understood," fortunately.

"Take all you require. I know that from a military point of view I am committing a fault, but . . ."

In due course the Colonel was court-martialed . . . and

acquitted, but by then "face-saving" was no longer necessary. So diplomatic had Türr been that the Colonel insisted on personally delivering to the General powder for 100,000 cartridges, 300 rounds of artillery ammunition and 6 cannon; the latter, however, could be classed as museum pieces.

The expedition resumed its course. Fifty red shirts were distributed. The artificers busied themselves making cartridges. Early on May 11 the vessels passed the island of Marittimo. The were approaching the Sicilian coast. One important point remained to be determined. By actual experiment Garibaldi had discovered that to land his force in small boats would require at least two hours. The prudent course was to make for some harbor and berth alongside of a dock. Marsala was therefore chosen. Being an important shipping point for wine it was abundantly provided with facilities. As soon as the Sicilian coast was sighted the semaphores on shore could be seen waving frantically. At 10.15 the harbor loomed in sight. Two frigates were noticed at anchor outside the mole. Bad news! An English schooner happened along. From her Garibaldi learned that the frigates were British. Good news! The *Piemonte* soon stopped a fishing smack and was informed by the skipper that a company of royalist troops that had been quartered in the town had left for Trepani the night before. Better news yet! A dash was made for the harbor which the *Piemonte* entered proudly flying the Tricolor of Italy with the White Cross of Savoy, not the republican banner of Mazzini. The *Lombardo*, unfortunately, ran aground on a bank 100 yards from the entrance. The Carabineers were landed to guard the harbor. Türr hurried to the telegraph station to stop that tell-tale signalling. A message had just been sent reading:

"Two steamers flying the Sardinian flag have just entered the harbor and are landing men."

An answer asking for further details had just been recorded.

With presence of mind Türr, who had taken the precaution of bringing a telegraph operator with him, sent the following correction:

"Please pardon my mistake. I find I was wrong. The two steamers are merchantmen from Girgento laden with sulphur."

"Idiot!" came the retort.

Meanwhile the volunteers, who had impressed every available small craft, were being landed. The crew of an English schooner lent a willing hand. Haste must be made, as two Neapolitan warships had left the harbor earlier in the day and might return at any moment. Sure enough, they did. Soon the *Stromboli* was sighted heading for the harbor with the *Partenope,* a sailing frigate, in tow. Noticing the commotion on shore, the *Stromboli* dropped her tow and put full steam ahead.

And now we come to an incident that has never been satisfactorily explained. Garibaldi, on seeing the *Stromboli* approach said: "I do not think they will fire." He was right. Instead of firing on the Garibaldians, who were marching along the mole, Captain Acton sent a boat over to the *Intrepid,* one of the British vessels, to inquire whether there were any British troops ashore. Had a few red shirts misled him? So outspoken had been British sympathy with the revolution that it is more likely that Acton feared an international incident. He therefore insisted on speaking to Captain Marryat (who, by the way, was not the novelist) and his colleague, Captain Winnington-Ingram. These two officers were on shore at the time, little suspecting that history was in the making. They promptly rowed out to the *Stromboli* and assured Acton that they would not interfere, but requested that the British-owned storehouses be spared. When finally the Neapolitans opened fire, Garibaldi and his men were safely inside Marsala. The British navy unwittingly had more than redeemed Nelson's hostility to the Parthenopean Republic sixty years previously.

Although the landing had countless witnesses, considerable divergence exists between the various reports. Such an easily verified detail as the name and number of the Neapolitan vessels present is variously reported. Alexandre Dumas may therefore be right when he stated that one of the vessels was commanded by a great-nephew of Admiral Carraciolo, an interesting suggestion and one that, if true, would account for many things. By another curious coincidence Captain Acton was a grandson of Ferdinand's prime minister who had been partly responsible for the hanging of the patriotic admiral.

The capture of Marsala did not become generally known until it was announced officially in Turin on May 14. The news fairly electrified Europe. Garibaldi with two wretched steamers had eluded the Neapolitan fleet and with less than 800 men had taken Marsala! It is interesting to compare the actual event with the Neapolitan *communiqué*. The art of distorting news is not as recent an invention as one might think. On the evening of May 13 the Neapolitan War Office announced that: "Two Neapolitan frigates opened fire on Marsala and killed several buccaneers. Their vessel, the *Lombardo*, was sent to the bottom." As a matter of fact both of Garibaldi's vessels had been scuttled to prevent capture. The total losses of the "buccaneers" had been one man wounded in the shoulder and one dog in the leg. No G.H.Q. during any World War has excelled that announcement.

The Garibaldians at once proceeded to advance on Palermo, striking due east, then northeast. On May 16 they met the Neapolitan army in the mountainous region of Calatafimi. In view of the scarcity of ammunition all except the Carabineers, who were trained marksmen, were ordered to hold their fire and rely on the bayonet. For a while the invaders were in a perilous position. Some of Garibaldi's staff advised retreat. "Italiani, qui bisogna morire!" was his answer. The words were hardly out of his mouth than a volley of stones indicated that the royalists were out of ammunition. A bayonet charge put them to flight. Now let us look at the *communiqué*. "The results of the engagement were not altogether decisive. The Neapolitan troops have retired to Palermo whence two columns of 3000 men each have been sent forward in pursuit of the enemy." How a retiring force can pursue one that is advancing is not explained.

After Calatafimi, Garibaldi announced to his followers that they "soon would be in Palermo or in Hell!" On May 19 they got their first view of the *Conca d'Oro*, the luxuriant valley that curls around Palermo, a lasting monument to the husbandry of the now vanished Arab. In the foothills, among groves of lemon and orange trees, they could see the spires and cloisters of Monreale, the priceless gift of the Normans to Mediterranean art. The prize was not to be theirs, however, without further fighting. The Neapolitans, under the leadership of a courageous Swiss officer, Colonel von Mechel, took the offensive. Fortunately, the Garibaldians had by now received the first of the many reinforcements that were to swell their ranks. The descendants of the Albanian colonists of Piano dei Greci and some 3000 Sicilians recruited by La Masa joined in the fighting, which from now on was intense. On May 27 the Garibaldians rushed into the city and reached the *Fiera Vecchia*, or Old Market. Two days of bloody street fighting ensued, a Neapolitan squadron doing very efficient work at long range. By the twenty-ninth, however, the Neapolitan generals were ready to talk terms and requested Admiral Mundy to call a conference on board the H.M.S. *Hannibal*. Commander James S. Palmer commanding the U.S.S. *Iroquois*, who attended the conference, has given an interesting account of subsequent events in his report to Isaac Toucey, Secretary of the Navy.

The Neapolitans began by ignoring Garibaldi and addressing themselves exclusively to the British admiral. When that officer refused to lend himself to such "farcical" behavior, they came out with their proposal which was nothing less than a suggestion that Garibaldi humbly petition the King for a liberal constitution. Garibaldi calmly announced that he was Dictator of Sicily and that for humanitarian reasons he would extend the armistice for twenty-four hours during which the Neapolitan authorities could think matters over. Then the meeting broke up. The next day at noon, much to Palmer's surprise, the Neapolitan garrison capitulated.

The sequel is quickly told. At Milazzo the Bourbon troops made a last stand, but a feeble one. Milazzo is, of course, the ancient Mylæ, where Caius Duilius perfected the *corvus*. Its citadel is the one whose importance de Ruyter had stressed. In the hands of a determined force it would have been a hard nut to crack. Discouragement, however, had undermined the morale of the Neapolitan army. Moreover, the Piedmontese government had now taken Garibaldi under its wing. Admiral Persano had appeared with a squadron, thereby rendering the relief of the fortress risky. There was no telling how the Sardinian admiral might "understand" his mission. He would probably be disavowed if he did anything rash, but that would not raise any Neapolitan frigate he might sink in the meantime. Milazzo surrendered; soon the entire island was in Garibaldi's hands. Entrusting the civil government to Crispi, Garibaldi now began planning to extend his conquests to the mainland. Volunteers were flocking to his standards. And here another navy comes into play, the United States Navy. "I have been careful to avoid anything like a breach of neutrality," Palmer informed the Navy Department under date of June 1, "and have refused protection to any but American citizens." He was soon to have his conception of neutrality put to a severe test! Let us have the Commander tell his own story.

"A few days since," he advises Secretary Toucey under date of June 21, "I received a letter, forwarded through the Sardinian Admiral, now in this port (Palermo) from a Mr. Wm. de Rohan, dated Cagliari, June 13, a copy of which I enclose. Its perusal will explain its purport. The Sardinian Admiral (the Count Persano) with whom I have been on the most friendly terms, is conducting (sub rosa) reinforcements from Italy for Garibaldi's expedition, though obliged by orders from his government to assume a seeming neutrality. He frankly told me that these steamers under the American flag, and with American names, had on board the long expected expedition of Colonel Medici, which were between 3000 and 4000 strong, and were only awaiting the coast to be clear for an opportunity of disembarking on the island.

"Thus, it was as I suspected, though the letter was my first intimation that the American flag was to cover this transaction. I took no notice, of course, of this cool piece of impertinence of Mr. Wm. de Rohan, but I learned the night before last that this party was safely landed from the steamers, in Castellamare bay, some twenty miles from this port. . . . Medici with the major part of his expedition has also arrived in town.

"The facts as far as I can gather, seem to be these: Three steamers were purchased at Marseilles, probably with the Garibaldi fund, a Mr. Wm. de Rohan (an American) assumes the position of proprietor, for which he was probably well paid [?], they arrive at Genoa, Mr. Patterson, the American Consul, furnished them with American papers, each individual has his passport, and these passengers profess to be going to work on the Suez canal. The Sardinian authorities doubtless winked at this proceeding, and they are formally cleared as American vessels. Mr. Patterson I presume to be cognizant of the whole transaction.

"What punishment is due the authors of this prostitution of our flag, the Department will best understand. As much as every lover of liberty must sympathize with the success of Garibaldi and [feel] disgust for the Government he hopes to overturn, I feel strongly tempted to seize them and put a stop to their illegal conduct, but it is too grave a step to undertake without instructions from the Government. Besides it would raise an outcry in Italy, and perhaps also in the United States and might not be an action the Department would approve. I learn moreover, they are to continue this passenger trade for some time to come.

"In my own judgment, the government of Naples will be subverted in a month, and then there will be more to complain."

The "cool piece of impertinence" was a request from Mr. de Rohan that the *Iroquois* meet his three steamers off Marittimo and escort them into Palermo. Mr. de Rohan also had the effrontery to assure the American commander that he was in no way connected with Garibaldi or other rebel leader. Admiral Persano, however, being "an officer and a gentleman" was unwilling to be a party to the deception the Yankee filibuster was trying to practice. We shall pass over the many extraordinary features of the situation, the apparent collusion of the American Consul at Genoa, the connivance of the Sardinian government, the "understanding" attitude of Admiral Persano, and come to one little-known fact. During the period between the sailing of the de Rohan steamers and the landing of Garibaldi on the coast of Calabria, an interval of about two months, the fate of Italy depended on the attitude one American naval officer might take toward three vessels whose right to American protection may well be questioned.

The American commander's understanding of the law applicable to the case was eminently correct, as his report of July 21 proves. "The soi-disant American steamers *Washington, Oregon* and *Franklin,* were busily engaged either in bringing reinforcements from Genoa to Garibaldi, or in carrying troops and munitions of war to different points on the coast of Sicily, hoisting, as it suited their convenience, the American or the Sardinian flag. One of them (the *Franklin*), arrived while I was in port. She, it seems, is the only one now commanded by an American, a reckless individual by the name of J. West Nevins, of Philadelphia. . . . These vessels are daily liable to be seized by Neapolitan cruisers, and will doubtless for protection hoist the American flag. In my judgment they will be lawful prizes, and yet, I must confess I should be embarrassed to see that flag attacked whatever were the provocation. By the law their bill of sale, endorsed by the American Consul at Genoa, makes them American property, entitles them to wear the flag and gives them a claim to protection; provided this sale to an American citizen be made *in good faith*, but nothing can warrant this privilege whilst engaged in their present occupation. The Department would oblige me by expressing their views on the subject." In the meantime, however, the *Iroquois* took no action.

If Commander Palmer had chosen the evening of August 18 to climb up to the majestic Greek theatre overlooking the eastern entrance to the Straits of Messina he would surely have been somewhat perturbed and probably greatly thrilled at seeing two steamers slip out of the little harbor of Giardini at the foot of the lofty rock of Taormina. To avoid the Neapolitan patrol they had laboriously steamed around the island from the Faro of Messina, where Garibaldi had established his camp. One was the *Torino*, commanded by Bixio, the other the *Franklin*, commanded by Garibaldi. The Liberator of Italy was about to land on Calabrian soil, a feat he surely would never have been able to accomplish had not Commander Palmer extended, impliedly if not actually, the mantle of protection over the "soi-disant American steamers."

Although somewhat cowed by the hostility they were encountering on all sides the Neapolitan cruisers had been ceaselessly watching Garibaldi's camp at the western entrance to the Straits at which point they are only two miles wide. The British had occupied the site fifty years before at the time

Murat was planning his futile invasion of Sicily. In fact, Garibaldi found the British earthworks practically intact. On August 8, however, Garibaldi succeeded in getting a small force of 200 men across in rowboats in the hopes of surprising the fort at Altifiumara which would would have given him command of the Straits. The attack failed and for the next ten days the band roamed about the bleak plateau of Aspromonte. The attempt, however, had served one useful purpose. It convinced the Neapolitans that any future attempt at a crossing would be made at the same point. Garibaldi skillfully utilized the situation thus created. Embarking some 3300 men on two vessels he circumnavigated the island, then made a bold dash for the beach near Melito. At this point the straits are thirty miles wide. As he had completely hoodwinked the Neapolitan patrol the crossing was safely made, the only incidents being a leak on the *Franklin* which Garibaldi, being a real sailor, located and some more unfortunate navigation by Bixio, who, being an amateur sailor, again ran his ship aground.

Garibaldi spent the whole morning of the nineteenth in a vain attempt to float the *Torino*. In the afternoon the Neapolitan cruisers appeared and the work had to be discontinued. His position was none too pleasant. The warships were firing on his force. In front of him were 16,000 Neapolitan troops. In the meantime, however, 1500 men commanded by Cosenz took advantage of the absence of the patrol and landed at Favazzina. The Neapolitan cruisers promptly abandoned operations against Garibaldi and rushed back to the Faro, where they had the hollow satisfaction of capturing the empty rowboats that were being towed back to the camp. The two Garlibaldian forces now proceeded to combine their movements so as to cut off the garrisons of the coastal towns from any help from the north. On the twenty-first, Garibaldi captured Reggio after considerable fighting in which the Red Shirts lost 150 killed and wounded. The two columns now converged on Villa San

Giovanni, whose garrison surrendered without firing a shot; Altifiumara and Scilla followed suit. Neapolitan resistance was over. The Bourbon troops were fraternizing with the invaders. Garibaldi had succeeded where Murat had failed. The march on Naples could now begin.

Past Pizzo, of tragic memory, the Garibaldians marched, their advance gradually assuming the form of a triumphal procession. Naples gave them a rousing reception, the Lazzari and the liberals for once being in agreement. Then a rapid pursuit of the Bourbon King, Francis II. One sharp battle along the Volturno and the descendant of a long line extending back to the Normans made for Gaëta and oblivion. Another liberator was approaching from the north, an Italian of the Italians, achieving the moral unification of Italy as well as the territorial.

In the Palazzo della Signoria at Sienna you can see two modern frescoes that may seem somewhat out of place in the old Tuscan hill town, the birthplace of Saint Catherine, a city of primitives, Gothic churches, narrow streets and sombre palaces. To those who believe that Italy has a future as well as a past the two paintings are all the more stirring because unexpected. In one Victor Emmanuel, a king for a few brief hours, having taken over the reins of government from the faltering hands of his father, Carlo Alberto, after Novara, is debating with General Radetzky the humiliating terms of peace the Austrians are imposing. The staffs of the opposing leaders are standing at a respectful distance in the courtyard of a Lombard farm. Radetzky calm and courteous but inflexible; Victor Emmanuel defeated but defiant. The incarnation of two irreconcilable principles whose conflicting aims can only be settled by the arbitrament of war. Nationalism and Liberalism on the one hand, Feudalism and Reaction on the other. In another fresco the same Victor Emmanuel clasping the hand

of the aging revolutionary on a country road between Caja-
nello and Vajrano.

"Como state, caro Garibaldi?"
"Bene, Maestà, e Lei?"
"Benone!"

Then they rode side by side, but not for long. Their victory won,
the Garibaldians were a problem. By now they numbered 20,-
000! The path of one leader was to take him to the Quirinal.
The path of the other ended in a humble hut on the lonely
island of Caprera. Working separately and necessarily with
different methods, the sum of their labors had created a great
Mediterranean power.

"Italia fara da se," Carlo Alberto had said in the early days
of his unhappy reign. True, but for Italy to make itself had
required a few heroes!

CHAPTER XX

"Aperire Terram Gentibus"

A T EIGHT O'CLOCK of the morning of November 17, 1869, with that punctuality that is the politeness of sovereigns, the Imperial Yacht *Aigle* slipped her moorings in the new harbor of Port Saïd, swung her graceful bow southward and headed for the narrow rift a modern Hercules had cloven in the rim that had imprisoned the waters of the eastern Mediterranean since time immemorial. A deafening roar of cannon broke the stillness. Between the flashes the cheers of 4000 seamen could be heard. The French frigate *Nemis* manned her yards, the other warships present followed her example. Under the awning that had been spread to screen the ardent African sun the Empress Eugénie, still in the full bloom of her matchless beauty, could be seen surrounded by the bright toilettes of her ladies in waiting. At a respectful distance stood the Empress' escort of officers in their tight-fitting uniforms glittering with gold braid and decorations. Winterhalter and de Dreux have perpetuated the memory of the period in their canvases, a *beau monde* such as we shall never see again.

Eugénie could safely embark on the journey that was to take her for a few brief hours into the Red Sea, once so far away, now so near at hand. The waterway which her kinsman, Ferdinand de Lesseps, had just completed had been duly consecrated the day before to the peaceful mission of opening the world to all people. To be sure that no precaution had been overlooked a Roman Catholic priest and an Orthodox pope had intoned the rites of their respective churches and a Ulema had invoked the blessing of Allah under a dais surmounted by a cross and a crescent. Besides the Empress and the Khedive Ismail, the Emperor of Austria and the King of Sweden had honored the occasion by their presence. The Emperor Napoleon III was unable to attend. The *année terrible*, alas, was but a few months off.

As de Lesseps had predicted, the task had been "simple enough, the smallest French railroads have greater difficulties," so while the *Aigle* led the procession of sixty-eight vessels to Lake Timsah all on board were undoubtedly convinced that correcting the oversights of nature was simple enough for French genius and French thrift. France had solved one of the oldest problems in history, one whose origin is lost in the haze of legendary times. According to Strabo, Sesostris thought of joining the Nile and the Red Sea in the year 1300 B.C. or thereabouts. Herodotus assures us that the Pharoah Necho sacrificed 120,000 laborers in the attempt. Darius, the Persian conqueror of Egypt, seriously contemplated renewing the endeavor but was dissuaded by the scientists of his time, who informed him that the level of the Red Sea was so much higher than that of the Inland Sea that an inundation of lower Egypt would ensue. Before scoffing at the ignorance of the geographers of antiquity it may be well to remember that Le Père, the engineer Bonaparte commissioned to draw plans for a sea-level canal, made the same objection. The Ptolemies, nevertheless, completed a Nile-Red Sea canal which Trajan later repaired. Remains of the embankments twenty feet high were discovered by Bonaparte and greatly fired his imagination. The Caliph Omar, after his conquest of Egypt, was urged to build a canal from sea to sea. Omar, however, saw in the canal a threat to the safety of his country, Arabia. One of his successors, El Mansour, blocked up the existing Nile canal in order to prevent the exportation of grain from Egypt to Mecca and

Medina, thereby starving those rebel cities into submission. Haroun-al-Raschid considered piercing the isthmus but abandoned the plan for fear of the Byzantine navy. Thus, as can be seen, at an early date the strategic importance of the Suez Canal had been discovered.

The engineering feat that was being inaugurated with pomp and circumstance was so much the work of one man that it is interesting to observe how the idea took root in his mind. The de Lesseps for several generations had served the French state. Ferdinand's father will be recognized as the consul who had helped Yusuf to escape to Algiers after his unfortunate nocturnal adventure in the beylical harem of Tunis. Ferdinand naturally followed in the footsteps of his father and entered the consular service in 1825 when only twenty years of age. After serving at Lisbon and Tunis he was sent to Alexandria in 1832. While in quarantine at that port he read Le Père's report. It made a profound impression on him. He was soon promoted consul at Cairo and there formed a friendship with Mehemet Ali and his son Saïd. In 1837 he was transferred. The year 1848 found him French Minister to Rome. There he incurred the displeasure of the republican government of France and was unceremoniously forced out of the service. In the meantime his friend Saïd had become viceroy of Egypt. Invited by that ruler he went to Cairo once more and began forming plans for the building of the canal. On November 30, 1854, he secured a valuable concession and set to work organizing the French corporation that still operates the waterway. De Lesseps was not an engineer but a financier of unusual ability. We need not go into the details of his labors except for one curious fact. The project met with the stubborn opposition of Great Britain. Disraeli attacked it in the Commons as "a project which will cause England to pay out large sums for armaments and at the same time do nothing more than produce some doubtful results of a cosmopolitan and philanthropic nature." "One Bosphorus gives us quite enough trouble," Lord Ellenborough exclaimed in the Lords, "but this proposal is to create another and to leave it in French hands!" British engineers were unanimous in predicting that the sands of the desert would soon convert the canal into "a stinking ditch." The climax came when Lord Carnarvon accused de Lesseps of bankruptcy, speculation and general turpitude. The Viscount de Lesseps wanted to challenge the Noble Lord but was persuaded to shrug his shoulders instead.

As a result British capital abstained from any participation in the enterprise, not that that made any difference. France was quite able to finance the work and did so. But England's opposition was not limited to tightening her purse strings. Diplomatic pressure was brought to bear on the Sultan. A large bloc of stock that had been assigned to the Porte was taken by Saïd nevertheless, a fact that later enabled Great Britain to solve a pressing problem. A hue and cry was raised in the British press about the *corvée*, or forced labor, used on the construction. Anglo-Saxons are always solicitous about working conditions, especially outside of their own country. The practice was regulated, thereby increasing the cost of the enterprise. The work continued in spite of British intrigue. De Lesseps overcame all obstacles, including an epidemic of cholera. That he should be the guest of honor on the *Aigle* was but a fitting tribute to his vision and perseverance.

The procession serenely steamed along the fifty-odd miles between Port Saïd and Lake Timsah. The correspondent of the London *Daily News* had the good grace to admit that "the word canal seemed misapplied. Here is a continuous sheet of water the surface of which is wider than the Thames at Richmond. It resembles more a broad and handsome river which runs straight to its destination." At Ismailia, a city named concurrently for Ismail, the son of Ibrahim Pasha, and Ishmael, the son of Hagar who had roamed the desert hereabouts in biblical times, the fleet came to anchor. The desert, of course, had disappeared. In its place along the lake front rose a modern town with boulevards, cafés, squares with trees and flowers, a viceregal palace, and the almost equally resplendent residence of de Lesseps. The native quarter was so commodious that Sir Henry Bulwer, the British resident, warned the viceroy that the French were treating the workers well in the hopes that they would transfer their allegiance from Egypt to France. The teamwork between Sir Henry and the British press was not of the best!

By creating Lake Timsah, de Lesseps had followed the pattern of nature's waterway, the Bosphorus-Sea of Marmora-Dardanelles. Had he done so in his next venture it is quite possible that the eulogistic term "canaliste" would never have degenerated into the epithet "panamiste." Seven years before the completion of the Suez Canal the waters of the Mediterranean had been admitted into the lake. Saïd, unfortunately, was dying and could not be present. His nephew Ismail, who, to quote his own words, was "plus canaliste que Monsieur de Lesseps lui-même," presided at the ceremonies in his stead. "In the name of His Highness Mohamed Saïd and by the grace of God," said de Lesseps as he broke the barrier, "I now command the waters of the Mediterranean to flow into Lake Timsah!" If the ghost of Bonaparte was by any chance watching from atop a pyramid he undoubtedly found that speech, like one of his own delivered many years before in the vicinity, "un peu charlatan." Bombast, however, was in the air and perhaps somewhat pardonable.

But to return to the ceremonies of 1869. At the halfway mark a pleasant surprise had been prepared by Ismail, who had hurried ahead in his yacht the *Mahroussa*, in the shape of a fantasia by the Bedouins followed by a review of the modernized Egyptian army among whom were numerous ex-Confederate officers. The next day the august assembly continued on to Suez, attended a grand ball and then dispersed. The Empress remained one day longer and steamed down the Red Sea as far as the Fountains of Moses in Arabia. During the opening months of the construction much of the fresh water used by the workmen had been brought in tanks from these springs. Later by rehabilitating the original canal, now 2500 years old, an abundant supply was secured from other sources, hence the garden that had supplanted the sand-swept wastes of Hagar's days. On the twenty-second, the *Aigle* was back at Port Saïd, the ceremonies were over. The motto de Lesseps had adopted, "Aperire Terram Gentibus," was a *fait accompli*. The consequences of that opening, however, were not to be exactly as he had expected. "I have done something for progress and peace," is how he modestly summed up his achievement. That he had done something for progress was evident. As for peace, that was another matter.

British opposition to the canal had not been due to any lack of enterprise, nor was it due to any lack of vision. On the contrary, the naval sense of the English had at once seen the strategic problem involved. Palmerston summed up the situation when he said: "The canal would open to the French in the event of war a short cut to India while we would be obliged to go round the Cape. The first thing the French would do would be to send a force from Toulon or Algeria to seize the canal. An expedition, naval and military, would steam away through the canal to India, sweep our commerce, take our colonies and perhaps seize and materially injure some of our Indian seaports, long before our reinforcements, naval and military, could arrive by a long sea voyage." All of which is, of course, sound Napoleonic major strategy.

The Suez Canal has undoubtedly complicated the problem of defending the Empire and greatly added to the expense that defense involves. Does the Panama Canal increase our problems of defense? No. Why? Because the United States is in permanent and undisputed possession of the territory through which the canal runs and can take all the requisite measures to protect it from sabotage or air raids, to say nothing of capture. The British position in Egypt calls for the Napoleonic touch, not the Nelson touch. This of course raises difficult diplomatic and military questions. All of that, however, was now water over the dam. The problem created by the canal had to be met and fortunately the advantages to British trade soon wrought a change in the British attitude. The London *Times* had espoused de Lesseps's idea from the start, so had Gladstone. When "the Great Frenchman," to use Gambetta's compliment, visited London the Queen bestowed on him the Grand Cross of the Star of India, the Prince of Wales presented him with a gold medal at a reception in Crystal Palace, and at a banquet at Mansion House the Lord Mayor in proposing a toast declared that "our eminent engineers made a mistake, Monsieur de Lesseps was right, and the Suez Canal is a living fact." The question of what to do in the presence of this "living fact" remained, however, in spite of the *amende honorable*.

The sensible thing to do was to "buy into" the company and secure a voice in the management if possible. How this was accomplished, with the help of the House of Rothschild, is well known. It furnished Mr. Disraeli an opportunity for a unique diplomatic *coup* and, more recently, furnished Mr. George Arliss with an equally good opportunity for a screen hit. It is hard to say which of the two performances was the more artistic. The Khedive was in such haste for his money. "Scarcely breathing time! But the thing must be done," Disraeli wrote Queen Victoria on November 18, 1875. "Mr. Disraeli perceives," he added, "that in his hurry he has not expressed himself according to etiquette. Your Majesty will be graciously pleased to pardon him." Her Majesty did, and well she might. There *was* no time to lose. "I have purchased for England the Khedive of Egypt's interest in the Suez Canal," Disraeli wrote

Lady Bradford on November 25. "We have had all the gamblers, capitalists, financiers of the world organized and platooned in bands of plunderers arrayed against us and secret emissaries in every corner, and have baffled them all and have never been suspected. The day before yesterday Lesseps, whose company has the remaining shares, backed by the French government whose agent he is, made a great offer. Had it succeeded, the whole Suez Canal would have belonged to France and they might have shut it up! We have given four million pounds sterling for his interest and run the chance of Parliament supporting us. We could not call them together for the matter, for that would have blown everything to Hades!"

As a matter of fact Disraeli had made an excellent investment. In 1929, the "boom year," the shares he had purchased were worth over seventy-two millions on the open market, and Great Britain had collected thirty-eight and one-half millions in dividends! What was even more important, England had secured ten directors on the board as against twenty-one French directors and one Dutchman. Parliament nevertheless gave its approval somewhat reluctantly to the transaction. England has never relished being forced into the Mediterranean, which, as its name indicates, is a landsman's sea. Landlocked waters are a poor place for the exercise of sea power. "A fair wind and plenty of sea room!" But the canal now being a "living fact," Britain could not afford to see it managed exclusively by potential enemies and actual rivals. Soon the British government was compelled to do something more than collect dividends and send directors to the meetings held at 1, rue d'Astorg. In 1882, the insurrection headed by Arabi Pasha necessitated intervention. In vain did England propose to France a joint occupation of Egypt. For some reason that is not quite clear de Lesseps was in sympathy with the Arabi movement. Perhaps he agreed with the obstreperous Egyptian that Egypt was not getting her share of the prosperity she was producing. Italy was next approached. Strange as it may sound to modern ears, the Italian government was not interested. England had to go it alone. One thing had meanwhile been pretty definitely "blown to Hades." It was de Lesseps' prediction that the canal would be an instrumentality of peace.

During the early days of the canal Great Britain was haunted by the fear that the waterway might be closed to her in time of war while kept open to her enemies. By the Convention of Constantinople, however, that danger was removed, theoretically at least. That treaty, which was an attempt to neutralize the canal in much the same manner as the Dardanelles had been, was entered into in 1888 by Great Britain, France, Austria-Hungry, Germany, Italy, the Netherlands, Russia, Spain and Turkey, and provided that the canal "shall always be free and open, in time of war as in time of peace, to every vessel of commerce or of war, without distinction of flag." At the same time strict rules were laid down to prevent the waterway being used as an asylum or base of operations.

Now the ability to interpret and enforce the rules in question, a police duty that theoretically belongs to Egypt, is what gives the canal such strategic value as it possesses. As long as the canal belongs to the canal company, Great Britain will claim the right to protect her investment, and by the same token use the waterway as her strategic needs require, rules or no rules. The "neutralization" of the canal is a legal fiction. On November 17, 1968, the concession given de Lesseps expires, after which date the title will revert to Egypt upon payment of "due compensation." What will happen then? Ask the Sphinx, unless of course the Duce makes that question a futile one long before then. That Egypt will ever be given any real control of the waterway is another fiction. The Suez Canal will continue indefinitely a bone of contention to be striven for by those seeking to supplant British naval supremacy. The profound naval sense of the British in opposing its construction is being abundantly vindicated.

That Egypt is still the "important country" Bonaparte attempted to conquer is more true today than ever, thanks to the Suez Canal; another illustration of the saying that the greatest force in the world is a Frenchman with an idea. We may well question, however, whether de Lesseps' creation will ever fully justify the motto he chose as embodying his idea!

CHAPTER XXI

"Marche Slave"

T HERE is something pathetic about the patient effort of the Russians to reach the oceans of the globe," Albert J. Beveridge once wrote. "There is something that wins our sympathy in the Russian's almost instinctive attempt to escape from his vast and mighty cage, unequalled in its own extent though that cage may be. . . . Turn where he would, the Slav could discern in the far distance the world's common oceans, which he felt to be his common right as well as the right of other peoples, but from which man and nature had conspired to bar him."[1] To possess one European port that is not ice-blocked or fog-bound for several months of the year seems a modest desire for so great a nation as Imperial Russia was, yet the only way it could be gratified was by taking the dangerous but dazzling "Road to Byzantium."

Until the end of the seventeenth century the Euxine had been a closed sea, the exclusive property of the masters of Constantinople, first the Byzantine Emperors, then the Turkish Sultans. "The Sultan considers the Black Sea," the envoy of Peter the Great reported to his master, "as his private abode into which strangers may not penetrate. It is a virgin confined in the recess of a harem, hidden from the gaze of strangers and he would prefer war rather than allow other nations to navigate this inland sea." Nothing daunted, Peter the Great decided to break into this seraglio by capturing Azov, to the

[1] *The Russian Advance*, by Albert J. Beveridge, p. 111.

246

great dismay of the Secretary of the Sublime Porte, who exclaimed that "when foreign ships obtain the right to navigate freely on that sea, the end of the Turkish Empire is at hand!" A somewhat pessimistic statement as subsequent events have proven. For over two months the Muscovites besieged Azov in vain. The reason for their failure is obvious. The Turks could keep the fortress supplied by sea. Peter retired, a defeated but wiser monarch.

A hurry call went forth. From Holland, Trieste, Venice, shipwrights were imported. Twenty-three thousand workmen were assembled at Voronezh, an inland city but one from which Azov could be reached via the river Don. The fleet they constructed consisted of two ships, twenty-two galleys, besides fire rafts and lesser craft. "Captain Peter Alexievich" commanded one of the flotillas whose flagship, the *Principium,* he had built himself. On July 18, 1696, Azov fell. The Russian navy had won its first victory. The "Marche Slave" had started.

Among Peter's many claims to the title of "the Great" his willingness to learn from foreigners was not the least. In March of the following year he accordingly set forth on the grand tour of western Europe that was to take him to Zaandam, Amsterdam and Deptford. Visitors to Zaandam are still shown the humble hut where Peter, disguised as a workman, spent a week working in a neighboring shipyard before, much to his annoyance, his incognito was discovered.

While on his travels Peter had written to the Patriarch Adrian: "We work to conquer the art of the sea effectively in order that on our return to Russia, being perfectly instructed, we may be victorious over the enemies of Christ." Although Peter may have attuned this statement to flatter his pious correspondent, he but restated the traditional Russian policy. Shortly after the capture of Constantinople by the Turks, Ivan III married Zoë Paleologue, the niece of the last Byzantine Emperor. From then on the Muscovite rulers assumed the role of Defender of the Faith and maintained a shadowy claim to the vanished empire of Byzantium. The task of internal consolidation, the incessant wars with Lithuania and Poland, the ambitious plans of Charles XII of Sweden, long prevented any active steps toward making good that claim. In fact the alliance between Turkey and Sweden enabled the Turks to regain Azov in 1711.

Peter the Great died in 1725 and the Russian navy came very near dying with him. It was not until the accession of Catherine the Great in 1762 that Russian sea power was to resume its development. The Empress Catherine, although a German princess who was placed on the throne by a palace revolution in which her husband, Peter III, lost his life, has been justly called the inheritor of the traditions of Peter the Great. One trait she undoubtedly had in common with her illustrious predecessor, a willingness to learn from the foreigner. Thirty younger officers were sent to England for training and foreign officers, mostly British and Danish, from now on frequently appear on the rosters of the Russian navy.

In the summer of 1764 the first Russian vessel to enter the Mediterranean, the frigate *Nadejda Blagopolutchia*, thirty-two guns, made a commercial voyage from Kronstadt to Leghorn and return, Catherine being a partner in the venture. Russia had joined the "deep blue" navies of the world.

The opening years of Catherine's reign were marked by an attempt to unite the nations of northern Europe in an alliance of which Russia was to be the leader, the plan being known as the System of the North. It is quite possible that the Byzantine mirage might have been forgotten had not Turkey been ill-advised enough in 1768 to take up arms against Russia at the instigation of France. Russia at once accepted the challenge in earnest. Two squadrons were prepared for Mediterranean service. The first, under command of Admiral Spiridoff, was to cooperate with the Greek and Slavic rebels, Russia's objective being nothing less than the liberation of the entire Christian population under Moslem rule. The second squadron was under command of Rear Admiral Elphinstone, a Britisher then serving in the Russian navy. Its mission was to prey on Turkish shipping in the Mediterranean and to prevent reinforcements and supplies reaching Constantinople from Syria and Egypt.

Admiral Spiridoff's instructions were prepared with considerable care as regards the international situation. Two of the provisions are curious. One was to the effect that the Barbary pirates were not to be molested unless discovered in the act of attacking a Christian vessel. Obviously, Russia had as yet no carrying trade. The other provision was that good relations were to be cultivated with the Knights of Malta. In fact, an envoy accompanied the expedition with a personal letter to the Grand Master from the Empress. One of the unexplained chapters of Mediterranean history is the interest Russia took in the Order. Many Russians, in spite of the difference in religion, were Knights of Malta and the chapel of the Imperial Naval Academy was formerly a Maltese chapel.

On August 6, 1769, the first Mediterranean squadron set sail from Kronstadt. It consisted of one 80-gun ship, three 66-gun ships, the frigate *Nadejda Blagopolutchia* and seven lesser craft. It was manned by 4995 officers and men. Admiral Spiridoff flew his flag from the *St. Eustaphy*. On October 20 the second Mediterranean squadron followed. It consisted of three 60-gun ships, two 32-gun frigates, and one despatch boat. It was manned by 2261 officers and men. Admiral Elphinstone flew his flag from the *Ne Tron Menea,* the "Don't Tread On Me," a name suggestive of the "rattlesnake" flags of the early cruisers of the American Revolutionary navy.

The first distant expedition of the Russian navy revealed many shortcomings both in personnel and equipment. The journey was a long chapter of accidents. The *Sviatoslav,* the largest unit of the first squadron, had to be left at Reval for repairs. She subsequently joined the second squadron. The *Lapomik*, a twenty-gun corvette, was wrecked in the Kattegat. Two ships, the *Severny Orel* and the *Europa*, and one gunboat, the *Grom*, were compelled to put into British ports for repairs. It may not be amiss to state at this point that the British at this time were far from showing the hostility to Russian expansion that characterized their later attitude. One corvette, the *Letoutchy*, had to put into Lisbon. It was not until the beginning of December that the first squadron straggled into Port Mahon, sadly reduced. It now numbered but nine vessels. The inexperienced crews, unaccustomed to such arduous journeys, had suffered severely, 392 men having died on the voyage. The sick list was in proportion. The second squadron fared better, although it too was minus one ship when it entered the Mediterranean, the *Tver* having been dismasted in a gale and forced to remain at Reval. Obviously the Russian navy was far from being so "perfectly instructed" as Peter the Great had hoped. One quality, however, the Russians did not lack, an eagerness to close with the enemy.

The first squadron lay at anchor at Port Mahon during January 1770; by February 22 it was off the island of Zante where two Greek insurgent frigates reported and were incorporated in the fleet under the Russian flag. On March 12 a force of 600 men, together with some field artillery, was landed on the mainland, at Vitylo, a small port on the eastern coast of the Gulf of Kalamata, while the fleet proceeded to bombard Korone. Some local insurgents, the Mainotes, joined the landing party and the entire force was divided into two detachments. One, the "eastern detachment," advanced boldly in the direction of Tripolitza, where the main Turkish army was located. In the ensuing battle the undisciplined Greek auxiliaries proved utterly unreliable. The small Russian force was completely destroyed. The "western detachment" was more successful. Proceeding to Navarino it succeeded, with the help of the squadron, in capturing that fortress on April 21 together with 7 standards, 42 cannon, 3 mortars, 30,000 pounds of gunpowder, besides a considerable quantity of small arms and ammunition. Passing on to Modon, the Russians laid siege to that citadel by land and sea. The Turks made a sortie. Once more the insurgents gave way. As a result the Russians lost their artillery, besides suffering heavy casualties. Thoroughly disgusted with their allies, whose inefficiency in action was only exceeded by their cruelty to Turkish prisoners, the Russians destroyed the fortifications of Navarino and retired to their ships.

In the meantime the second squadron had arrived off the eastern coast of Morea where the Turkish fleet was believed to be. On May 27 Admiral Elphinstone sighted a Turkish fleet of ten ships, five frigates and seven lesser craft at anchor near the island of Spetsia. In spite of the disparity in numbers Elphinstone attacked. The Turks declined battle and withdrew toward Nauplia, the Russians to Cerigo, where Admiral Spiridoff assumed command. On June 6 the Turks were once more sighted cruising between the islands of Spetsia and Hydra. Owing to lack of wind they again could not be brought to action. The pursuit continued for three days, the Turks, however, making good their escape.

At this stage of the proceedings Count Alexis Orloff, who had been appointed Commander-in-Chief of the Russian forces in the Mediterranean, arrived on the scene and on June 22, off the island of Milo, hoisted the Imperial Standard on the *Tri Ierarka*. Though not a sailor himself, Orloff had the benefit of the sound advice of a British officer serving in the Russian navy, Commodore Samuel Greig, the first of a line of three Greigs to hold commissions in the Russian navy. The combined fleet under Orloff's command now consisted of nine ships-of-the-line, three frigates, one gunboat, and four lesser craft. The pursuit of the elusive Turkish fleet was resumed toward the island of Chios. There it was finally located, anchored in a disorderly line extending across Chesme Bay, a deep indentation in the coast of Asia Minor opposite Chios. It was an impressive affair commanded by a noted Algerine admiral, Djeyzairmo-Hassan-Bey, whose flagship was a 100-gun vessel, the *Capitana-Ali-Bey*. Another, the *Capitana-Pasha*, mounted 96 guns. Besides these powerful units the Turks had four 84-gun ships, one 74, one 70, six 60's, two large frigates, and numerous small galleys. On paper, they were far superior to their opponents, yet once more disregarding numbers the Russians boldly prepared to attack.

On July 5 at 11 A.M. the battle of Chesme, surnamed by the Russians "the Russian Lepanto," began. At the foremast each Russian vessel flew a battle flag with the "Jerusalem Crosses," a cross whose four arms are likewise crossed. To their crews it was to be a battle of Christian against Infidel, the Cross against the Crescent. The *Europa* led the way followed by Admiral Spiridoff's flagship, the *St. Eustaphy*. Soon the *Europa* found that she was heading for some rocks and was obliged to tack. Admiral Spiridoff continued on, making for the Turkish flagship until he found himself under a cross fire from five Turkish ships. The wind being light it was some time before the other Russian ships could get into action. Nothing daunted, the Russian admiral ordered the ship's band "to play to the last" while he grappled the Turkish flagship. Boarding parties went over from both sides and a hand-to-hand struggle ensued. Soon, however, the Turk caught fire. Her burning mainmast fell across the *St. Eustaphy* setting fire to that ship. The Turk blew up. Seeing that a similar fate awaited his vessel, Admiral Spiridoff prepared to abandon ship. He had already lost over one hundred men killed. While he was transferring his flag the *St. Eustaphy* flew into the air. The Turks thereupon proceeded to massacre such survivors as they could reach in the water, to the rage of the Russians, who from then on took no prisoners. The losses on the Russian flagship reached the ghastly total of 600 or more, only sixty being saved.

The destruction of the two flagships put an end to the first phase of the battle, the Turks at two in the afternoon cutting their cables and retreating to the shelter of their batteries along Chesme Bay. The Russians sent their light draught vessels into the bay to bombard while a council of war assembled on the *Tri Ierarka*. There it was resolved to attack the Turkish fleet by means of fireships. Four ships, two frigates, and a despatch boat were selected to cover the operation, which was entrusted to Commodore Greig.

The Turkish fleet was huddled together in Chesme Bay "like birds in a net," to quote one eyewitness. At 1 A.M. with a light wind and a full moon the Russian detachment got under way and anchored at assigned stations. The Turkish fleet and batteries opened fire, the Russians answered. Soon two Turkish ships were in flames. The signal for the fireships to advance was then given, three rockets from the *Rotislav*. The fireships were four in number commanded by Lieutenants Dugdale, Mackenzie, Ilyin and Gagarine: two Britishers and two Russians. The light of the moon and the glare of the burning ships made them easy targets.

Dugdale led off and soon met with a brisk fire but managed to run his craft into the middle of the Turkish fleet. There he set fire to his fuse and swam back to his squadron. His fireship, however, was sunk by Turkish gunners before it had done any damage. Mackenzie ran his ship aground. The Russians were more fortunate. Ilyin, after coming unscathed through a withering fire, ran against a Turkish 84, grappled, and soon had the Turk ablaze. Gagarine set fire to his craft before reaching the enemy, allowing the wind to carry it against a Turkish vessel. Soon Turk after Turk caught fire and with deafening explosions flew into the air. When the crews of the fireships had made their escape, Ilyin having calmly rowed back in a rowboat, Greig opened up once more with his guns. All night long the inferno continued. When dawn broke the entire Turkish fleet was a confused mass of smoking wreckage with the exception of one ship-of-the-line, the *Rodos,* and six galleys, all of which had been abandoned by their crews. Besides the warships countless merchantmen, transports and auxiliaries had been destroyed. Such had been the force of the explosions that the land batteries had been seriously damaged as well. The Turkish casualties were over ten thousand men.

The Russian navy had won one of the most devastatingly thorough victories of history. No wonder the Empress bestowed on Orloff the title of his exploit, together with the right to add the Cross of Saint Andrew to his arms and to fly the Imperial Standard during his life. Greig was promoted to Rear Admiral. The seven captains and four lieutenants who had participated in the night attack were decorated. All present received one year's pay, besides dividing 170,000 rubles in prize money, and were awarded a medal bearing on the obverse the effigy of the Empress and on the reverse the burning Turkish fleet, with the legend: "It existed, Chesme!" and the date.

The victory of Chesme, far from resulting in a relaxation of Russian naval effort, was followed by a "mopping up" such as the Ægean had not seen since the days of the Romans. The first step was to secure a base of operations. After an unsuccessful attempt to seize the island of Lemnos, during which the *Sviatoslav* ran aground and was lost, the island of Paros was selected. Although somewhat distant from the Dardanelles, as a result of which the blockade of the straits was far from air-tight, it had the advantage of possessing the best anchorage in the Archipelago, Port Nausa on the northeastern coast of the island.

Paros has changed but little since the days when it was the

headquarters of Russia's imposing but little known Mediter-ranean venture. Primitive but spotless, it is still an island of little flat-roofed white houses, of monasteries, chapels and huge round windmills. Not a carriage wheel is to be seen in Paros, all transportation being done on donkeys. The storehouses the Russians built at Port Nausa are probably the most modern buildings on the island; until a few years ago the Russian inscriptions on them were still legible. Of course, the island offered no facilities for repair work, the Russians being com-pelled to send their vessels to Leghorn or Port Mahon when-ever overhauling was needed.

The Russian fleet, nevertheless, was kept up to the original strength by constant reinforcements. A third squadron, com-manded by Admiral Arth, a Danish officer serving in the Russian navy, left Kronstadt on July 11, arriving at Paros on November 5, 1770. With it came some much-needed infantry-men, 2600 in number. Orloff now had a force with which to garrison conquered territory and proceeded to take possession of practically the entire Archipelago, the Christian population welcoming the Russians as liberators. Soon a fourth squadron arrived on the scene. Orloff was now in a position to harass the Turkish possessions on the mainland. Mytilene, Beirut and Tyre were captured. None of these places, however, was held for longer than necessary to destroy the Turkish war mate-rial. In November 1772 a fleet of twenty-four Dulcignote cor-sairs were decisively defeated on the historic site of Lepanto, seventeen of their vessels being destroyed. To climax a series of brilliant raids, Lieutenant Alexiano, with two small vessels, surprised a Turkish squadron in the harbor of Damietta and captured the newly appointed Commander-in-Chief of the Turkish forces, Selim Bey. Among the trophies was the great standard of Mahomet, which was sent to the Empress.

And then, disquieting news from headquarters began filter-ing through. First one, then another armistice was granted to the hard-pressed Turks, much to the disgust of Orloff, as the Turks did not hesitate to take advantage of the respite to slip supplies and reinforcements to threatened points. What was going on behind the scenes?

On the mainland the Turks were faring but little better than at sea. Turkey was being invaded by three Russian armies simultaneously. One was attacking the principalities of Moldavia and Walachia, the other two were advancing in the Crimea and in Kabardia. Chesme coincided with Roumianzev's victory at Kagul, which opened the way for the occupation of the principalities. Here Austria grew nervous. The Balkans were too near home for comfort, but how to stop Russia's victorious advance was a problem. It was solved by drawing a diplomatic red herring across the trail. Why indulge in further costly warfare against Turkey, when an easy accretion of territory could be obtained by joining with Prussia in splitting Poland three ways? The ruse worked and Turkey had the first of a series of miraculous escapes. To be sure, according to the treaty of Kuchuk-Kainardji, Turkey was compelled to acknowledge the independence of the Crimea and to cede to Russia Azov and Kilburn and to allow Russia to assume the protection of orthodox Christians in Turkish territory. Moldavia and Walachia and Bessarabia, which Russia had occupied, were to be returned but the right to navigate freely on the Black Sea was accorded to Russia, the most galling of all the provisions.

What became of the conquests the Russian navy had achieved? They melted like an iceberg in tropical waters after the Russian fleet weighed anchor on the long homeward journey to Kronstadt. A few of the Christians retired with the fleet and were given lands in the newly acquired territories. Those who remained soon had cause to rue it; the usual reprisals followed. The "Marche Slave" had not failed; it had been "called off."

Peace between Russia and Turkey was of short duration, however. The next campaign is of interest to Americans as it brought to the fore John Paul Jones, who, by the capture of Otchakoff in 1788, made the definite annexation of the Crimea possible. Such naval activities as the Mediterranean saw were limited to a few Russian corsairs. By the treaty of Jassy, January 9, 1792, Turkey reluctantly confirmed Russia's title to a large strip of the northern coast of the Black Sea. The wars of the French Revolution which soon followed brought about a better understanding between the two countries, who were both alarmed by the doctrines the French were preaching. The Czar sent his fleet to protect the Sultan when Bonaparte made his dash for Egypt, thereby creating a precedent Russia was to invoke at a later date. At Tilsit the two emperors seemed about to divide Europe between them. The stumbling block proved to be Constantinople, so ardently desired by Alexander. To Napoleon, thoroughly imbued as he was with the notions of eighteenth-century diplomacy, Constantinople seemed the Key to the Empire of the World. The inability of the great powers to agree again saved the Sultan in 1807, as it was to save him many times thereafter.

The Napoleonic victories, however, had enormously increased the prestige of France. In order to offset the activities of the French ambassador, General Sebastiani, the British sent Admiral Duckworth into the Sea of Marmora. Sebastiani bestirred himself, with the result that the English fleet beat a hasty retreat and was compelled to run the gauntlet of a brisk Turkish fire as it sailed back through the Dardanelles. The rivalry of Russia, France, and England had brought the strategic value of the waterway into sharp relief.

The first perfect working model of an inter-oceanic canal was not the work of any engineer. Mother Earth supplied it, two relatively short passages connecting a small inland sea. In the hands of a strong nation the Dardanelles might have proven a source of prestige and influence. In the hands of nineteenth-century Turkey, the possession of the straits merely amounted to giving a decrepit jailer the key to a brig in which a thoroughly husky sailor was impatiently awaiting an opportunity to "crash the gate." To avoid becoming the battleground for a struggle in which she no longer had any real interest or influence, Turkey appealed to the powers to formulate the regulations under which she was to operate the waterway. Such a document was the treaty of 1809, in which the powers interested agreed to a "neutralization" of the straits. If Russian warships were thereby denied access to the Mediterranean at least Russia was assured, theoretically, that no hostile fleet would menace her newly acquired Black Sea possessions. Far from being the key to the "Empire of the World," the strategic importance of the Dardanelles had made Turkey the object of an international tutelage.

The Greek War of Independence sounded the death-knell of such naval strength as Turkey had left. On October 27, 1827, the Turco-Egyptian fleet was quietly riding at anchor in Navarino Bay, awaiting the outcome of the peace negotiations then pending. Navarino, of course, is the harbor formed by the island of Sphacteria where the Athenians had defeated the Spartans. Suddenly a shot rang out. How or by whom it was fired has never been determined, although the weight of evidence points to some over-zealous Moslem. Immediately, Admiral Codrington, who was the Senior Officer Present, opened fire. Admiral de Rigny, who commanded the French squadron, and Admiral de Heyden, who commanded the Russians, followed the example of the British. The allied vessels were far superior to the Turks in armament, although inferior in numbers. After three hours of cannonading the Turkish fleet of eighty-one vessels was destroyed, with the exception of one frigate and fifteen smaller vessels. The allied losses amounted to 177 killed and 480 wounded. The Turks lost over 6000.

The allies heralded their performance as a great victory. Can we blame a modern Turkish historian, Youssouf Fehmi, for calling it "un odieux guet-apens"?

Russia was not allowed to achieve Greek independence single-handed, but she was soon to have an opportunity of bringing Turkey within her "sphere of influence." It was a sadly weakened Turkey that faced the Egyptian rebellion headed by Mehemet Ali. In 1833, the viceroy decided to make a bid for independence and sent his son, Ibrahim Pasha, who had distinguished himself in his campaign against the Greek insurgents, to invade Turkey. Once more the Czar came to the rescue of the Sultan. A Russian fleet sailed into the Golden Horn and landed 50,000 men at Scutari, thereby disposing of any threat of invasion. Services of this sort have to be paid for. Russia was henceforth to be the guardian of the straits, according to the Treaty of Unkiar-Skelessi. As might be expected, Great Britain would not rest until the rights Russia had acquired were limited in such a way as to exclude Russian warships from the Mediterranean. Realizing that she was faced by another coalition, Russia bided her time and made her plans.

In 1853 the omens were propitious. The revolution of '48 had shaken the old Austrian Empire to its foundations. Russian bayonets had put the Emperor back on the throne of Hungary. France had just come through a gruelling ordeal of civil war. It would seem as if Napoleon III had too many problems facing him at home to engage in a foreign war. As for England, why not tempt the "nation of shopkeepers" with a bargain; England to take Egypt, Russia to take Constantinople? "The best laid schemes o' mice and men . . ." England was not interested. Napoleon, in spite of his declaration: "l'Empire, c'est la paix," was looking for a war to consolidate his dynasty. As for Austria, gratitude is as rare among nations as among individuals. When Nicholas boldly took the "road to Byzantium" every man's hand was against him. Even Piedmont joined in just to show that she too was a Mediterranean power.

The ensuing war began with purely defensive operations intended to protect Constantinople from the threat of Russian capture. The coalition of England and France, with Austria mobilized and ready to intervene, caused Russia once more to pause. The Allied armies encamped at Gallipoli and Varna, however, found an enemy more deadly than the Russians to combat, the cholera. Here the war might well have ended but for the fact that the destruction of the Turkish fleet at Sinope on November 30, 1853, had alarmed the Allies, who thereupon determined to render another such attack impossible by destroying the Russian base at Sebastopol. The British participation in that siege was certainly not "la guerre" in the modern acceptation of the word, except for the mortality. It is doubtful whether it was "magnifique," except for the bravery of all concerned. The British blundering subsequently inspired Sir William Gilbert, usually the most kindly of critics, to indulge in a scathing bit of satire, far more damning than any criticism made by the "grovelling" newspaper correspondents who, thanks to a new invention, the telegraph, were able to give their readers, also the enemy, a daily account of the errors committed.

In fact, when I know what is meant by "mamelon" and "ravelin,"
When I can tell at sight a chassepot rifle from a javelin,
When such affairs as sorties and surprises I'm more wary at,
And when I know precisely what is meant by "commissariat,"
When I have learnt what progress has been made in modern gunnery,
When I know more of tactics than a novice in a nunnery,
In short, when I've a smattering of elemental strategy,
You'll say a better major-general has never sat *agee!*

Thus does Sir William in one of his inimitable "patter songs" describe Major-General Stanley, the mythical "very model of a modern Major-General." The only symptom of efficiency was displayed by a frail Victorian gentlewoman. At Scutari, opposite Istanbul, you can still see the hospital she organized. You will have no difficulty finding it as it is close to the burial ground which, in spite of Miss Nightingale's efforts, is well tenanted.

How about the French? Well, they at least knew a mamelon when they saw one, as Pelissier proved by capturing the Mamelon-Vert on September 8, 1855. On the same day MacMahon stormed the Tour Malakoff and stayed there in spite of desperate counter-attacks. "J'y suis, j'y reste!" It was a grand day for the old African army with its zouaves, turcos, spahis, vivandières. On the tenth Sebastopol capitulated after three hundred and twenty-two days of siege, three pitched battles, and three assaults. On entering the fortress, the French discovered some curious metal containers filled with explosives to which were attached some electric wirings. Just like the Russians to expect such contraptions to explode under water and damage a vessel! No wonder they had not been used. They did, however, prove most useful in blowing up the Russian dry-docks, which were literally hoisted on their own petards.

As a diplomatic blunder the Treaty of Paris nearly equals the Treaty of Versailles. Russian naval forces were thereby limited in the Black Sea to a few cruisers. Sebastopol was to remain dismantled. The Russian people are too great a force to be humbled with impunity. "Ils me le paieront bien un jour!" Gortchakoff was heard to mutter between his teeth as he came out of an interview with Buol in Vienna, where he had vainly pleaded with Austria to use her influence and prevent France and Great Britain from putting Russia back to where she had been before Catherine the Great came to the throne. Austria paid for her shortsightedness at Sadowa, France at Sedan. For a long while it seemed as if England, who had been the prime mover in the conspiracy to hamstring Russia, was to escape her share of the penalty. But she ultimately paid, with compound interest, at Gallipoli and Munich.

"Turn where she would . . . man and nature had conspired against him." One friend, one only, did the Slav find. "In the present crisis," Nesselrode wrote, "Prussia is the only one of the powers that has consistently manifested an intention not to be hostile to us." The Prussian victories over Austria and France were therefore not unwelcome to Russia. What was more, she intended to make use of them. On October 31, 1870, Gortchakoff calmly announced to Europe that "His Imperial Majesty no longer considers himself bound by the Treaty of Paris." What form this unilateral denunciation was to take was not apparent for some time. Russia, however, had learnt by bitter experience that her only chance of breaking the coalition that was blocking her attempts to reach the Mediterranean was to place herself on higher ground than her own interests. Panslavism was to furnish the opportunity for a "moral issue."

After the Crimean War, Turkey promised to reform her administration of the Christian states under her rule. The situation, however, called for a change of régime rather than a reform of the existing one. By 1875 conditions had become intolerable once more and Bosnia-Herzegovina, Montenegro, Serbia pluckily took up arms in an attempt to secure complete independence. A wave of enthusiasm swept over Russia. Russian volunteers flocked to the Serbian standards. A Russian general, Tchernaieff, was given supreme command. The insurgents, however, succumbed to superior numbers. On October 29, 1876, the Turks scored a decisive victory at Djunis, whereupon Alexander II intervened and formulated demands that would give the Balkan states a certain degree of autonomy. Again the fear of Russia was to cause the powers to support Turkey. A conference was held at Constantinople in December. In less than a month it dispersed, having accomplished nothing but convince Turkey that Russia stood alone. Another meeting in London was equally fruitless. Russia declared war on April 23, 1877.

The Russian army at that time was in process of reorganization, but the Russians made up in numbers and courage what they lacked in efficiency. Over 300,000 men crossed the Roumanian frontier. All the Balkan states joined the invaders, including the Roumanians, who were not Slavs but Latins. True to their traditions, the Turks put up a stubborn resistance. They were, however, face to face with a great nationalistic surge, also a dynamic leader who for picturesqueness has seldom been equalled, General Skobelev. Wearing a gray overcoat and mounted on a white charger, he seemed the incarnation of the North. After three months of intense fighting around Plevna, Osman Pasha surrendered with 40,000 men. In spite of the bitter cold, Skobolev crossed the Schipka pass in January and captured another army of 36,000 men and ninety guns. By the thirtieth, the Russians were before the Chataldja lines. The Turks requested an armistice, which the Russians granted only on the surrender of the positions defending Constantinople. The Turks could surrender them without rendering their plight any the worse. Disraeli, although predicting the defeat of Russia, had taken the precaution of sending a fleet to defend the Turkish capital.

The Turks and Russians met at the little town of San Stefano to discuss terms. When the chancelleries of Europe read the peace victorious Russia had dictated the statesmen gasped. The Asiatic conquests of Russia were of minor importance in the days before oil became standard. Not so the other provisions. All the Balkan states were granted independence and received considerable accretions of territory. Bulgaria was raised to a principality and given an outlet to the Ægean at Kavalla. Failing to secure Constantinople for herself, Russia had made a detour and secured a Mediterranean port for her client. The Slav had marched to the sea!

Again Russia was to know a bitter disappointment. Bismarck, now that France and Austria had been beaten and German unity achieved, began scanning the horizon for the next probable enemy and the next possible ally. He recognized Russia as the former and Turkey as the latter, as far-seeing a bit of statesmanship as Europe has ever known. A hurry call went out from Berlin. The powers met. The pretensions of Russia and her allies were drastically cut. Austria was given Bosnia-Herzegovina to "administer." England, as the price of her naval co-operation, received Cyprus from which to watch the straits. Turkey was restored to the possession of her Balkan seacoast. Man had once more conspired to keep Russia from the sea.

Kronstadt, Archangel, Vladivostok; Russia is still a quasi-Arctic naval power. The warm waters of the Mediterranean seem farther off than ever. If and when, in the dim future, she makes another attempt to break through, it will unfortunately not be under the banner bearing the Cross of Saint Andrew. "Holy Russia" died at Brest-Litovsk. Skobelev, "the White General," will be replaced by some Red commander, an ominous change of color.

Marche Slave! Who has not felt a thrill on hearing the opening bars of that stirring paean, first performed at a concert in aid of the Slavic soldiers wounded in the Turkish war? The solemn dirge of the Russian peasant, stolid, patient, loyal; Russia of the plains. Then a brisk Cossack tune, visions of wild cavalrymen singing as they beat time on their tambourines; Russia of the steppes. And then the Anthem! Russia of the Czars, the might that for centuries saved Europe from the Asiatic hordes that still menace her. That was the Russia Europe conspired to crush. Well, let us hope Europe knew her business. The *Internationale*, however, seems a poor substitute for Tschaikowsky's immortal work.

CHAPTER XXII

In Which the Black Cross Reappears

AT DAYBREAK on August 4, 1914, the inhabitants of Bone were aroused by a sharp report followed by an explosion. The German light cruiser *Breslau* was bombarding the waterfront. At the same time the battle cruiser *Goeben* was bombarding Philippeville. The material results were negligible. The strategic results, however, were considerable and worth the risking of two vessels, one of them, the *Goeben*, a valuable one. Not that the bombarded seaports could make any effective answer, but the wireless alarm that was sent crackling through the air was picked up by a force so overwhelmingly superior that the performance of the two Germans might well have proved suicidal.

Let us dismiss at once the legend that the German navy at any time indulged in wanton acts of barbarism. A sound military reason can be assigned for all their moves, including the bombardments by Admiral Souchon's squadron. The French mobilization plan called for the transportation of the XIX army corps from Algeria to Cette in a convoy to which some obsolete armored cruisers had been assigned. The sudden appearance of so formidable a vessel as the *Goeben*, eleven-inch armor and ten eleven-inch guns, was enough to make the French admiral at Toulon, Vice-Admiral Boué de Lapeyrère, pause. What was more, the German had a speed of twenty-eight knots and had just undergone a refit at Pola. From intercepted wireless despatches the French knew that the two

German ships on the evening of August 2 were near Messina. Admiral Lapeyrère therefore took it upon himself to telegraph to Bizerta and Algiers to hold the transports until a suitable escort of battleships could be secured. The effect of thus upsetting the time-table might have been disastrous. As a matter of fact, it did prevent the arrival of the XIX army corps in time to participate in the opening battles.

Having succeeded in his mission of delaying one French army corps, the next problem facing Admiral Souchon was to make good his escape to Messina, the rallying point for German warships according to the plans of the Triple Alliance. His success in raiding the Algerian ports was due to his promptness and boldness. His escape was due to the hesitancy of his opponents. Great Britain had not yet declared war, the time limit given in the British ultimatum did not expire until midnight of August 4–5. That war between the two nations was unavoidable must have been apparent to the British Admiralty, since they hurriedly despatched the two battle cruisers *Indomitable* and *Indefatigable* from Malta to Gibraltar to head off the *Goeben* should she make a dash for the Atlantic. At 9.32 A.M. of August 4 the two British vessels were accordingly steaming west, well off the African coast, when they sighted the two Germans heading east. Captain Kennedy of the *Indomitable*, the senior officer, immediately changed his course, and the two Britishers followed the Germans. Each side trained its guns on the other and in this strange formation the whole procession proceeded at top speed toward Messina.

In the meantime Captain Kennedy was frantically calling the commanding officer at Malta, Admiral Sir A. Barkeley Milne, for orders. Milne, in turn, was vainly requesting London for permission to act. The answer he received was to "hold" the *Goeben*, but not to open fire unless the German attacked French transports and even in that event to warn him first. How to "hold" an enemy who had four knots the advantage in speed, the Admiralty did not attempt to explain. Nelson would have concluded that the best way to hold an enemy was to sink him, but that was before the days when radio ear-muffs formed part of an admiral's equipment. By 4.35 P.M. the Germans were hull down, so at 6.40 Admiral Milne radioed to Kennedy to proceed west once more, slowly, still believing that the *Goeben* would try to waylay French transports.

Admiral Souchon's difficulties, however, were only just beginning. An unpleasant surprise awaited him at Messina. Italy had proclaimed her neutrality and the Germans were given the usual twenty-four hours to leave port. Hurriedly taking on coal from a waiting collier, the German admiral put to sea expecting to be met by a superior force. Some of his officers are said to have made their wills and to have posted them at Messina, a wise precaution but unnecessary, as we shall see.

Where to go was the question. After vainly trying to decide the matter from headquarters, the German high command left the decision to the man on the spot, a sensible but outmoded way of handling such situations. Curiously enough, no one wanted the *Goeben*, in spite of the powerful reinforcement she represented. Austria was most unwilling to risk her fleet now that England was an enemy. The *Goeben* might draw the British into the Adriatic. The uncertainty concerning Italy made it essential to keep the Austrian fleet intact. The Turks were not as yet ready to throw off the mask of neutrality. Nevertheless, Admiral Souchon decided to make the dash for the Dardanelles. It was the only chance the Central Powers would get to throw a capital ship into the Black Sea. Moreover, it was probably the last thing the Allies were expecting. So on August 6, at 6 P.M., Admiral Souchon, his decks cleared for action, bravely passed through the southern entrance of the Straits of Messina.

To his surprise, no enemy was in sight. Off Cape Spartivento, however, a tough customer was awaiting him, the light cruiser *Gloucester*, Captain Kelly. Try as he would, Admiral Souchon could not shake off that Irish terrier whose incessant radioing might, for all he knew, bring a whole fleet down on him. In vain did the *Breslau* turn on the pursuer, Captain Kelly opened an accurate fire and the *Breslau*, after sustaining several hits, desisted. Finally the *Gloucester* drew off, recalled by orders from Malta. There was no use calling, the British had no ships within reach.

Souchon had made a fantastic escape from the opponents who came in contact with him. The failure of the other Allied vessels to find and destroy the two German vessels is even more astonishing. On the evening of August 2, Admiral Lapeyrère received orders to "stop" the *Goeben* and the *Breslau*, as soon as news of hostilities reached him, orders as indefinite as Milne's orders to "hold" them. The puzzled Frenchman did not put to sea until 4 P.M. on the third. His fleet was an imposing one, seventeen armored vessels, six cruisers, thirty destroyers, and six submarines. The fleet soon separated into three divisions. One headed for Oran, one for Algiers, and one under command of Rear Admiral Cocheprat, consisting of six battleships of the *Danton* class, besides six cruisers and some destroyers, headed for Philippeville. Had the destroyers been sent ahead, they could not have failed to establish contact with the Germans. They were, however, retained with the fleet. As it was not until 1.20 A.M. of August 4 that the French fleet received news of the declaration of war, the French commander was probably justified in keeping them in leash.

At 4.50, news was received of the bombardment of Bone and Philippeville. Lapeyrère at once headed his eastern division toward Bone then, at 7 A.M., concluding that the Germans could not be overtaken, he ordered it to proceed to Algiers. As a matter of fact, had that division continued on toward Bone it would have fallen in with the Germans within two hours.

What caused the change of course to the west? The only explanation possible is the extreme nervousness of the French high command for the safety of its convoys. In view of the number of other French warships in the neighborhood, sufficient to protect the main harbors and transports, it would seem that the Chocheprat division might have kept on its course on the chance of the *Goeben* turning east instead of west. The French have sought to shift to the British the blame for not bringing the Germans to action once they turned east. Two wrongs, unfortunately, do not make one right, especially in war. Allied naval operations in the Mediterranean during the early days of the war were characterized by a lack of co-ordination that is quite understandable if we stop to consider how recent the *entente cordiale* was. That the two nations who had fought so long and so bitterly should ever be called upon to co-operate in the very waters that had witnessed so many of their battles was indeed a situation that Suffren and Nelson would have considered quite beyond the range of possibility.

We have seen how the British initiative was held up by the ultimatum. It was to be further held up by an exaggerated respect for Italian neutrality. Though most authorities agree that a passage between two seas may be traversed by belligerents, the British Admiralty instructed British vessels to keep out of the Straits of Messina. These instructions were subsequently revoked, but too late to help the pursuit of the *Goeben* and the *Breslau*.

When Admiral Milne heard from the *Gloucester* that the Germans were entering the Ionian Sea, his best chance of picking up the trail was by coming through the straits with his two ships, the *Inflexible*, flagship, and the *Indefatigable*, which had been guarding the entrance to the Tyrrhenian Sea, the *Indomitable* being absent coaling. He was obliged to make the long detour around Sicily. Had he steamed at full speed he might even so have caught up with the Germans. Kelly was certainly doing his part by giving their exact position every hour. Instead, he proceeded to Malta at cruising speed, expecting Rear Admiral Troubridge, who was watching the Otranto Channel with four armored cruisers and eight destroyers, to intercept the two Germans. Troubridge, however, declined to make a Roman holiday by fighting a daylight engagement with the *Goeben* and the opportunity for a night action did not present itself. His conduct was severely criticized by Mr. Churchill and Admiral Milne and he was subsequently brought to trial. In the meantime, however, one of his ships, the *Defense,* had been destroyed at Jutland so quickly as to justify his statement that the *Goeben* could have "sunk the whole lot" of cruisers constituting his command. One Coronel was enough, so Troubridge was acquitted.

Admiral Milne, be it said, was hardly in a position to bring charges against his subordinate. Had he actively resumed the chase after coaling at Malta, he might have disposed of the *Goeben.* On August 8, Admiral Souchon arrived at the island of Denusa, near Naxos, where a collier awaited him. There, he received disquieting news. Turkey was still hesitating about permitting him to enter the Dardanelles. It was only after many anxious hours of delay, during which he could hear the wireless of the Britishers grow stronger as they leisurely steamed through the Ægean, that Admiral Souchon finally received permission and anchored safely off Seraglio Point. He had run through a broken field for a touchdown!

After an absence of many centuries, the Black Cross of the Teutonic Knights was once more making history in the waters that had first seen it unfurled. Cut off from any base, single-handed save for one small consort, the *Goeben* had delayed France's African contingents and was about to turn a vacillating neutral into an active ally. All this, of course, ran counter to the rules of the game. History abounds in examples of corsairs who have caused enormous damage to their opponents and diverted squadrons who have spent months bringing them to bay when they were required elsewhere. Germany was to furnish several notable corsairs. Such tactics, though exasperating, have not had much effect on the final outcome. They are the usual recourse of the weaker maritime power. But here was a corsair who was directly affecting military operations miles inland.

Although Turkey's entry in the war on the side of the Central Powers was probably inevitable, the presence of the *Goeben* and the *Breslau,* plus their brilliant commander, undoubtedly hastened that event. The opportunity for settling old scores with Russia in the Black Sea was too tempting to resist. On October 27 the two German cruisers, now dubbed with outlandish Turkish names, sailed through the Bosphorus under command of Admiral Souchon. The names of the ensuing actions evoke varied memories: Sebastopol, Balaclava, to say nothing of Trebizond, the city where Xenophon rested after his Katabasis, where Alexius Comnenus founded his fabulous empire after the capture of Constantinople by the Latins and from which his successors waged war against the Genoese when, backed by the Paleologues, the Ligurians attempted to capture the trade of the Euxine.

Admiral Souchon's operations in the Black Sea added greatly to the problems of hard-pressed Russia. As a result plans of all sorts to relieve the pressure were forced upon the British cabinet as early as January 1915. Lord Fisher tells us there "must have been a baker's dozen of 'em going around." Most of them were what the First Sea Lord called "wildcat expeditions." They finally boiled down to two, a landing in the Baltic or an attack on Constantinople. The latter appealed to Mr. Winston Churchill although it was opposed by all experienced officers. Duckworth, in his time, had warned against repeating the experiment. Sir Percy Scott, the *enfant terrible* of the British navy, called it "crazy." If Alcibiades was the originator of the "side show" it remained for the British amateur strategist to father the greatest of them. That the Dardanelles expedition did not end in another Achradina was due to the superb skill with which the Anzac army was re-embarked, but then embarkation work was a specialty of the British navy. Lord Fisher tells a story of how he embarked 8000 men in nineteen minutes. On that occasion one apoplectic major complained to the admiral that a bluejacket had shoved him into a boat saying: " 'Urry up, you bloody lobster, or I'll be 'ung!" "Quite right," answered the admiral, "the man would have been hanged had he not filled his boat in so many seconds." Curiously enough, this maneuver, which was carried out in the Mediterranean, earned for the British navy the congratulations of the Sultan Abdul Hamid!

"Der Geschichtsschreiber ist ein umgekehrter Prophet" (the historian is an inverted prophet), Hegel once remarked. Viewed in retrospect it is easy to see why an attempt to "force the Dardanelles" was a futile undertaking. Far from pleasing Russia the move aroused her suspicions. Had it succeeded it would have added one more threat to Allied harmony. The situation of the Allies, once in Constantinople, would have been so insecure that it is doubtful whether they would have been able to render Russia any assistance. That Turkey would have sued for peace is by no means certain. The occupation of the city after the armistice did not compel Turkey to accept peace terms that gave the northern shore of the Sea of Marmora to Greece. Let us assume, however, that by penetrating into the Black Sea the Allies would have "taken Europe in the rear," to quote the instructions given Bonaparte by the Directoire, what were the chances of success?

The opportunity for a surprise attack was thrown away by a premature bombardment intended to "test the range of the Turkish guns." This bombardment was delivered by an Anglo-French fleet on February 19, 1915, the British being commanded by Vice Admiral S. H. Carden, the French by Rear Admiral Guépratte. It demonstrated that, to quote the British commander, "the effect of long range bombardment by direct fire on modern earthworks is slight," which is merely a restatement of Thomas Jefferson's dictum about breaking glass windows with guineas. Nevertheless the bombardment was resumed on the twenty-fifth and this time the British expected great results. The new battleship *Queen Elizabeth* had been somewhat reluctantly sent to add her 15-inch guns to the uproar. They proved imposing but no more effective than the lesser one of her consorts.

At this stage of the proceedings Admiral Carden's health broke down completely and he was relieved by Vice-Admiral J. M. Robeck. This officer decided to send his older battleships into the straits for short range firing after a preparation by the entire fleet at longer ranges. The results were sickening. By this time the Germans had had time to mount heavy howitzers. Even at long ranges the hits were accumulating on the Allied vessels. When the "third-class battleships," that marine "cannon fodder," closed in to short ranges the Turkish fire became deadly. The *Bouvet* blew up, being hit apparently simultaneously by a mine and a heavy caliber shell. She sank carrying over 700 of her crew with her. The *Ocean* and the *Irresistible* had to be abandoned in a sinking condition. The *Gaulois* was saved from foundering by beaching on Rabbit Island. The *Suffren* and the *Inflexible* were so badly damaged that they had to be withdrawn, the *Charlemagne, Agamemnon, Albion* hard hit. The Turkish losses had amounted to twenty-four killed and seventy-nine wounded. One barracks had been destroyed, three guns dismounted, but numerous ones had been compelled to cease firing because of the earth that was choking their muzzles. The Allied navies on March 18 had sustained a defeat, the brunt of which fell on the French, whose sound professional sense had caused them from the first to object to naval bombardments unsupported by an adequate landing force. "Damn the Dardanelles," Lord Fisher wrote to Mr. Churchill, "they will be our grave." A story was circulated after the war to the effect that had the Allies resumed the attack they would have found the Turks short of ammunition. Recent investigation, however, disproves this yarn. The Turks had plenty of ammunition reserves though not of as modern a type as what they had been using but quite effective, nevertheless, at the short ranges at which the battles were being waged.

The Dardanelles were to be the grave of many a British soldier. There was no blinking the facts. Naval action had failed. An expeditionary force was accordingly gotten together and entrusted to General Sir Ian Hamilton. Besides the Anzacs, who constituted the bulk of the force, it consisted of a French colonial contingent, a naval division and three British infantry divisions, in all about 70,000 men. For reasons more political than military Lord Kitchener ruled Asia "out of bounds." On April 25 the first landing took place, the British on the European side, the French on the Asiatic side, the latter being merely a feint. Had that army accompanied the original expedition it might have accomplished results. Now it was too late. The Germans had prepared trenches that made advance impossible save at hideous cost. The Turks were doggedly defending every inch of ground against the new invaders from "down under," whose bravery was quite on a par with any who had fought on the shores of the Mediterranean. Nor were the British at the end of their naval troubles. Stationary warships are easy targets for torpedoes. Protection is practically impossible outside of secure harbors. On May 13 a Turkish destroyer fired three torpedoes at the battleship *Goliath*. All three hit. The vessel blew up with a loss of 570 men. The *Queen Elizabeth* was at once recalled to England. On the twenty-fifth the *Triumph* was torpedoed by the *U–21*. She sank in ten minutes with seventy-one of her crew. The same submarine a few days later sank the *Majestic*. The "third-class battleships" were proving first-class coffins. As you go up the Dardanelles today the charts and the "Pilot" tell you where to beware of wrecks.

Now it must be apparent from even so fragmentary an account that something was radically wrong with British methods. England was not "muddling through." Had the British possessed a general staff to prepare war plans in advance they would surely have conducted their operations differently or, better yet, the professionals would have been in a position to squelch the glib amateur who had proposed so "crazy" a plan. "Never in the history of the world," General Liman von Sanders afterwards wrote, "has any such expedition sailed, never has a big campaign been so hastily organized and gotten together and never has such an undertaking had so little consideration from home." The General has overlooked Sebastopol. Gallipoli was the Crimea, plus the Germans. The General's remarks apply equally well to the former campaign with this qualification. Information concerning the Crimea was difficult to obtain in the 50's, whereas information concerning the Dardanelles was easily procurable in 1915. The British on both occasions had simply fallen into the same fatal error, a reliance on sea power to see them through, to offset their military unpreparedness. One plan for taking Constantinople by an advance through Thrace, which had been carefully worked out by General Metaxas, the German-trained Greek strategist, was completely and complacently ignored, a blunder that undoubtedly accounts for some of the hostility to the Allied cause displayed by Greece during the early stages of the war. To sum up. At Sebastopol England had the leading military power as an ally; at Gallipoli she had the leading military power as an enemy. We need seek no further why one venture succeeded and the other failed.

The appearance of the Black Cross as an ally of the Crescent was perhaps the most unexpected event of the first World War. Although Turkey was included in the debacle that overtook the Central Powers she promptly arose from her defeat a greater power. Much of her increased prestige is undoubtedly due to the self-confidence she acquired by her successful campaign under German leadership. As far as Turkey is concerned the first World War was a "war of liberation." Europe is now faced with a rejuvenated Turkish nation determined to be the master of its own destinies once more. Few vessels, therefore, have influenced history more than did the two gallant cruisers of Admiral Souchon when, after eluding the numerous opponents who could have blocked their way, they dropped anchor in the Golden Horn.

CHAPTER XXIII

"The Bitter Sea"

ONE OF the requisites for a great leader is the ability to sum up the emotions of his hearers in a few concise words. "The bitter sea" is how Mussolini has described the Adriatic, a trenchant expression that epitomizes regrets and resentments whose roots strike deep into Mediterranean history. The stranger who attempts to weigh the conflicting claims to the western shore of the Balkan peninsula soon finds himself lost in a maze of contradictory statements. Certain factors, however, are so apparent that no amount of propaganda can dispel them; certain historical facts so uncontrovertible that even a peace conference cannot deny them, it can only disregard them as having lost their vitality.

Let us begin by assuming that Dante was correct when he said that the Gulf of Quarnaro "closes Italy and bathes her borders."[1] Dante's boundary is now a *fait accompli* thanks to another poet, d'Annunzio, so we may pass on to the country beyond the Istrian peninsula, the radiant "seacoast of Illyria" where Shakespeare laid the scene of *Twelfth Night*.[2] Since Dante excluded it from his conception of his fatherland what arguments can present-day Italians advance for including it in their conception of "Unredeemed Italy"?

[1]*Sì come ad Arli, ove 'l Rodano stagna,*
Sì come a Pola, presso del Quarnaro,
Che Italia chiude e suoi termini bagna.
— *Inferno*, ix, 112–114.

[2]In *The Winter's Tale* Shakespeare speaks of "the seacoast of Bohemia," which would indicate that he knew the Slavs had reached the Adriatic.

Fascist Italy is somewhat inclined to overestimate the archæological background in staking out "Italia Irredenta."
Pushed to its extreme conclusion the Roman argument would
justify designs on everything between Britain and Bithynia.
The Italian claim to Dalmatia rests on more solid ground than
the ubiquitous remains the Empire has sown broadcast over
the lands it once governed. In the first place it rests on the
omnipresent evidence of a long Venetian occupation.

The sentimental appeal of Venice, the firmly governed state
that spread Italian prestige over the length and breadth of the
eastern Mediterranean, is difficult to resist. No sooner are we
beyond Trieste that we are greeted by reminders of the Queen
of the Adriatic. The pleasant grin of the Lion of Saint Marc
beams on us continually. As we proceed down the Dalmatian
coast the surroundings suggest northern Italy. At Zara we
enter the town through a gate surmounted by a most imposing
lion. The cathedral might be in Lucca or Pisa, so far as the
purity of its Tuscan architecture is concerned. A certain medieval atmosphere pervades Sebenico. The cathedral has the
Gothic style to be found in the hill towns of Umbria. At Spalato we are suddenly reminded of Rome itself by a monumental relic of imperial days, the palace of Diocletian. Himself
a Dalmatian, Diocletian preferred Spalato to Rome as a residence and after abdicating retired to enjoy the few remaining
years of his life in his luxurious retreat, parts of which are in
excellent state of preservation.

At Trau we get our first impression of something non-
Italian. The romanesque cathedral suggests southern Germany,
we shall see why presently. Two lions, one in the *loggia* or
courthouse, the other over the town gate, and the windows of
the palaces again bespeak a Venetian builder. At Ragusa the
dominant note is more Venetian than ever, which is remarkable
in view of the fact that Ragusa was really never more than an
ally of Venice. No more charming examples of transplanted

architecture can be found anywhere than the Rector's palace and the buildings along the Stradone. The Gothic arches and lace-like trefoil at once evoke memories of the Doge's palace and the Grand Canal. The massive fortifications, however, are a foretaste of those we shall see at Corfu.

Last but not least we must mention the Bocche di Cattaro, one of the world's most perfect natural military harbors. Castelnuovo, the fortress defending the entrance, has at various times been seized by Turkey, Venice, Russia, France, England and Austria, a high compliment to its strategic importance. After a long and stormy attempt at independence, during which it underwent Hungarian and Serbian domination, the little republic whose towns cluster around the picturesque inlet of Cattaro submitted to Venetian rule in 1420. Needless to say, the impress of Venice is the one that is the most pronounced.

Taken as a whole, the outward signs that meet the eye along the three-hundred-odd miles of coast we have been skirting (the total length of the Adriatic being slightly under five hundred miles) are essentially Italian and predominantly Venetian. Whatever other rulers may have held sway have left but few stone documents to attest their passage. If the hallmarks of a culture may be taken as a criterion, if architecture can be accepted as a muniment of title, then Italy prevails beyond question. In vain do we search for footprints that indicate a trail leading away from Italian civilization. The eye can read only one word emblazoned on every monument and reflected in many small details of life and customs: Italia.

So far we have been considering only the evidence of our eyes. When we come to consider the evidence of our ears we find that the Italian language is seldom heard outside of the towns. Reliable and up-to-date statistics are unfortunately difficult to obtain. The Austrian figures published in 1910 are the last official ones available showing ethnic proportions. In Dalmatia they allow the Italians only 3 per cent of the population, or some 18,000 souls. Italian authorities have vigorously denied the accuracy of these figures, claiming that even according to Austrian computations they could muster before the first World War 10 per cent of the population, or some 80,000 souls, if Italian subjects residing in the country be included. Since that war the proportion of Italians has undoubtedly greatly increased. The Italian government has encouraged a steady infiltration of its citizens into that strategically important region separated by a scant 110 miles of water from the Italian peninsula.

As we travel inland, however, the peasantry are invariably non-Italian both in language and appearance. As soon as we enter the Dalmatian countryside we approach a strange world, the Balkans. Once across the narrow strip of territory that separates the hinterland from the sea the change becomes very marked. The traditional Balkan dress with baggy trousers and round skullcaps, the "cheese-box" coiffures of the women give a fantastic, opera-bouffe air to the country folk. Soon we get our first contact with Islam; some Moslem woman in a muddy-brown dress still wearing a *yashmak*; a Turkish café in which thick black coffee is being served in copper cups; a slender minaret overtopping the neighboring belfry.

In Bosnia-Herzegovina you have the feeling that it is only thanks to Montenegro that Mohammedan Albania has been prevented from overrunning the land. A curious mixture of people who refuse to fuse surrounds you. The truth suddenly dawns on the traveller that the nations who wielded sea power in the Adriatic never extended their authority beyond the range of their guns. They may have occupied strategic points, fortified important harbors, controlled sea-borne traffic; they may have marched their armies across the back country occasionally, but the underlying population they have left undisturbed, as far as manners and customs are concerned. In order to understand the situation obtaining today we must turn back the pages of history.

The early history of Dalmatia is the normal one of a Roman province. It was attacked by the legions for the first time in 156 B.C., but was not definitely conquered until the reign of Augustus in 14 A.D. Between 476 and 535 it was under Gothic domination. Justinian added it to the Eastern Empire. With the Slavic invasions of the first half of the seventh century, Dalmatia began to assume a prominent part in history. The latinized populations of the Balkans took refuge in the seacoast towns. The cleavage we see now is therefore one of long standing; the Italian elements hugging the shore and leaning on the mother country, the invaders occupying the mountains and plains and maintaining a hostile attitude toward the urban population they were unable to subdue. No wonder the visitor today gains the impression of an Italian civilization clinging to a coast whose hinterland is controlled by an entirely alien people.

Between 535 and 1102 Dalmatia was under Byzantine rule once more, a purely nominal rule, however, as the Eastern Empire was unable to afford any real protection. As a result piracy flourished on a grand scale. The Saracens ravaged the coast in 829. A republic of Serbian pirates established themselves at the mouth of the Narenta and waged war against Venice for more than a century while their allies, the Croats, exacted tribute from the Dalmatian cities. The pirates were finally crushed at Curzola and Lagosta by Doge Orseolo in 998, thereby relieving the hard-pressed Dalmatian coast, a victory that was thereafter celebrated annually in the picturesque ceremony of the Wedding of the Adriatic. At the same time the Doges assumed the significant title of Dukes of Dalmatia. In 1073 the Venetians again came to the rescue of Dalmatia and drove off a fleet of Norman corsairs. From that time on the influence of Venice in the Adriatic steadily increased. Soon Venice was brought into contact with a newcomer, Hungary.

Between 1102 and 1105 the Hungarians, under the leadership of King Coloman and aided by the Croats, invaded Dalmatia and established headquarters at Trau. It was at Trau that Bela IV took refuge when the Mongols invaded his kingdom in 1241, pushing their raid as far as the Adriatic. As Hungarian ecclesiastical architecture was largely the work of German artists it is not surprising that the cathedral at Trau should show German influence. The Hungarians were careful to respect the franchises of the Dalmatian cities though not their maritime trade. As a result the country was divided into two factions. The shipping interests favored Venice while the landowners sided with Hungary. Venice made several attempts to reassert her authority over Dalmatia, notably in 1125 and again during the Fourth Crusade, on both of which occasions Zara was recaptured. This rivalry between Hungary and Venice continued until the growing power of the Turks rendered it impossible for Hungary to protect her Dalmatian possession. Between 1420 and 1444 the whole of Dalmatia came finally under Venetian rule with the exception of Ragusa, whose position in the Adriatic has always been an exceptional one.

The history of Ragusa is as colorful as the city itself. It came into prominence in the middle of the seventh century when the Latin colonists of Salona and Epidavrum took refuge there after their cities had been destroyed by the Avars, one of the Hunnish tribes then ravaging southern Europe. A goodly number of Slavic refugees joined the new settlement, so that at an early date Ragusa became the center of Slavic life in the Adriatic. Ragusa was always hospitable. Although Ragusa reflects Venice more than any Dalmatian city, Venetian tutelage ceased in 1358 when Ragusa dismissed the Venetian resident and established a republican government whose head bore the curious title of Rector. An astute government was that of Ragusa.

A timely treaty with the Turks saved Ragusa from the fate of more powerful states. Between 1358 and 1526 it enjoyed the protection of Hungary. Caravans brought abundant trade to the city from Hungary and Roumania at a time when other Dalmatian cities were suffering from a diversion of traffic. Ragusan galleys were present at Lepanto. Twelve Ragusan ships went down with the Armada. Ragusan commerce was widespread at that time, ranging from India to America. Our English word "argosy" is a reminder of the fact that Ragusan carricks visited England. Strongly fortified in the Venetian manner, tenaciously defending her independence, Ragusa was the only Mediterranean state to remain neutral between 1800 and 1805 when Napoleon seized the city. Nevertheless the Congress of Vienna gave Ragusa to Austria.

To the Slavs, however, Ragusa remains Dubrovnik, "the Woodland City." If you have ever breathed the balsam of the forest that still covers Lacroma, the island enclosing the harbor, you will understand the poetry of the Slavic name. From the fifteenth to the seventeenth centuries Dubrovnik sheltered Slavic culture from Turkish molestation. The Serbs have called the city "the South Slavonic Athens." Whatever intellectual life the eastern Adriatic could boast of was confined to Dubrovnik. All of which, however, did not affect Venetian hegemony in those waters.

The naval preponderance Great Britain acquired during the Napoleonic Wars has exercised so marked an influence on Mediterranean affairs of late that we are apt to overlook the fact that for many years Venice played an equally important part in that sea. The rich harvest of commerce and the imposing array of trading posts Venice gathered during the Crusades started her on the road to wealth and power but the passing of the Crusades did not curtail the activity of this hardy maritime state. A glance at the chart of the Mediterranean as it stood in the latter part of the fourteenth century will show that

Venice had also occupied a string of islands in the Ægean and the Ionian seas and fortified many strategic positions in the Peloponnesus and the Gulf of Corinth. For some unaccountable reason the history of these seas during the Middle Ages has been neglected. The romantic appeal of Catherine Cornaro has saved only Cyprus from the oblivion that has enshrouded the other Venetian colonies. A far-flung empire could Venetian seamen have contributed to the national patrimony had a united Italy been in existence.

The most valuable of these outposts strategically was Corfu, commanding the entrance to the Adriatic, an idyllically beautiful island in spite of the grim-looking Venetian citadel dominating the harbor. If the Adriatic was spared Turkish invasion it was thanks to the Venetian base at Corfu. In spite of five gruelling wars against Turkey, Venice had enough energy left to reconquer Morea in 1685 and occupy Athens. The rally, however, was short-lived. Unaided, Venice could not successfully resist the Turks in the long run. At the outbreak of the Wars of the French Revolution the once mighty maritime state was a mere façade. Completely exhausted, Venice surrendered to Bonaparte without as much as firing a shot. A glorious tradition did the Venetian navy transmit to the Italian navy nevertheless. At Lepanto Venice had rescued Christianity.

Obviously the Venetian colonial system could not have lasted as long as it did had not the "life line" along the eastern Adriatic remained intact. It is a high tribute to the administrative ability of the Venetians that during the entire period between the annexation of Dalmatia in 1444 to the final disruption of the Venetian system at Campo Formio in 1797 not one serious insurrection occurred in the Dalmatian cities. As a result of the effective protection Venice had afforded, relations between the republic and her Slavic neighbors had been most friendly. The *Riva degli Schiavoni* on the waterfront of Venice still re-echoes that friendship based on a community of interests. The desire of present-day Italy to revive the Venetian precedent by taking Dalmatia into her system should therefore not be regarded as a new venture in imperialism. It is but an endeavor to return to a *modus vivendi* that existed for over eight hundred years.

The "Duchy of Dalmatia" disappeared at Campo Formio together with Venetian independence. Venetian territory was used to make change in the give and take between the Directoire and Austria. France needed Corfu in her fantastic designs on Egypt and accordingly annexed it as well as the other Ionian Islands. They were, however, soon captured by England and many years later ceded to Greece. Austria fell heir to the Venetian mainland. Manin's heroic effort to liberate Venice in '48 ended in a tragedy. It was not until 1866 that united Italy was in a position to challenge the Hapsburg title to Venetia successfully, Austria being then at war with Prussia. An attempt to bring the status of Dalmatia forcibly before the peace conference signally failed. The Italian fleet went down to a decisive defeat at Lissa. Persano was no match for Tegetthoff, one of the really great admirals of history. Italy must perforce bide her time. Meanwhile she strengthened her position in the Balkans by a marriage between the Prince of Naples, later King Victor Emmanuel III, and Princess Helena of Montenegro.

The first real chance came with the first World War. The recognition of Italian claims to the eastern shore of the Adriatic was the *sine qua non* of Italy's entry into the conflict on the side of the Allies. The Treaty of London unreservedly allotted to Italy all of Istria, except Fiume, and the Dalmatian coast as far south as Cape Planca. The remainder of the coast was to be "neutralized"—whatever that may mean—with the exception of Ragusa which was to be assigned to Croatia, Serbia and Montenegro, together with Fiume and San Giovanni de Medua in Albania. The treaty, however, recognized

Italy's special interest in the remainder of Albania generally and specifically approved the Italian occupation of Avlona effected in the closing days of 1914. By implication it recognized Italian interests in an extensive territory containing a large and varied Slavic population. The reasons for this recognition are more important now than ever. If they were valid in 1915 they at least create a presumption in favor of Italian claims today.

As might have been foreseen, the Treaty of London turned out to be a trouble breeder, owing to the vagueness of some of its provisions and the definiteness of one of them. Immediately after the armistice it became apparent that Italy's allies were seeking an excuse for not living up to their agreement, a matter in which the United States proved most useful. Zara was the only Dalmatian city the peace conference was prepared to deliver to Italy. The rest of Dalmatia was to be included in a new fiat state, Yugoslavia, in which Montenegro lost its identity and Croatia was subjected to Serbia, an unexpected interpretation of the word "neutralize," to say the least. Moreover, an independent Moslem state was soon set up in Albania which promptly became the object of plots organized across ill-defined borders by factions who were casting covetous eyes on Albanian territory. Matters came to a dramatic head in 1923 with the murder of some Italian commissioners who were locating the boundary between Albania and Greece. An Italian fleet bombarded and occupied Corfu in reprisal, a move that may well have cloaked a plan to recapture that island, which Venice had first captured in 1386. As the evidence of official Greek connivance in the crime was far from conclusive, the powers intervened. Italy, by her recent annexation of Albania, has probably removed that country from the international scene, diplomatically if not militarily. Dalmatia, however, remains an unsolved problem. Rapallo has repeated one of the major grievances created at Campo Formio.

The United States, obviously, was not bound by the Treaty

of London and was therefore at liberty to throw its weight on the Slavic side at Versailles. In so doing, however, we gave an unfortunate illustration of a well-meaning persistence in a theoretic, academic illusion: the idea that Slavic unity is possible. The animosity between Czechs and Slovaks greatly facilitated Nazi plans in Czechoslovakia, as we now know. The Kingdom of the Serbs, Croats and Slovenes ignores several fundamental differences that have long divided the southern Slavs, differences that cannot be overcome by invoking memories of the "South Slavonic Athens." The Serbs are Orthodox Catholics, the Croats and Slovenes are Roman Catholics. The language spoken in the new realm is essentially the same throughout, to be sure, but the script used is different. The Serbs adhere to the Cyrillic alphabet. From the outset the difficulties that beset Yugoslavia sprang, not from minorities, but from "a house divided," and pretty evenly divided.

We need not go into the history of the conflict. It culminated in an atrocity, the murder of King Alexander and Jean-Louis Barthou, the French Minister of Foreign Affairs, at Marseilles in 1934. The assassin proved to be a Slav, a member of the Ustassi, a group of terrorists bent on "liberating" the Croats from Serbian rule. The pan-Serbs retaliated with repressive measures, in vain. They could not muster more than 50-odd per cent of the votes. By 1939 even the pan-Serbs were ready to admit that if the new state was to hold together it could only be on a federated basis in which the Croats were given a capital and a parliament of their own.

The early relations between the Croats and the Dalmatians had been far from cordial, as we have seen. It is impossible to avoid the conclusion that the reasons now impelling the Dalmatians to align themselves with their kinsmen the Croats, with whom they are usually grouped, rather than with the Serbs are more than sentimental. Both Dalmatians and Croats take readily to the sea; neither can resist the economic attraction of the Adriatic. The Serbs, on the other hand, gravitate toward the Danubian basin. Their only appearance in the Adriatic was one hundred years of piracy, a form of navigation in which landsmen frequently excel. By putting a warlike inland race in control of the coastal area the powers created anew the same situation that formerly prevailed when Hungarian kings governed Dalmatia.[3] The overland trade routes, not the high seas, are the means of communication favored by Hungary and by Serbia. The sullen quarrel now in progress is another manifestation of the age-old rivalry between land power and sea power that has now chosen the Adriatic as its duelling ground. It was Venice that once rescued Dalmatia from intolerable stagnation. Why should not Italy do the same today? The economic interests of Italy and Dalmatia do not clash.

Why, indeed, the Italians ask. The Serbs do not need the Adriatic coast, the Dalmatians are not strong enough to defend it. If federation is to be the fate of Dalmatia, why not federation with a sea power? How long must the *Riva degli Schiavoni* wait for the Slavic traders that once thronged the Venetian waterfront?

The explanation the Italians give for this state of affairs is not likely to lessen their resentment. France and England at Versailles were playing power politics. No "moral" or "racial" issue was involved. The growing might of Italy was upsetting the sacrosanct balance of power in the Mediterranean. The best way of checkmating Italy was to install a strong hostile state on the eastern shore of the Adriatic. There, say the Italians, is the real explanation of Rapallo. The remedy is obvious. Patiently must Italy pick up the shattered fragments of Venetian glory, regain the control of the Adriatic that once made Venice great. The alternative is to reject a heritage.

Venice, *la République Sérénissime!* When next you stand

---

[3]One of the grievances of the Dalmatians and Croats prior to the first World War was that they were dependent on Hungary, not Austria.

before the Basilica of Saint Marc gaze at the quadriga brought from Constantinople by Doge Enrico Dandolo in 1204. Then walk across the Piazetta and look at the two columns brought from Syria by Doge Domenico Michele in 1126. Now turn and contemplate the three flagstaffs that once flaunted the banners of Cyprus, Morea, and Crete. Unless you are in too great a hurry to get out to the Lido you might ask your gondolier to row you to the Arsenal instead. Its portals are guarded by two marble lions that once adorned Porto Leone, as the Piræus was called in the Middle Ages. The jewels have long since been pried from the crown of the Queen of the Adriatic. Can Fascist Italy redeem them? Or is Nazi Germany about to produce a "missing heir" to some of the assets of the Venetian estate?

The Adriatic, the bitter sea!

CHAPTER XXIV

In Which *Weltpolitik* Goes into Reverse[1]

WE HAVE come a long way and as our story draws to a close we find the Mediterranean the scene of another conflict originating far from its shores, one that is gradually resolving itself into a duel between British sea power and Axis land power. If *Weltpolitik* brought England into the Mediterranean, it is now being invoked by England's enemies to justify their attempt to oust her from that sea.

Great Britain's position in the Mediterranean has been defined by Italian writers as "an artificial one." She has no territory to defend outside of a few bases; she has no population to protect except some "natives"; she has no vital trade derived from that region; her long-range commerce can be equally well served by resorting to the more circuitous route around the Cape of Good Hope. In this connection it is interesting to note that only 20 per cent of Britain's imports are normally routed through the Mediterranean, largely due to the fact that whereas the distance from Liverpool to Bombay is approximately 80 per cent longer around Africa this difference dwindles to a scant 10 per cent for the run from Melbourne to Liverpool. No wonder that at the first appearance of war clouds in the Inland Sea the British Admiralty prudently reroutes all shipping.

The British Mediterranean "life line" is a military not an

[1]This estimate of the situation is made as of December 1, 1941.

economic institution, besides being an afterthought. Great Britain entered the Mediterranean in 1704 when she seized Gibraltar with a view of being in a position to impede the junction of the Toulon and Brest fleets. By progressive involvement she continued on, deeper and deeper, in order to exert pressure on France, then on Russia and finally on Italy. She has always used her control of that sea as a means of securing objectives elsewhere, of which the defense of India is but one. Great Britain may be a power in the Mediterranean but she is not a Mediterranean power. Her influence in the Inland Sea has been coercive, never constructive. As a result there is only one legitimate Mediterranean power who would not welcome her withdrawal: Greece. Even when the "entente cordiale" was in full bloom France was endeavoring to confine the British navy to the eastern Mediterranean. The presence of British warships off the French European and African shores was always deeply resented.

Greece, like England, is essentially a maritime nation. As such she was bound to fear the land-based policies of Germany which necessarily spell ruin for Greek carrying trade. An economy in which sea-borne traffic is relegated to second place and such Mediterranean trade as is maintained is allotted to Germany's partner Italy would prostrate the Greek shipping interests. Whatever prosperity Greece enjoyed was mainly the work of her traders. With over six times the population of Greece, Italy has only slightly better than 10 per cent more merchant shipping—figures that speak volumes for the relative importance of sea-borne commerce in Greek life. Economically as well as strategically Greece's future is indissolubly linked with that of England. There is nothing Byronic about their relations today. They are in the same boat.

It was however the Adriatic, "the Bitter Sea," that was the proximate cause of the spread of the present war to the Mediterranean. No sooner had hostilities started on the Continent

than Great Britain began interrupting the free transit of condi-
tional contraband between Dalmatian and Italian ports. No
self-respecting nation can tolerate a blockade operating almost
within sight of her shores. During the first World War President Wilson had protested against a British blockade well off
our Atlantic seaboard, a blockade for which some precedent
could be found, be it said. The British blockade in the Adriatic,
however, was as incompatible with Italian self-respect as one
say in the Gulf of Mexico would be to our self-respect.

Delicate though the Adriatic situation undoubtedly was, it
could probably have been settled by mutual concessions. Italy
stood in urgent need of some British exports—notably coal—
which the British government could have justifiably embargoed
as a war measure. Unfortunately Fascist Italy has for some
time been harboring certain aspirations which represent the
most bewildering confusion of romanticism and realism in all
history. Nothing about the aims of modern Italy is simple.
They radiate in every direction, but underlying them we find
a belated recognition of the historic past of the Italian people.
The invocation to Imperial Rome is somewhat far-fetched,
suggesting archæology not history. When, however, Italians
move on to the feats of their trading republics they can make
out a rather convincing historic case. If there is one thing that
impresses the traveller in the Adriatic, the Ionian, the Ægean,
it is the continually recurring reminders of Venetian domination, with occasional vestiges of Genoese occupation to vary the
picture. Most of the islands of the Ionian and the Ægean have
been under Italian rule at one time or another and Dalmatia,
as we have seen, was Venetian for eight centuries. Rhodes and
the Dodecanese were annexed after the Italo-Turkish War
together with Tripoli. Italian plans to complete the collection,
however, were bound to run foul of British interests. Great
Britain does not propose to allow Italy to dominate the eastern
Mediterranean. The "life line" is insecure enough as it is.

The Italian claims on Savoy and Nice are purely sentimental, Savoy being the cradle of the Italian ruling house, Nice the birthplace of Garibaldi. Both, nevertheless, are essentially French. Corsica, on the other hand, is not. I have yet to find a Corsician who did not speak Italian. After the expulsion of the Arabs in 930, Corsica came under Genoese rule, with occasional stormy interludes of independence. In 1764 both the Genoese and the "patriots" headed by Paoli appealed to France to settle their differences. This France did by annexing the island. Today, however, Italy will find a brand of romanticism in Corsica far more potent than any she can supply. In spite of its strategic importance to Italy, guarding as it does the approach to Genoa and Leghorn, the Duce will have a hard time persuading the world that he is entitled to Napoleon's birthplace.

When we come to Italian claims on Tunis we find a genuine case of *Italia Irredenta*. Owing to its proximity to Sicily, Tunis during the past one hundred years or more has seen a heavy overflow of Italians. Today they outnumber the French 90,-000 to 70,000. The French occupation of 1881 was bitterly resented by Italy, who claimed that France had agreed to respect the independence of the Regency provided Italy did likewise. The excuse that Tunisian territory was serving as a starting point for Arab raids on Algeria did not allay Italian irritation. The French occupation was supported, reluctantly be it said, by Great Britain, who, with her usual far-sightedness in naval matters, did not want to see both sides of the Malta passage in the hands of one power. Italian protests fell on deaf ears. The Italians in Tunis today constitute a veritable *urbs in urbe* with schools, churches, and hospitals of their own. On a recent visit to the colony General Balbo considered himself so completely at home that he did not bother to call on the French resident! All attempts to settle the status of the Italians in the Regency have failed, the troublesome problem, of course, being the question of military service. In 1935 an agreement was reached whereby all children born after 1965 were to be considered French. Three years later Italy denounced the agreement.

Tunis, however, is not the only grievance Italy has against France and England. The sanctions imposed on Italy during the Abyssinian war, inspired as they were by two nations whose pockets were literally bulging with colonial loot, infuriated the Italian people. They had no influence on the campaign, as the Italian high command was shrewd enough to foresee that the sanctions might include a closing of the Suez Canal and had accumulated in Italy's East African colonies sufficient men and supplies to see them through. Their only effect was to focus the attention of Italy on Egypt. In 1936 Italy was contributing 20.2 per cent of the tonnage transited through the canal. Once the Abyssinian war was over Italian tonnage dropped, to be sure, but in 1938 it was still 13.4 per cent of the total. The tolls Italy has contributed since entering on her Abyssinian venture have been a heavy drain on her gold reserves. No wonder Italy regrets that her only contribution to the canal at the time of its construction had been the opera *Aïda!* All endeavors to secure relief and a voice in the management of the waterway were fruitless.

An ambitious program, to say the least, and one that was bound to bring Italy into a bitter conflict with both France and England. Moreover Italy was engaged in plans of internal and colonial development that were taxing her resources to the utmost when the sudden revival by Nazi Germany of the *Drang nach Osten* put her on the horns of a dilemma. She had either to resign herself to seeing Dalmatia slip through her fingers or join the "new order."

A volume could be written on the subject of the Balkan peninsula and yet, when all is said and done, the story resolves itself into a vain and never-ending search for political leadership just, strong, yet flexible enough to co-ordinate the heterogeneous populations huddled together in that area. It would be unfair to the Turks to deny that they made an effort to assist the various peoples they conquered. Unfortunately, the Turks were and remained Asiatics. Add the irreconcilable religious differences and the reason for the failure of the Turks to maintain themselves except by the persistent use of force is apparent.

For a while Russia seemed cast for the part of Balkan moderator. We have seen how the Treaty of San Stefano withered under the fierce glare of *Weltpolitik*. The *Drang nach Osten* has been made all the easier for the obliging way the Congress of Berlin played into the hands of Austria, without disposing of Russian ambitions however. It is interesting to speculate as to what might have happened in the Balkans had Austria been equal to the role Franz Palacky had envisioned nearly one hundred years ago. "If Austria did not exist, Europe in its own interests would have to create it,"[2] he declared when asked by his fellow-countrymen to head the movement for an independent Bohemia. But Palacky's dream of a Danubian Confederation headed by Austria and opposed to Russia required a flexibility of which the Hapsburgs were incapable. The persistence of certain ideas in history is truly impressive. Austria, as Palacky had correctly sensed, was primarily an idea. Once the Reich had succeeded the Empire it was to be expected that the Fuehrer, himself an Austrian, would take up where the Emperor had left off. Palacky would not recognize his idea today. It has grown into a vast confederation extending from the Mediterranean to the Arctic, from the Black Sea to the North Sea.

Italy's interest in the Balkans is not a new development. It is the logical outgrowth of her Venetian past, part of her inexorable strategic needs. When, however, united Italy began

[2]This remark is frequently but erroneously attributed to Metternich.

casting her eyes across the Adriatic once more it was to find Russia and Austria busily conspiring for the territory vacated by the Turks. The refusal of Austria to admit any Italian rights in the former Venetian possessions, to say nothing of the hinterland, was the main reason for Italy throwing in her lot with the Allies during the first World War, with the meagre results we know. Wars today usually resolve themselves into a struggle between the "haves" and the "have-nots," to quote Admiral Mahan's now hackneyed classification. Italy has been aptly called "an economic poorhouse," and her recent defeats may be partly due to her industrial deficiencies. British officers were amazed at the antiquated material they captured in Libya. On this basis it is difficult to see how Italy could fail to go over to the German camp; but the Balkan problem, now as before, undoubtedly forced Italy's hand and is responsible for her taking action she would gladly have deferred to a more propitious time.

Once the decision was made, the Italians approached their objectives with intense realism. Leaving Germany to dispose of France, Italy selected England. Regardless of the ultimate outcome the Italian attack on Egypt is sound Napoleonic major strategy. It is the only way the Duce can redeem "unredeemed Italy." The fate of these regions hinges on the outcome of the larger conflict being waged in the Mediterranean. To win, however, Mussolini must succeed where Bonaparte failed, a stupendous assignment especially in view of the fact that the Italians have more than Mamelukes to deal with. That being so, it is somewhat astonishing that Italy should have engaged in a "side show" which, even had it been successful, was certain to hinder the prosecution of the attack on Egypt. Until the records of the present war are thrown open it will be difficult to account for what seems on its face an egregious blunder. Certain facts, however, are apparent.

No sooner had Italy entered the present war than the Italian government began protesting the use of Greek waters by British air and sea forces. The controversy soon grew acrimonious. Finally, on October 28, 1940, the Italian government served an ultimatum on Greece demanding the right to occupy strategic points on Greek territory. An invasion of Greece followed forthwith, with results so unexpected as to lend credence to the Italian contention that Greece and Britain had long been secret allies. Italy had sadly underestimated the extent and promptness of British aid. It is difficult, however, to avoid the conclusion that an obscure motive prompted the Italian move into Greece and that the alleged violations of Greek neutrality were only a pretext. Germany in taking over Austria failed to get the Adriatic ports that once belonged to the Dual Monarchy. That Germany is aspiring to become a Mediterranean power, as Austria was, is more than likely. A mutually advantageous bargain seemed all indicated. In exchange for a renunciation of all claims on Trieste and Fiume, Italy may have hoped to deliver Saloniki to the Reich, after a little Blitzkrieg of her own.

The Italian collapse placed Germany squarely "on the spot." Effective aid had to be given Italy if she were to remain an active belligerent. Here the age-old Balkan hatreds furnished a ready-made solution. The Bulgars are more Turanian than Slavic in origin and consequently have little in common with the Serbs and nothing, of course, with the Greeks. Their relations with both have been embittered by a long-standing feud arising out of conflicting claims to Macedonia. Historically the Bulgarian claim is as good as any other—which is damning it with faint praise. The Parisian *chef* who first applied the name *macédoine* to any hodge-podge of fruits or vegetables was an embryo ethnologist as well as a *cordon bleu*. A desire to recover the port of Kavalla, held for a brief period after San Stefano, may well be influencing Bulgaria now as it did in 1915. It would not be accurate, however, to attribute Bulgaria's pro-Axis attitude to sentimental reasons, much less to a vendetta. If Greece is bound to Britain by a similarity of interests, Bulgaria is bound to the Reich by equally impelling motives.

In 1938 nearly 54 per cent of Bulgaria's imports came from the Reich and nearly 59 per cent of her exports went to that country. Bulgaria is essentially an agricultural state, approximately 80 per cent of her population being farmers. In a close co-operation with industrial Germany, Bulgaria's best chance of prosperity is to be found. The relations between Bulgaria and Germany are pretty good evidence of the fact that, so far as the Danubian Basin is concerned, the "new order" Germany is championing fills an economic need. If it is obvious that Bulgaria cannot successfully oppose German plans in the Balkans it is equally obvious that there is no good reason why she should want to do so. Bulgaria can ill afford to see Germany lose; hence her refusal to yield to British blandishments or threats and the assistance she gave the German invaders.

The German drive to the Ægean is undoubtedly the most momentous event of the present war in that it has introduced some formidable new elements into Mediterranean strategy. The first is a purely technical development the importance of which cannot be overestimated: the unexpected efficacy of the *Luftwaffe* in carrying out invasions involving the crossing of open water. When the "inter-bella" period is objectively considered one man will stand out pre-eminently, General Douhet,[3] and it would not be surprising to find the great Italian exponent of air power ranking with the great American exponent of sea power, with this difference. Mahan showed how it *had been done*. Douhet showed how it *would be done*. One was an analyst, the other a prophet. Like Mahan, Douhet wrote mainly for foreign consumption. When Mahan began writing we had no real navy. When Douhet began writing no

[3]Giulio Douhet, 1869–1930. His outstanding work, *Il Dominio del Aria*, was published in 1921.

nation, least of all Italy, had any real air force. Douhet's great contribution to history lies in the fact that he convinced the Germans that they need not fear British navalism or French militarism provided they developed their potential airplane production. Curiously enough, the two latter nations placed Douhet in the same category as H. G. Wells or Jules Verne. He taught his own countrymen the value of Italy's aeronautic position which, cutting as is does the Mediterranean practically in two, could seriously threaten England's hold on the Mediterranean. Douhet, however, would probably be amused to find his predictions not only fulfilled but surpassed. That Germany could occupy islands at will in the Ægean under the very nose of the British navy is almost as astonishing as seeing Italy—with German help to be sure—do likewise in the Ionian. As a result, in a few weeks' time Italy recovered most of the outposts lost during the wars of the French Revolution and, passing on to Africa, rapidly re-established the Libyan front gravely compromised by the energetic advance of the Anglo-Colonial army. It would now seem as if the Axis never contemplated bucking the formidable British "life-line" but, as the sports writers would say, had always intended "taking to the air." The monotonous regularity with which the Italo-German forces completed their forward passes constitutes the real surprise of the war at sea.

On the political side the Italian collapse set in motion an avalanche. The German invasion of Yugoslavia, Greece and Crete raises the question whether Europe may not be faced with the presence of a strong Teutonic naval power in the Mediterranean—a position Austria never achieved. As the Mediterranean is blocked at both ends by Great Britain we may be witnessing the beginning of a fight to a finish that will decide the fate of Europe for centuries. If the threat to the British Isles is less serious today the threat to the Empire is more so. With Germany in possession of an extensive Mediterranean coast line the British position in that sea may become untenable.

Several interesting subjects for speculation naturally present themselves at this point, the first being of course the distribution of the spoils in the event of an Axis victory. Just at present the immediate need of defeating Great Britain is holding the Axis partners together. The solvent of unsatisfied claims, of mutual recriminations as to the value of services rendered, has yet to make its appearance. Predictions on that score are entirely premature at present, other than to point out that in the last analysis Germany would be the arbiter and that the permanence of the results obtained would depend on the fairness of the allocations made. This is difficult in all regions. In the Balkans no settlement distantly approaching permanence has ever been made.

Another interesting feature of the present war—one that distinguishes it from most of the recent wars in the Near East —is the fact that Russia and Turkey have taken no part in the proceedings as yet. In the case of Russia the reason is obvious. In view of Hitler's openly declared intention of attacking the Soviets at the first good opportunity it was but natural prudence on the part of the Kremlin for once to stay out of the Balkan imbroglio and prepare for the invasion of the Ukraine that is now in progress. Russian declarations that her abstention from interference in Balkan matters was due to a desire not to exert pressure on her weaker neighbors should therefore be taken with a grain of salt. She had no compunction about attacking Finland, Poland and the Baltic States. Recent events have abundantly justified Russia's change of policy. She will have trouble enough maintaining her position in the Black Sea. Her interest in the Mediterranean today is subordinate to her Euxine problem.

The position of Turkey is more difficult to analyze. The traditional policy of the Porte has been to ally itself with the power offering the surest guarantees against Russian aggression. Today Turkey's problem is to pick the winner. If Germany, reinforced by her Balkan allies,[4] can succeed in putting Russia back to where she was when Peter the Great started for the Sea of Azov and establish herself on the Black Sea Turkey, at her peril, must be in on the death. The age-old problem of the Straits may well be developing into a larger and novel problem. British financiers did more than pipe oil from Baku to Batum. They brought a prolific source of future intrigue and strife. Turkey's position has been further complicated by an understandable desire to be rid of the French and British mandates in Syria, Lebanon and Palestine, which to her are "lost provinces." Moreover, Turkey still fears Italian designs on Anatolia, a relic of the last World War. Now, as in 1915, Germany would seem Turkey's natural ally. The Reich may be seeking access to the Asiatic oil fields but apparently has no territorial ambitions at Turkey's expense. "Berlin to Bagdad" has shrunk to a railroad survey.

With France definitely out Great Britain does not seem to have an ally who is not as much of a liability as an asset. From now on she must wage the fight for the commercial and maritime hegemony of Europe alone, except for such aid as the United States may be willing to extend and the very useful diversion her new ally, Russia, has been making. How much longer Russia will be able to divert German equipment—especially aerial equipment—may well be questioned. What form Mediterranean warfare will now assume is, however, still uncertain. The long-deferred attack on Gibraltar seems as remote as ever. However much Spain may desire to recover "the Rock," she is too dependent on food imports to risk a blockade by the British navy and consequently is not encouraging Axis plans for another siege of that fortress. It would seem

[4]Roumania seems to be actively participating in the operations against Odessa.

rather as if Great Britain might soon be faced with a resumption of the original Italian plan, now entrusted to German leadership and operating from German-controlled bases, and that the present offensive in Libya is an attempt to forestall another attack on Egypt. In spite of an impressive naval superiority, Great Britain has been unable to prevent the Axis from maintaining contact with Libya. What is more serious, it would not be surprising if the Vichy government were induced to grant the Germans transit facilities through Tunisia. Cape Bon, it should be remembered, is only ninety miles from Sicily. French good will has been badly shattered by the British salvos at Oran, an arbitrary exercise of sea power that justifies French distrust of British warships in the western Mediterranean. Moreover, the assistance France can render is not limited to giving Germany the run of her north African possessions. France possesses a highly developed system of inland waterways. French torpedo boats have on several occasions been sent from the channel ports to the Mediterranean through canals. It is quite possible for the average coastal submarine to travel from the North Sea to the Mediterranean via the Rhine-Rhone canal. The strategic importance of these "interior lines" is obvious and may prove a trump card in the hands of the Vichy government. Last but not least, Turkey might be prevailed upon to open her land route through Asia Minor to Suez, in which event the British in Egypt would have two fronts to defend.

On the other hand, predictions that Italy would "slip a bolt" across the Malta passage have not been borne out. Malta is still intact and British convoys to Egypt have been getting through. The Mediterranean is in no immediate danger of becoming "nobody's sea." Both sides are using it quite as freely as in the last World War, more so if aviation be included. It is more likely to become "everybody's sea." A new chapter in the long story of Mediterranean strife is undoubtedly in the making, thanks largely to the *Luftwaffe*. In this connection it should be said that Britain's adoption of the air arm will rank with Hamilcar Barca's switch to land power as one of the most remarkable adaptations in the annals of warfare. Unfortunately for the British, war is still a question of positions, as Napoleon once declared. What England cannot duplicate is Italy's position, the facilities she offers land-based aviation. It was to offset this natural advantage that Great Britain sought Greek aid. "On a souvent besoin d'un plus petit que soi!" The Balkan peninsula, taken in conjunction with Morea and Crete, is a fairly acceptable substitute for the Italian peninsula and Sicily and would have enabled the British seriously to hamper Axis movements, both naval and aerial, besides subjecting Italian embarkation ports to intensive bombardment by the R. A. F. All of which is now water over the dam.

As regards strategy, however, the situation has not changed since the days of Leibniz and Baron Tott. Whoever has a foothold on Egypt has a strangle hold on England, now as of yore. A threat against Suez is Germany's best chance of securing a recognition of the "new order" she hopes to establish just as it is Italy's best chance of securing a recognition of her claims to *Italia Irredenta* and obtaining the *Lebendsraum* her rapidly growing population requires. The community of interests between Germany and Italy is complete in so far as strategy is concerned. It would be a grave mistake on the part of the German High Command to treat Italy's Egyptian campaign as a local, limited affair intended to facilitate communications between Libya and her East African colonies. The demolishing of the British bastions in the Mediterranean is an indispensable preliminary to the rearing of the Axis structure. What *Weltpolitik* did, *Weltpolitik* must undo. Viewed from this angle Egypt still complies with Napoleon's definition: "the most important country in the world."

The Sea of Memories

A BUSY CROSSROAD by which throughout the ages many people have passed, jostling and elbowing each other as they hurry in pursuit of their goal; a restless region despite the serenity of its coast line, the scene of countless bitter struggles often waged amid incredibly beautiful surroundings; a sea along which merchant and soldier have alternated, where men have battled and died for gain, for glory or for their God, where adventure soon turns into tragedy: the Mediterranean!

A legendary sea that has attracted men from all corners of the globe. Some came and went, others stayed and mingled with those whose coming none can trace today: Persians and Arabs from the Near East, strange tribes from the North, Asiatic hordes, even Mongolians from the Far East and, stranger yet, the venturesome seamen of a young republic determined upon demonstrating to the Old World that the New World had grown to man's estate. Some came to plunder, others came in the hopes of finding a home on the sunlit slopes of its shores; some came from distant seas in pursuit of an enemy, others because beyond its eastern portals lay the El Dorado of their dreams. A sea where men have hunted each other, where the pirate has sought the riches others had created; where friars have not only prayed but fought, where knights have not only fought but prayed; where feudal lords have carved out realms, have ruled, then vanished; where mercenaries have served, betrayed, prospered, then failed; where trading states have accumulated fantastic wealth, only to lose it in time: the Mediterranean!

A sea whose early annals are lost in the haze of fable, where every island and headland suggests some myth or deed of valor until every chart seems a page from an open book of romance or history; a sea along whose shores the noblest of man's works still stand, some bearing the scars of war, others intact, the inspiration yet the despair of succeeding generations. The austere column of Greece, the compelling grandeur of feudal battlement, the splendor of Byzantium's dome, the grace of Italian Gothic, the flight of the minaret—that arrow Islam points heavenward; all that art ever envisioned and craftsmanship perfected, all that cunning ever planned and daring accomplished, all that faith ever dreamt and devotion realized, you will find it all in the Mediterranean.

The records of the past stand revealed to those who have the love and the patience to study them. How about the future? That is in the lap of the Gods. Economically, the future of the Mediterranean seems secure, thanks largely to the growing importance of the riparian nations. It is still the shortest distance between more than two points. Politically, however, the situation is as confused as ever. Moslem and Christian are still daggers drawn and the rejuvenation of Turkey has demonstrated once more the wisdom of the maxim of the Civil Code that "nemo est haeres viventi." Russia has apparently ceased sniffing the salt breezes of the Mediterranean for the time being but the ambitions of her powerful neighbor have given a dangerous interpretation to the prophetic remark of Palacky. The aspirations of Italy to the empire once held by her trading republics will not down, the plans of England for the recapture of the trident that has slipped from her grasp in the oldest of the seas are meeting with an unexpected opposition and after forty-one centuries the Pyramids are awaiting the advance of another invader. Distressing as it may be to admit, the chances of peace in the Mediterranean are as slim as ever.

Will the Mediterranean witness another Mylæ, Actium, Lepanto or Chesme? It would seem rather that it has become the scene of daily encounters between contestants bent on making some sea lane impassable and others who must keep it open. No one engagement can give the victor command. Instead of pitched battles between galleys or ships-of-the-line we are witnessing a war of ambuscade, the sudden dash of some mysterious craft from behind a rocky inlet, a dripping whale-back rising to the surface to survey the havoc it has caused, the treacherous blow of some hidden force detonating beneath the waters of the sea, whirring airplanes emerging from a cloud or out of the "sun gauge" with grim-looking projectiles ready to drop; a three-dimensional war has driven the stately battle-ships to cover.

It would seem as if strife had played an inordinate part in the story we have been telling. Granted; but is not strife the rule rather than the exception in the life of nations as well as in the lives of individuals? Therein lies the great fascination that the Mediterranean exerts over those who know her past and are following the course of her present crisis. Not but that she lends herself to placid contemplation as well. Whoever has lapsed into a reverie at the sound of a serenade fading away along the waters of the Grand Canal or has been startled by the song of Islam rising from the moonlit terraces of an Arab town; whoever has seen the brilliant colors of the sails on the lagoons of Venetia or the more delicate coloring of the Greek barks as they glide into some tiny haven hedged in by glistening white houses while monstrous-looking windmills wave their arms frantically in the fresh breezes of the Ægean; whoever has strolled of an evening on the beach of a bottle-necked harbor in the Balearic Isles upon which the Catalan fishermen have drawn their sturdy boats and has watched them untangle the brown nets they are setting out to dry; whoever has seen the Saracen Towers of the Calabrian Coast peering out for an enemy who will never appear again, at least not in the shape their builders knew; whoever has admired a Turkish felucca as she comes about, using oars when in stays, and dashes for the narrow mouth of the port of Rhodes behind which stands the intrepid citadel of the greatest of military companies; whoever has felt the spell of the Prophet envelop him as he wanders among the crumbling tombstones of Scutari or stops to rest a while in the mystical half-light of a mosque; whoever has heard the call of the muezzin descend like a voice from that distant seventh heaven or has listened to the bells of Monreale drift out at vesper time over the bountiful Conca d'Oro will join with me in a prayer that the Mediterranean may some day know the peace she has hitherto been denied.

And so as outward bound we once more pass the Pillars of Hercules let us take a last glance at the winged grace of a lateen sail, the rig under which Pagan, Moslem and Christian, trader and warrior, pirate and Crusader have sailed. Until they vanish below the horizon let us gaze at the headlands that were parted in days beyond the reach of mythology. What deeds have not been enacted behind that portal!

Salve atque vale! To those who in the past have striven in yonder sea, to those who are now striving there, to those who will in future be called upon to do so. Whatever the issues, whoever prevails, the days of heroism are surely not over. The Mediterranean has not given its last contribution to history. May the successors be ever worthy of the noblest among their forebears who have made the Mediterranean

THE SEA OF MEMORIES!

Index

DATE DUE

THE EASTERN MEDITERRANEAN